From CREWE
to the CAPE

Copyright © Mark Potts, Tony Marks and Howard Curran
Published in the United Kingdom by MPire Books of Crewe
email: mark@markpotts.wanadoo.co.uk
ISBN 978-0-9556733-5-1

All rights reserved. This publication may not be reproduced, stored in a retrieval system, or transmitted, in any form or by any means electronic, mechanical, photocopying, recording or otherwise, without the prior permission of the publishers. Every effort has been made to contact present copyright owners to any photographs that appear in this book which are not properly credited. We will do our utmost to include any acknowledgments to all parties and amend any errors or facts that are not correct, in subsequent reprints of this book.

From CREWE to the CAPE

Diary of a Railway Town During the Boer War 1899-1902

Mark Potts, Tony Marks & Howard Curran

Contents

Chapter One 1899 - FROM CREWE TO THE CAPE 19

Chapter Two 1900 - RELIEF BUT NO VICTORY 58

Chapter Three 1901 - MORE RAILWAYMEN REQUIRED! 91

Chapter Four 1902 - WELCOME HOME TOMMY ATKINS 124

Chapter Five 1903 - HONOUR THE CITIZEN SOLDIERS 154

THE MEN WHO SERVED 174

IN MEMORIAM 187

RAILWAY VOLUNTEERS MEDAL ROLL AND DRAFTS 193

DIARY OF SAPPER ARTHUR WILLIAM MAYBURY 200

SUMMARY OF EVENTS 206

Disclaimer & Acknowledgments

Every effort has been made to make this book as accurate as possible. The primary sources used for letters and local events were *The Crewe Chronicle* and *The Crewe Guardian* and we have taken these as being factually correct. Names of the serving service personnel are as spelt on the Boer War Memorial situated in Queens Park, Crewe, unless proven otherwise. The story and events of the war are only briefly touched upon, but can be further researched by reading either *The Boer War* by Thomas Pakenham (ISBN 0-349-10466-2) or *The Great Boer War* by Byron Farwell (ISBN 1-84022-217-4), both highly regarded books on the subject. Place names in South Africa are spelt as recorded on the map on page 20. Finally, we would like to thank Diane Dyer for her time and efforts during the production of this book, the staff of Crewe Library who contributed articles and photographs, to Noel Hannon, an authority on the Railway Volunteers, to Colin McLean for the loan of his letters written by Sapper Arthur Henry Foy, Lucy McCann of the Bodleian Library of Commonwealth & African Studies at Rhodes House, to Peter Wray and Peter John for the information given for the Royal Engineers Medal Roll, Bournemouth cemetery staff, also David Sadler who copied out the diary entries of his grandfather who served, Brian Edge for proofing the final draft, and all who donated their treasured photographs, including the South Africa War Graves Project, who provided the majority of the cemetery images which appear at the back of the book.

Preface

The Boer War was fought between the British Empire and Dutch settlers, who resided in South Africa in the independent Boer republics of the Transvaal and Orange Free State (which bordered the two British self governing colonies of Cape Colony and Natal). The war ran from October 1899 until May 1902 and ended in a British victory, although the brutal way this victory was achieved, brought worldwide condemnation. It turned out to be the longest, costliest, bloodiest and most humiliating campaign fought by the British Empire between 1815 and 1914 and according to Rudyard Kipling, gave the British 'no end of a lesson.'

Relations with the Boer nation had been strained since the First Boer War in 1881, especially after a British force suffered an embarrassing and crushing defeat during the Battle of Majuba Hill. This reversal alone had many on home shores thirsting for military revenge. After this short campaign, the British government granted the Boers self-government in the Transvaal under theoretical British overseeing.

Pressure on the Boers intensified in 1885, when gold was discovered in the Transvaal and the area was swamped by mainly British fortune seekers (known as Uitlanders). These new settlers were poorly regarded by the Boers, but despite paying a considerable amount of tax, they were denied any political rights. In 1896 Britain tried to improve these rights but the disastrous 'Jameson Raid' only added fuel to the fire, and this was used as an excuse to justify a major military build up in the Cape. The Boers eventually lost patience with the British government and issued an ultimatum about the withdrawal of troops from their borders. Threats and counter-threats ensued, until the Boers struck the first blow by invading Natal in October 1899. Within a short time, the Boers successfully besieged the garrison towns of Ladysmith, Mafeking and Kimberley, and in one week in December 1899, defeated the British on three separate occasions. It was not until vast reinforcements arrived in South Africa that counter-offences began, to relieve the garrison towns and enabled the capture of both Boer capitals by June of the same year. Even with the war effectively over, Boer guerrillas continued hostilities to great effect, attacking British garrisons, plundering war-laden trains and disrupting communications, for a further eighteen months until the British responded with their blockhouse, barbed wire and land clearance policy, which saw them destroy Boer farms, confiscate and destroy food stocks, crops and animals and place civilians in over fifty ill-equipped concentration camps, where thousands died, including many women and children. This episode remains one of the darkest chapters in British military history. The last of the Boers finally surrendered in May 1902 and war ceased with the signing of the Treaty of Vereeniging, which ended the existence of the Boer republics. A total of 21,942 British Empire troops lost their lives during the war (the majority from sickness and disease) and around 26,000 Boers died, mainly in the poorly run and unhygienic concentration camps. Britain eventually paid out compensation for restocking and repairing Boer farmlands and promised eventual self-government, which was granted in 1907. In 1909 plans to unify the four territories into a self-governing state became reality in 1910 when a united South Africa came into being. Just four years after their formation, they would fight side by side with British Empire troops during the First World War.

·Introduction·

Nobody could have thought on July 4, 1837, when the first train stopped at Crewe that, 62 years later, the town would play such a significant role in a major military campaign. That inaugural journey by the Grand Junction Railway Company from Warrington to Birmingham, using Crewe as its halfway point, turned out to be the beginning of the town.

It has been stated in several military journals and publications, that the Cheshire railway town provided more men, per head of population, than any other town in England or Wales for the 1899-1902 Boer War. The 500 men listed on the local Boer War memorial in Queens Park in the town (plus others who are not commemorated) certainly supports the claim, and among the names are the 26 who lost their lives, through accidents, disease and in action.

The proud military heritage attached to the town of Crewe saw signs of life as early as 1859, when the scare of a French invasion prompted a Volunteer Movement all over the country which saw 160,000 men enrol by the summer of 1860. In October 1864, a public meeting in the Mechanics Institute was held to form a Crewe Corps, and in January 1865 the application was finally granted by the War Office. One month later, 146 men were sworn in to what would become the 36th Cheshire Rifle Volunteers, with the officers drawn from railway company officials. No.1 Company was initially commanded by Captain Francis William Webb and No.2 Company by Captain Spencer. Drilling took place in the Market Hall, Corn Exchange and later above the saw mills in the Deviation Shop, and the early highlights for the Corps were to be guard of honour for H.R.H. Prince of Wales and the Duke of Edinburgh on their respective visits to Crewe Works. By 1878 it numbered 401 men, but just two years later, this unit unfortunately disbanded, but the idea for a new formation gathered pace in the latter months of 1886. The Locomotive Superintendent, Francis William Webb, along with senior officials and prominent local Conservatives, helped to raise an entire Corps of Royal Engineers from the ranks of the railway workers of the town. Webb had spoken about the idea to the Secretary of State for War, Mr William Henry Smith, regarding the working and maintenance of railways in time of war, and raising a Volunteer Engineer Corps composed exclusively of railway men, with a view to them being ready for active service if required. Smith was in favour of the idea, and further talks by Webb with Sir Richard Moon, the then Chairman of the LNWR (London & North Western Railway), saw the scheme approved. At the time of their embodiment on April 1, 1887 (the official date given), they held the distinction of being the only Reserve military unit in the British Army recruited entirely from a single employer. This unit would eventually become the 2nd Cheshire Royal Engineers (Railway) Volunteer Corps, but would be better known in the immediate area as 'The Railway Volunteers' or 'Crewe Works Army.' To show the connection with the railways, their smart new uniform sported inwardly facing collar dogs depicting the 3,000th loco to roll off the Works production line, which had occurred in the same year as their formation.

    Initially in its early conception, over 800 men applied to join the unit, which gave the opportunity of picking only the finest men from the ranks of engine drivers, firemen, cleaners, boilermakers, riveters, fitters, smiths, platelayers, shunters, pointsmen and office workers, with their early drilling taking part in a large room at the newly built Gas Works. Within twelve months, the unit consisted of six companies, totalling 24 officers and 610 men, with each company comprising of staff from a specific department. For example, "A" Company was commanded by George Whale and were drawn from the running department and "C" Company were nearly all office staff. The make-up of the Railway Volunteers soon after formation was as follows:

No.1 ("A") Company - Captain G. Whale, 1st Lieutenant F. R. Oke, 2nd Lieutenant J. Dick, Surgeon-Major J. Atkinson, Assistant Surgeon T. C. Bailey, Quarter Master G. Martlew, Chaplain Reverend A. H. Webb, Quarter Master Sergeant G. R. Gibson, Bandmaster E. Chapman, Bugle-Major G. Hope, Armoury Sergeant J. Bellyse, Orderly Room Clerk W. Davey, Company Sergeant Major T. Ouldcott, Sergeant J. Slight, Sergeant A. Billington, Sergeant J. Rowbottom, Sergeant H. Haughton, Corporal C. Thorpe, 2nd Corporal W. D. Heeler, Bugler W. H. Guest.

No.2 ("B") Company – Captain A. M. Thompson, 1st Lieutenant W. Dandison, 2nd Lieutenant J. T. Roberts, Company Sergeant Major J. J. Latham, Sergeant A. Billington, Sergeant W. B. Latham, Sergeant E. Stephenson, Sergeant F. Jenkins, Corporal G. Wytcherley, 2nd Corporal W. Costin, Bugler T. Plant.

No.3 ("C") Company – Captain W. Norman, 1st Lieutenant A. Hignett, Company Sergeant Major C. Nield, Sergeant H. Osborn, Sergeant J. N. Jackson, Sergeant J. Heeler, Corporal J. Dyson, 2nd Corporal J. Wyton, Bugler H. Settle.

No.4 ("D") Company – Captain A. G. Hill, 1st Lieutenant W. W. G. Webb, 2nd Lieutenant H. Constable, Company Sergeant Major C. Stapley, Sergeant R. Sandham, Sergeant R. J. Wilson, Sergeant A. Taylor, Corporal E. Taylor, 2nd Corporal G. Surridge, Bugler W. J. Morgan.

No.5 ("E") Company – Captain H. D. Earl, 1st Lieutenant E. P. W. W. H. Warneford, 2nd Lieutenant J. S. S. Mowbray, Company Sergeant Major J. Thomasson, Sergeant J. Simon, Sergeant W. Billington, Sergeant M. R. Cross, Corporal T. Halsall, 2nd Corporal J.W. Smith, Bugler I. Conway.

No.6 ("F") Company - Captain J. Tandy, Lieutenant C. B. H. D. Dent, Company Sergeant Major F. Eastwood, Sergeant W. J. Badger, Sergeant J. W. Heaton, Corporal H. Roberts, 2nd Corporal W. Conquest.

From 1888, the Crewe Engineers were commanded by Colonel Sir Edward Thomas Davenant Cotton-Jodrell (born June 29, 1847), a former Captain in the Royal Artillery, who resided at Reaseheath Hall in Nantwich, but also owned estates at Yeardsley in Cheshire and Shallcross in Derbyshire. He was the only son of the Rt. Rev. George Edward Lynch Cotton and Sophia Ann Tomkinson, daughter of the Rev. H. Tomkinson - former vicar of Acton (he added Jodrell to his name by Royal Licence in 1890). His military instincts were inherited from his grandfather Captain Thomas Davenant Cotton of the Royal Fusiliers - a staff officer who had fallen at Nivelle during the Peninsular campaign.

After parading several times in the town, usually to a large audience, one of their first major engagements was to proceed to York (Knavesmire) in the early hours of June 20, 1887, to take part in Queen Victoria's Golden Jubilee Review. Out of a total of around 4,000 men, of which the majority were regulars, 563 men of the Railway Volunteers took part, which included field exercises and a march past. They were commanded on the day by Colonel Loyd, Adjutant Gossett, Captain A. M. Thompson, Captain J. Tandy, Captain George Whale, Captain A. G. Hill, Captain W. Norman and Captain H. D. Earl. Three times during the day Colonel Loyd (formerly of the Grenadier Guards and the 2nd V.B. Royal Warwickshire Regiment) was called aside by the reviewing officer to commend the 'Volunteers' on their excellent show and his comments that they could easily have passed off as regulars went down well with the attending officers. On June 9, 1888, they took part in a local parade, when Queens Park in the town was opened to the public for the first time. Among the attending dignitaries was H.R.H. The Duke of Cambridge, who was Commander-in-Chief of the British Army. On September 16, 1889 a total of 408 Railway Volunteers marched through Chester city centre and again their smartness and togetherness were noted by the large crowd. In June 1897, Captain Tandy, one Sergeant and 20 men represented the Corps, when travelling to London to take part in Queen Victoria's Diamond Jubilee.

Track laying and bridge building exercises honed their skills at yearly training camps, firstly at Conway, then in the sand dunes at Rhyl and Blackpool, and their musketry practice was undertaken at Holmes Chapel (close to the viaduct), to where the Corps would march from the Market Square in Crewe. During their training regime, a total of 245 of the unit enlisted in the British Army for one day, which qualified them for the Royal Engineers Railway Reserve, where they would remain for six years and be liable for active service at any time. This Crewe unit comprised of 60 firemen, 25 cleaners, 25 boilermakers and riveters, 60 fitters, 7 strikers, 7 smiths, 50 platelayers, 5 shunters and 6 pointsmen.

Along with other town Reservists and regulars, they would not have long to wait to test their skills in a hostile environment, as the rumblings from South Africa would soon see these men of Crewe in the thick of the action.

(**LEFT**) Francis William Webb (1836-1906), Chief Mechanical Engineer of the LNWR, 1871-1903. He was the Mayor of Crewe, 1886-87 and 1887-88 and was one of the main founders of the 2nd Cheshire Royal Engineers (Railway Volunteers). (**BELOW**) The official opening of Queens Park on June 9, 1888, although it had been dedicated some twelve months earlier on July 4, 1887. That date coincided with Queen Victoria's Golden Jubilee, the 3,000th locomotive built in Crewe Works and 50 years since the first train had stopped at Crewe. Amongst the many dignitaries pictured below is James Middleton, who had driven that first train, and to him was afforded the honour of unveiling the clock. (Inset) Colonel Cotton-Jodrell.

(**ABOVE**) The official programme for the grand opening of Queens Park. (**BELOW**) The Railway Volunteers line-up on Volunteer Fields ready for inspection by the Duke of Cambridge, Commander-in-Chief of the British Army. In the background are the houses of West Street and St. Barnabas Church.

(ABOVE) Crewe Engineers laying standard and narrow gauge railway lines in the Rhyl sand dunes, Whitsuntide 1889.

(LEFT) Sapper Jack Walley, Rhyl 1890.

*(**ABOVE**) June 1894. Children inspect a trestle bridge built by the Railway Volunteers. The camp can be seen to the right. (**BELOW**) Sharpshooters at Bisley from No.4 Section, "F" Company, who were among the best shots of the Corps. They are (back row, left to right) Captain W. F. Black, 2nd Corporal J. Glover, Sapper William Spilsbury, Sapper J. Jardine and CSM W. Johnson. (Front row) Sapper J. Rowley, Sapper W. Ferrington and Sapper A. Bailey.*

Four photographs from the Rhyl encampment in 1895. (**ABOVE**) The Railway Volunteers Band. Far left is believed to be Bandmaster W. Coen and centre stage is 'Major' the dog. (**BELOW**) A posed shot outside the mess tent.

(**ABOVE**) Morning ration party of "C" and "F" Companies.

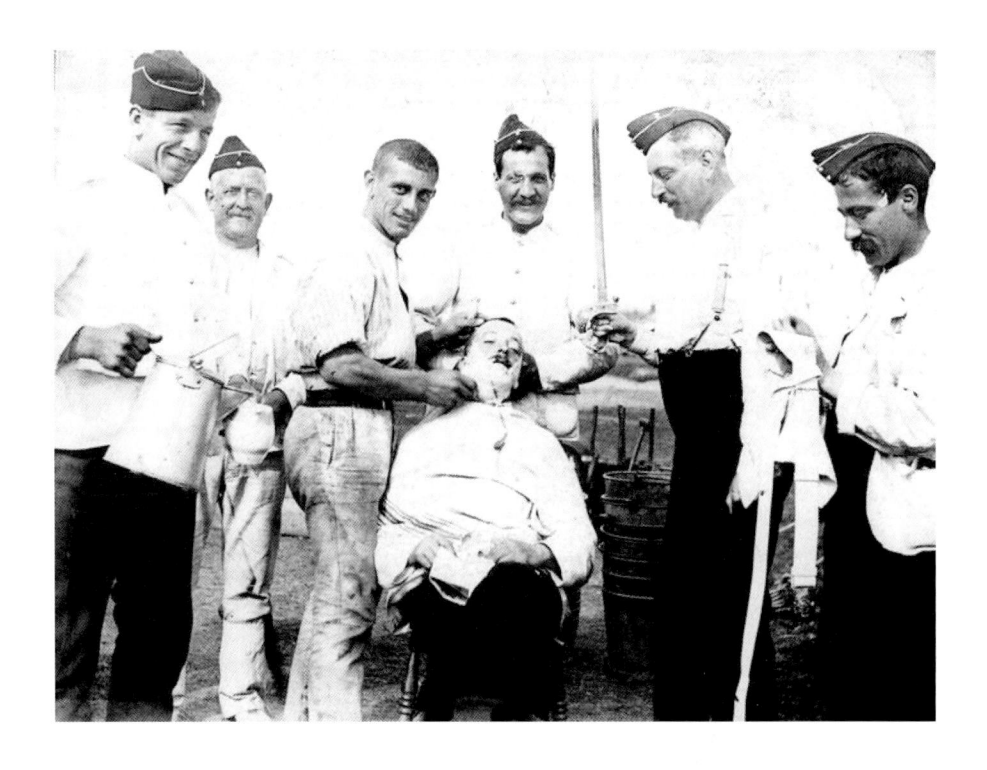

(**ABOVE**) Fun and games in camp. George Riddle Gibson receives a shave from H. Stafford.

(ABOVE) Railway Volunteers at Holmes Chapel rifle range in 1895. *(BELOW)* The advance party of the Crewe Engineers on parade on the Market Square in 1897, just prior to leaving for the annual encampment at Rhyl. Behind them are the houses of Market Terrace. The sign on the far left house reads 'Thomas William Lovatt - Registrar of Births & Deaths.'

(**ABOVE**) *The main party on the Market Square in 1897, probably before the departure to Rhyl. This time the houses in the background are in Delamere Street.* (**BELOW LEFT**) *Mary 'Poppie' Gibson (later Chesworth), pictured here at Rhyl in 1897. She was the daughter of QMS George Riddle Gibson of 276, Hungerford Road.* (**BELOW RIGHT**) *George's young son Harry, standing to attention.*

(LEFT) Francis William Webb on the Earle Street Sports Stadium cricket pitch on May 14, 1898. In the background is the banked cycle track, which in 1969 would form part of the speedway track.

(RIGHT) Sapper Percy Powell of the Railway Volunteers. (ABOVE) A Crewe Engineers tunic button.

Chapter One · 1899
·From Crewe to the Cape·

There was an air of excitement on the streets of Crewe towards the end of September, as war with the Boers in South Africa seemed inevitable, and this reached fever pitch when the Army and Reserves were mobilised on October 7. Crewe members of the Railway Reserve waited patiently for news of their involvement and this was received early Sunday morning on October 8. Initially, 105 men (over 40% of the Reserve) received their warrants from the Paymaster of the School of Military Engineering at Chatham to proceed to Brompton Barracks, and these would include drivers, firemen, cleaners, blacksmiths, platelayers, boilermakers and riveters. Others eligible for the call-up faced a nervous wait, as all were eager to be a part of the first draft, as the main tabloids predicted a swift end to the war and the troops home to enjoy Christmas festivities. Colonel Cotton-Jodrell and other senior officers including Adjutant Major Fullerton and Captain Tandy were kept busy preparing for the departure which was to commence no later than Tuesday, October 17. As stated in the local newspapers, the Railway Reserve would be required for special work during the war and although they would undoubtedly be in the thick of the action, their tools would be the pick axe, sledge hammer, jim crow and screw jack and not the rifle and bayonet, even though many in the Corps were excellent shots following years of practice at Holmes Chapel. The key to the war would be the transportation of the troops and war-materials across the vast and empty veldts (open grassland) of South Africa and these Crewe Engineers would play a major part in the upkeep of the railway network.

In times of peace, a Reservist was paid the princely sum of 6d a day, but when mobilised this increased so a Sergeant was paid 3s 3d, a Corporal 2s 6d, a 2nd Corporal 2s 2d, a Lance Corporal 1s 6d and a Sapper 1s 1½d. In the case of a married man, his wife would receive 8d a day, plus 2d for each child.

Just prior to war, there were 4,268 miles of single line railway in South Africa, with 3,267 miles in British territory. In Cape Colony the lines were in three sections. The Western Section started from Cape Town and passed through De Aar Junction, Orange River Station and Kimberley, before joining the Rhodesian Railway at Vryburg, continuing to Bulawayo. The Midland Section started from Port Elizabeth and had two branches which joined at Rosmead Junction. Then after passing

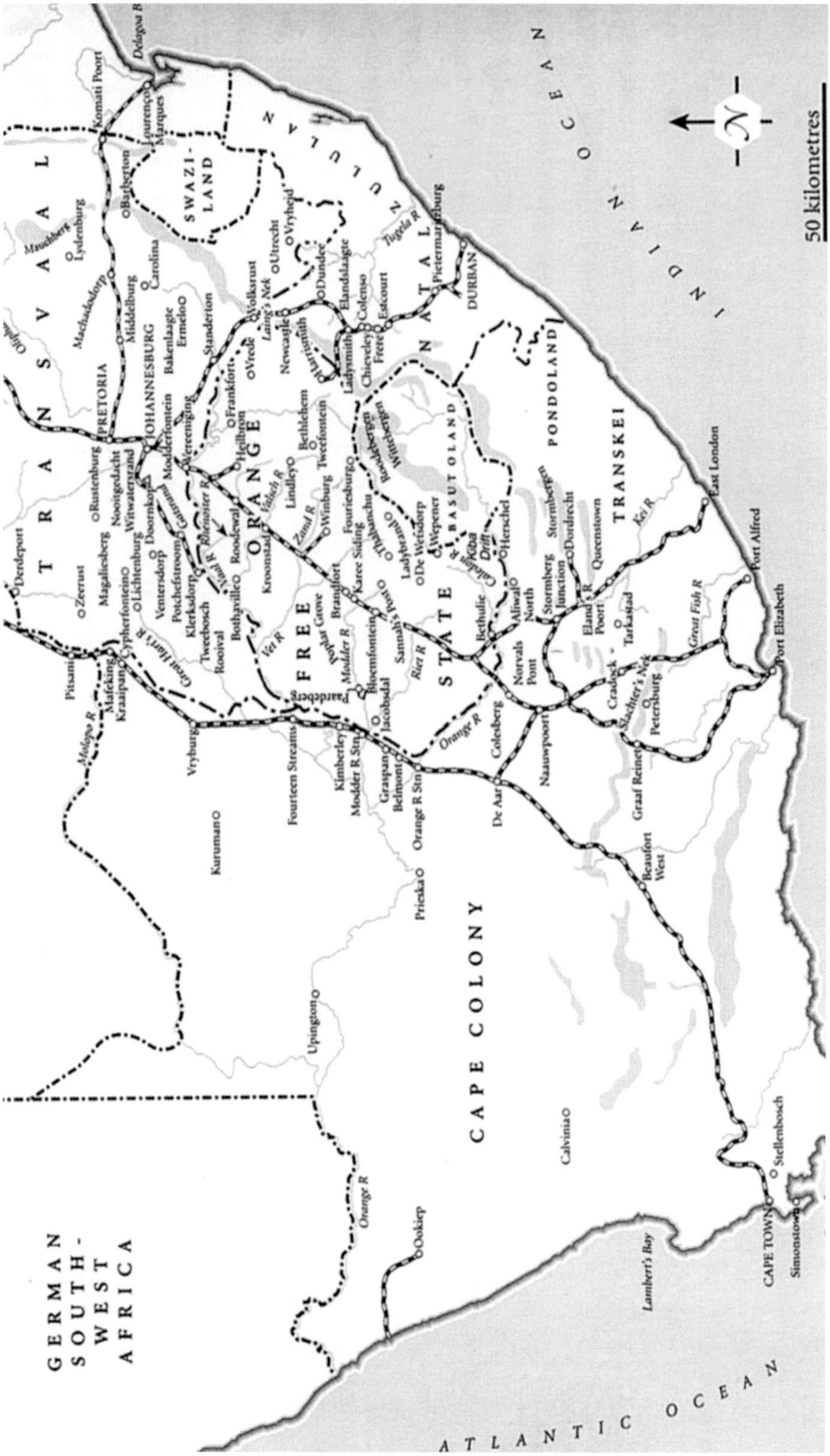
GERMAN
SOUTH-
WEST
AFRICA
CAPE COLONY
ORANGE
FREE
STATE
TRANSVAAL
NATAL
ZULULAND
SWAZI-
LAND
BASUTOLAND
PONDOLAND
TRANSKEI
INDIAN OCEAN
ATLANTIC OCEAN
50 kilometres
N
Delagoa B
Komati Poort
Lourenço Marques
Barberton
Lydenburg
Machadodorp
Middelburg
Carolina
Ermelo
Bakenlaagte
Standerton
PRETORIA
JOHANNESBURG
Rustenburg
Nooitgedacht
Witwatersrand
Modderfontein
Vereeniging
Heilbron
Frankfort
Vrede
Volksrust
Laing's Nek
Utrecht
Vryheid
Newcastle
Dundee
Elandslaagte
Ladysmith
Colenso
Chieveley
Frere
Estcourt
Tugela R
Pietermaritzburg
DURBAN
Bethlehem
Lindley
Kroonstad
Winburg
Zand R
Vaal R
Vet R
Rhenoster R
Roodewal
Bothaville
Potchefstroom
Ventersdorp
Lichtenburg
Zeerust
Derdepoort
Klerksdorp
Tweebosch
Rooival
Magaliesberg
Mafeking
Kraaipan
Pitsani
Molopo R
Vryburg
Fourteen Streams
Kimberley
Modder R Stn
Paardeberg
Poplar Grove
Brandfort
Karee Siding
Bloemfontein
Jacobsdal
Graspan
Belmont
Orange R Stn
Riet R
Sannah's Post
Thabanchu
Ladybrand
Wepener
Dewetsdorp
Bethulie
Aliwal North
Norvals Pont
Herschel
Colesberg
Orange R
Naauwpoort
De Aar
Stormberg
Stormberg Junction
Dordrecht
Queenstown
Tarkastad
Cradock
Elands R Poort
Graaf Reinet
Petersburg
Great Fish R
Kei R
East London
Port Alfred
Port Elizabeth
Beaufort West
Kurumani
Prieska
Upington
Calvinia
Ookiep
Orange R
Lambert's Bay
CAPE TOWN
Stellenbosch
Simonstown

Naauwpoort Junction (where a branch line connected it with the Western Section at De Aar), it reached the Orange River at Norvals Pont, where it joined the Orange Free State Railway, leading to Bloemfontein and the Transvaal. Finally the Eastern Section led from East London to Stormberg, where it connected with the Midland Section by a branch to Rosmead, reaching the Orange River at Bethulie, and joined the Orange Free State Railway at Springfontein. In Natal, the main line ran from Durban through Pietermaritzburg, Ladysmith and Newcastle, joining the Transvaal railway system at Charlestown, while a branch led from Ladysmith west to the Orange Free State. These location names would soon be familiar to the Crewe men on their way to the war zone.

It had been obvious that the South Africa rail network would play a major part in the war, so the British Government formed a Department of Military Railways. They appointed Major E. P. C. Girouard D.S.O. as the Director of Railways for the South African Field Force, after he had successfully supervised railway operations during the Sudan campaign. His main role was to oversee the railways in British territory; make arrangements for the rapid repair of lines damaged by the enemy; and eventually take control of the lines in Boer territory, which when in British hands, would be known as the Imperial Military Railways.

Early indications noted that a proportion of the Crewe Railway Reserve going to South Africa would be attached to the 8th Railway Company of the Royal Engineers, who were already in South Africa, occupying positions at Ladysmith and near the Transvaal border. They had been despatched in July 1899 (landing on August 5) to patrol the Cape Government Railway in two armoured trains specially constructed at Cape Town. The rest of the men would be in the 10th Railway Company who were still on home shores, and the 31st and 45th Fortress Companies, who were also units in the Royal Engineers.

Monday, October 16, was the confirmed day for departure, and the townsfolk of Crewe started preparations for the 'send-off.' Part of the official order read:

> 'With reference to the special order of the 10th instant, the detachment Railway Engineer Reserve, now under order for Chatham will parade in full order, without arms, but with rolled greatcoats on Monday the 16th instant as follows: Market Square 10.30am, Crewe depart 11.30am (special), Victoria arrive about 3.30pm, Victoria depart 4.20pm, Chatham (Central) arrive 5.21pm. No kits should be taken as military kits will be issued at Chatham. Captain Tandy and Lieutenant Bowes will accompany the detachment, returning to Crewe after handing over to the O.C.R.E. Reserves.'

The remainder of the Volunteers were invited to parade on the day in their 'walking out' dress. Sergeant Major Williams and Sergeant Jones were also invited to accompany the men to Chatham in order to bring back all property belonging to the Corps, as the men would be supplied with fresh uniforms and military kits upon arrival. A proposal was also put forward for Crewe Works to be closed from breakfast until 2.00pm so the men could give their colleagues a 'hearty send-off.'

News about the call-up saw one household in the town receive four sets of papers. The head, who was a member of the Railway Volunteers, received his, as well as his three lodgers, who were all members of the Shropshire Light Infantry.

On October 11, following threats and counter-threats, war was declared when the Boers invaded Natal.

Three days later, 19 more Crewe Engineers received their 'blue paper' to proceed to Chatham, bringing the total leaving for war to 124. Later in the afternoon a further 58 men were notified that they too could receive the call in the very near future. These 77 men were to be attached to the 31st Fortress Company, who were to work in conjunction with the Railway Companies.

Others members of the Crewe Engineer Corps keen to be a part of the action volunteered their services, including Lieutenant Nash, who was accepted into the Royal Engineers at Chatham. First Class Army Reserves from Crewe, who numbered around 50, received no big 'send off' and most left immediately to join their respective regiments. On Friday, October 13, twenty men belonging to the Shropshire Light Infantry made their departure, after spending an evening with their workmates at the Swan Hotel.

At the Lyceum Theatre on the Friday night, one member of the Railway Volunteers got up on stage and recited a comic verse composed by several comrades. As expected the ditty brought the house down and the young Sapper left the stage to deafening applause. The words of the verse were:

> 'It seems we've got to thrash the Boers,
> To Avenge Majuba Hill;
> Our Crewe Reserves in Britain's cause
> Will give old Kruger a pill.
> He'll have to swallow it whether or no,
> Our prestige to maintain,
> And Kruger's state will have to go,
> So says Joe Chamberlain.'

On the Saturday morning (October 14) notices were posted in Crewe Works, to the effect that the factory would indeed be closed on the Monday until 2.00pm so workers could attend the departure and the Mayor also requested the town's tradesmen to close their shops from 10.00am until 2.00pm. The request was met with general favour. On Saturday afternoon a large contingent of the men leaving for South Africa attended the Lancashire League match between Crewe Alexandra and Horwich and were given a magnificent ovation from the crowd of around 4,000. At half-time the Temperance Band played several military airs, including *The British Grenadiers* and *The Death of Nelson*. For the record the home team did not disappoint and won the game 4-1 to go top of the league table. Later in the afternoon a section of the men attached to the 10th Railway Company underwent their medicals. Of the 40 who attended, only one was deemed 'unfit for foreign service.'

In the week before departure, a number of presentations by workmates were made to Reservists leaving for war. On the Friday lunchtime, a large gathering of Crewe Works employees congregated in the Boiler Shop Smithy as Sappers Coleman, Butt, Sanders, Harris (all of the Railway Reserve) and Sergeant George Allman (Shropshire Light Infantry) received their gifts from Joseph Ellis, one of the oldest and most respected workmen in the department. The Fitting Shop employees held a similar gathering on the same night. Here Sapper George Wearne of "D" Company of the Railway Volunteers received several gifts, including a purse of gold coins. At a lodge meeting of the Loyal Britannia Order (Crewe) also on the Friday night, lodge members Sappers S. Wolfe, W. Barnes and William Champion were presented with leather pocket wallets. At noon on Saturday some 800 men in the Fitting Shop witnessed the presentation of a gold ring and a purse of gold coins also to Sapper Wolfe. In the Wheel Department, gifts were bestowed on Private T. Baystone of the 23rd Royal Welsh Fusiliers and Sapper A. Forrest of the Railway Reserve. Sapper H. Thompson received a silver mounted walking stick from the men of No.2 Erecting Shop and in the Tender Shop, Private R. Jones of the Royal Welsh Fusiliers and Sappers Fairbrother and Tirrell of the Volunteers were presented with their gifts. William Cunningham, the popular trainer of Crewe Alexandra F.C. received several items from men in the Axle Box Department. Premium apprentices raised £3 which was presented to Sapper J. Evans, who was the main support for his widowed mother. Early Saturday evening, employees of No.3 and No.4 Erecting Shops assembled at the Old Vaults in High Street, where gifts of silver-mounted pipes, pouches of tobacco and a purse of money were presented to Sappers J. Brookes, H. Hubbard and W. Godkin. Sapper E. Broach, employed in the Loco Stores Office, and the only member of staff of the General Offices currently called up, received his gifts on Saturday afternoon from fellow clerks. He too received a pipe and tobacco pouch, as well as a pen-knife.

At 8.30pm on the Saturday night, a boisterous party was held for the departing men at the Royal Hotel. About 120 Railway Volunteers assembled as guests of the Corps. Among the attending officers and dignitaries were Mr H. D. Earl (Crewe Works manager), Mr K. Macrae, Captains Tandy, Warneford, Jackson, Beaumont and Stones, Lieutenants Bowes, Nash, Collins, Tweedy, Godson, Davenport and Brierley, Sgt. Major Williams, Quarter Master Sgt. Gibson, Bandmaster Coen, Bugle Major Brennan, Sergeants Robbe and Jones and Royal Engineers Company Sgt. Majors Nield, Stapeley, Eastwood, Osborne, Billington and Fleet. The only officers absent were Colonel Cotton-Jodrell and Adjutant Major Fullerton, who were busy preparing for the departure. An excellent meal was served and a unique feature of the night was that the officers acted as waiters. At the conclusion of dinner, the chair was occupied by the second in command of the Corps, Lieutenant Colonel Kennedy. After the men had sung *Rule Britannia* for the umpteenth time, Sergeant Swinwood, one of the men bound for South Africa, became so stirred with enthusiasm, he mounted his chair and delivered an impromptu speech, which was wound up with:

"Well lads, wait till we get there, we'll show them what we are made of!"

This received round after round of applause. Lieutenant Colonel Kennedy then arose to propose a toast to the health of the Queen, whose cause he said, the Reservists of the Crewe Corps were going to South Africa to defend. The toast was drunk and the National Anthem sung with much enthusiasm, accompanied by Mr W. Galley on piano. Kennedy then delivered a rousing speech and commented that the Reservists, apart from a few men from the Tower Hamlets Engineer Battalion belonging to the Great Northern Railway, had the unique honour of being the only Volunteers presently proceeding to serve Queen and country. A telegram was then read out which had been received from the 1st Bucks Volunteers at Wolverton. It read:

'The officers and non-commissioned officers of the Wolverton Volunteers, dining together tonight, congratulate their Crewe comrades selected for active service and heartily wish them goodbye and good luck.'

This was met by a loud and prolonged cheer. A comic verse by Lieutenant Bowes then caused endless amusement and the night drew to a close with much handshaking between men and officers. As the party left for home, a group of well-wishers cheered them all the way down Mill Street, with cries of *"Bravo the Engineers"* and *"Success to the Reserves."*

Meanwhile on the same day, a sea of people turned out at Southampton Docks to bid farewell to General Sir Redvers Buller and his Army Corps of 47,000, bound for South Africa. Buller sailed on the *Dunottar Castle*, with his men aboard a fleet of civilian liners, chartered by the Admiralty. It was the biggest expeditionary force to leave Britain for over a century.

By early Monday morning on October 16, the townsfolk of Crewe started final preparations for the day that would live long in the memories of the many thousands who attended. A great display of bunting and Union flags coloured the streets and the sun broke through the early morning clouds as the bells at Christ Church rang out. By 8.00am the crowds streamed from the railway station and an hour later the approaches to the Market Square were packed, with many arriving on bicycle. As the minutes ticked by, even the side streets on the route to the station were overflowing and cabs and traps had to take a circular route while proceeding to and from the station. Every public building and business establishment displayed the Union flag and in High Street and Mill Street, there were many streamers of flags linking the rooftops. The men going to war started to assemble around 9.30am, as mayhem ensued in the nearby streets, choked with a throng of people from all over the area (who had poured into the town by road and rail from Chester, Northwich, Winsford, Middlewich, Congleton, Sandbach and Nantwich, as well as a large number from the Pottery towns) eager for a glimpse of the 'Crewe Works Army.' The balconies over the Birmingham Bank, the Post Office and the shops at the far end of the Square were converted into temporary grandstands. Points of vantage were soon all taken as people clambered on top of the Post Office roof, neighbouring shops, walls, lamp posts, chimney stacks and other less stable viewing areas. The windows of the houses in Market Terrace presented a sea of faces as did those of the Manchester & Liverpool Bank. Young boys perched themselves in tree branches and on street lamp handles. The police present experienced great difficulty in forming a square sufficient for the men to be drawn up for inspection, but with the help of around 100 Railway Volunteers (not going to war) the task was soon completed. The Mayor John Jones witnessed the incredible scenes from the balcony above the

Post Office entrance, with the crowd estimated at around 30,000 in the Market Square and immediate area, with a further 45,000 lining the route to the station. After family exchanges, the men fell in at the sound of the bugle, promptly sounded at 10.30am, assembling in two separate detachments - the 8th and 10th Railway Companies (plus a few members of the 31st and 45th Fortress Companies). Around 400 other members of the Railway Volunteers had turned out in their walking out dress and assisted the police in controlling the vast crowd. Travelling warrants were handed out to the departing men, resplendent in their scarlet coats, field caps and red-striped trousers. Francis William Webb, Chief Mechanical Engineer of the LNWR, shook hands with every man with the words *"Good luck and God speed"* and every handshake was greeted by a cheer from the crowd. Webb also promised every man going to war that their jobs were safe and would be there when they returned. At 10.35am the men were photographed and ten minutes later were inspected by Colonel Cotton-Jodrell. Two bands were present to help whip up the fervour of the crowd, not that they needed any further encouragement. The Regimental Band, under the direction of Mr W. Coen and the Carriage Works Band under Mr J. Delves, played several patriotic tunes. After all formalities had been carried out, the crowd hushed as Mayor Jones addressed the men:

> *"Colonel Cotton-Jodrell, officers, non-commissioned officers, the men of the 2nd Cheshire Railway Engineers, this magnificent demonstration we witness today, the like of which has never been seen in the town of Crewe before, creates in some of us a degree of wonder and surprise. We may have been a little pessimistic in the past in regard to the loyalty of the townspeople, but after the enthusiastic display of today, surely we can never have any misgivings for the people of Crewe (Cheers). To all of you, our fellow townsmen and loyal subjects and soldiers of our Queen (Cheers), who, in answer to the call of duty, are leaving your homes today to join with other of your comrades of Great Britain and the Colonies to go out to South Africa to help to secure for our people there, the just rights and privileges to which they are entitled (Cheers) and also to help defend the fair name and honour of our beloved country (Renewed Cheers). On behalf of the town I wish you God speed (Prolonged cheering). Everyone must admit the British government has been patient in this matter (Here Here). But there is a time when patience ceases to be a virtue (Applause) and that time has now arrived (Here Here). The Boers have thrown out the challenge, and have madly unsheathed their swords and shall we stand still and see our people oppressed and our nation insulted and not offer to them a helping hand? (Cries of No). With the Boers must lie the responsibility whatever may be the ultimate result of the war (Loud Applause). This is a day*

unique in the history of our town and we are proud to know that you are amongst the first of the Volunteer Reserves that England has called out. So you are not only bringing credit to our town and the great railway company to which you are proud to belong, but it also redounds to the credit and honour of the commanders and officers of your Corps (Cheers). This is not a time to play with your emotions and feelings, but rather a time to help and encourage and cheer you. We feel confident that you will give a good and creditable account of yourselves whether in preparing the way for action or engaged in fierce conflict with the enemy (Loud Cheers). We rely on your bravery, we feel sure that you will quit yourselves as men, never forgetting the motto of your town, to some of you the town of your birth – 'Never Behind' (Renewed Cheers). We hope and pray that we may have the further honour in a very short time of welcoming you back again to the embrace of your friends, and that you may return with honour and receive the plaudits of your countrymen's 'Well Done' (Loud and Prolonged Cheering). And now again once more, I wish you God Speed and only a short time I trust it may be, before we see you all back again. So I say to you Goodbye! Goodbye!! (Great Cheering)."

At the conclusion of the Mayor's address, he called for three cheers for the departing men. A marvellous outburst of enthusiasm followed and for every cheer, hats, handkerchiefs and other items were tossed wildly into the air. Cheers were then afforded for Colonel Cotton-Jodrell, the other officers of the Corps, the LNWR Company and the Queen. The Regimental Band then played the National Anthem and at this point the majority of the male portion of the crowd removed their headwear as the Volunteers and their officers stood proudly to attention. The Mayor's speech was then followed by words from Colonel Cotton-Jodrell.

"I am taking leave of you today with the full and proud conviction in my heart – and I know it is shared with every one of your officers – that you will do your duty to the utmost of your ability in whatever position you may be placed (Cheers). I have watched the formation, growth, and progress of this Railway Reserve with very great interest and the last two or three years of its history have afforded me a great deal of satisfaction (Here Here). I want to tell you that I feel proud myself today, in having contributed even in a very small way to the sending out of such a fine and skilled body of men in the service of their country (Loud and prolonged Cheers). Let me offer you one word of advice. You are going to enter into the regular Army. You will find, even at Chatham, things strange and different to what you have been accustomed to here. But all will go well if you remember that the first duty of a soldier is obedience and the second, the control of his own temper (Here Here). In the distant land to which you are going, I know you will often think of this old Corps. We are parting with you this morning with the full conviction that you will do everything you can to keep up

the reputation of your old Corps and of the town and Borough of Crewe to which his Worship the Mayor has just alluded, and also that you will never forget to maintain all that is noblest and best traditions when fighting under the glorious flag under which we are so proud to serve (Loud Cheers). I only wish I was going with you myself (Ringing Cheers). I wish that the whole Corps was going out and I believe in expressing that wish, I am only expressing one which is shared by every officer and man whom you are leaving behind today. I do not believe there is one of us but what envies you in the position that you now occupy. Goodbye men, good luck, a safe return and God bless you all (Hearty Cheers)."

During the proceedings the crowd was entertained by the Regimental Band. Just before the march away from the Market Square, Colonel Cotton-Jodrell handed over command to Captain Tandy who immediately called the men to attention. Then to an enormous cheer, the column finally began their trek to the railway station. At the head were approximately 100 of the Corps, plus a large force of policemen, whose specific aim was to clear a path for the departing troops. Then came the Carriage Works Band followed by Bugle Major Brennan, the Bugle Band and the Regimental Band under the direction of Bandmaster Coen. Preceding them were the officers of the Corps with the rear brought up by the Band of the Gordon Boys Brigade, who had been performing all week at the Lyceum Theatre. As the men took their first steps the Regimental Band struck the opening chords of *The Girl I Left Behind Me,* an air associated with the departure of troops for active service. This sparked scenes of wild celebration in Coppenhall Terrace. The procession moved towards High Street, but there were doubts whether they could progress, such was the density of the crowd. But somehow the men, despite halting several times, slowly forced their way through to the bottom of the street and eventually under Mill Street bridge. The crowd here, if possible, was even greater and again every vantage point had been utilised, including a high hoarding near to the railway bridge which had been taken over by a group of young boys. At this stage, the Carriage Works Band took over musical duties and commenced to play *The British Grenadiers.* At the station top mayhem ensued. A large force of policemen and railway officials did their best to keep back the crowd intent on witnessing the departure of the special train taking the men to Victoria. The procession successfully made it through the station doors but suddenly a cry of "*Rush the fort*" saw a number press forward, and with the sliding door unable to take the strain, it was forced off its runners. The crowd then rushed down the slopes and steps leading to the platform and their excitement reached a crescendo when the special train drew up to the departure platform. Cheer after cheer followed as the men took to their compartments, with many in attendance reduced to tears. The Mayor managed to get onto the platform and shook hands with men hanging out of carriage windows. Then punctually at 11.30am the guard's whistle blew and the train slowly steamed away from the platform. The bands struck up with *Auld Lang Syne* but this was drowned out by deafening cheers. No sooner had the train cleared the platform, dozens of the attending Railway Volunteers rushed to cross the line, followed by hundreds of civilians, who mounted the down platform in order to see the departing loco pass out of view up the London line. *"Bravo the Engineers"* they shouted as the train slowly disappeared from sight. With this the station soon emptied, and the two bands, followed by 200-300 members of the Railway Volunteers, marched back to the Market Square to the tunes of *Men of Harlech* and *Soldiers of the Queen.*

The excitement of the day continued until late in the evening and the event passed off without a single injury, although several women and children fainted during the day. The men of Crewe Works were slow to take up their posts in the afternoon and when the buzzer sounded at 2.00pm, many did not bother to return at all. In one shop only 17 out of 700 turned up and in the Moulding Shop only one returned from a total workforce of 400. This absenteeism was not only in Crewe factories. In Nantwich, many had travelled to witness the send off and several clothing firms in the town closed for the morning. In the afternoon however, one establishment reported up to 500 hands had failed to show for the afternoon shift.

By now, the special train was well on its way to Chatham and along the way, the men were still afforded cheers and applause. A large crowd had gathered at Stafford and the fog signals placed on the track just before the station, signalled the arrival of the loco, which slowed considerably so the crowd could show their appreciation. At Rugby the train stopped for five minutes for light refreshments and again the crowd was large. Here there were touching scenes of reunions of apprentices and 'ex-Crewe-ites' who had once worked side by side in the Works. The band of the Rugby Steam Sheds was also present. Yet another sizeable crowd was waiting at Willesden Junction and here to greet the men and accompany them to Victoria Station was Lieutenant Colonel Harrison, General Manager of the LNWR, who was dressed in full uniform.

When the train finally arrived at Victoria the men were allowed thirty-five minutes of 'free time' before the train left for Chatham at 4.22pm. Arriving at 5.30pm, the men were welcomed by the Colonel and Captain of the Royal Engineers and Adjutant Weekes. Headed by a fife and drum band, the body of men marched through the Chatham streets to their barracks. Again a crowd of well-wishers had lined the route. After entering the barracks square, the Crewe Engineers were given a tremendous welcome from their colleagues of the regular force, before they were handed over by Captain Tandy and Lieutenant Bowes. After formalities, the men enjoyed a meal, then fell in for an early night. On the Tuesday morning they received their new equipment, which included two khaki uniforms, puttees, white helmet, two red frock coats, one pair of cloth trousers, two pairs of boots, one pair of slippers, belts, sea kit and a quantity of bandages. Next day they proceeded to Gravesend for two days of musketry instruction. This consisted of 7 rounds at 200 yards standing and then kneeling, followed by 7 rounds at 500 yards kneeling and lying down. Four points were scored for a bullseye, 3 points for an inner and 2 for an outer. The rifles used in the exercise were the Lee Enfield pattern, the latest model served to the troops. The most notable scores among the new contingent were from Sapper W. Spilsbury 83pts, Sapper R. Calderbank 83pts, Sapper H. W. Butt 72pts and Sapper Alfred Coleman 71pts. At the conclusion of the day's shooting, 7 rounds were fired at 500 yards in volleys and 7 rounds of independent fire to acquaint the men with the new magazine rifle. The permanent staff at the rifle range were hugely impressed by the shooting skills of the Crewe men. According to a letter sent home by old campaigner Sapper Coleman of the 10th Railway Company, those who scored over 70pts were entitled to a marksmen's badge - a decoration that warranted a penny per day extra payment. On Friday, October 20, the Crewe Engineers, now settled to life at Brompton Barracks, received a surprise visitor when Colonel Cotton-Jodrell turned up to check on the morale of his men.

At this stage, it was reported in *The Crewe Guardian* that a total of 129 men had in fact been called up. Of these one had failed his medical at Crewe and two at Chatham (this total of 126 men in the first draft is substantiated by an interview in *The Railway Magazine*, February 1900 by Francis William Webb). Several men had married before the October 16 send off and one member - Sapper Phillips - married at St. Mary's Roman Catholic Church on Tuesday, October 17, at 8.00am, then left on the noon train for Chatham.

Back in Crewe there was disappointment for the 58 men of the Railway Reserve eagerly awaiting their papers, when the War Office reported that there would be no more demands on the Corps for the time being. Men in the Army Reserve in the town however, were still receiving the call to arms. One such man was Private George Tonks of the Steel Works Forge, who was attached to the 23rd Battalion, Royal Welsh Fusiliers, and 27 others also received papers to proceed to their respective units.

On Saturday, October 21, the men of the 8th and 10th Railway Companies and 31st Fortress Company, plus other detachments of the Royal Engineers, left Chatham for Southampton, for the long voyage to South Africa. Despite the dense fog, thousands lined the route to the station to cheer them on their way. Accompanying them were the brass bands of the Corps and the band of the 2nd Lancashire Fusiliers. Among the crowd to see them off were Colonel Cotton-Jodrell and Major Fullerton and a number of their Crewe Engineer comrades. The 10th Company set sail on the same day (5.00pm), with the 8th and 31st starting their journey the following morning (9.00am).

Back home a fund for the families of men away at war, instigated by the Mayor John Jones, gathered pace and on Thursday, October 26, a meeting in the Mechanics Institute was well attended. The idea of the fund was for the families to receive a weekly allowance to augment the sum received from the War Office. All churches, workplaces and public institutions were urged to take up a fund box and many in the town obliged. The LNWR donated £100, the Earl of Crewe £25, F. W. Webb promised £1 a week until Christmas, and the Mayor donated £10, as did Councillors C. H. Pedley, A. G. Hill and Dr. Wilson. Many others in the audience promised weekly subscriptions ranging from a few pence to a few pounds. On the following Saturday a fund raising concert was held at The Lyceum Theatre by 'The Sign of the Cross' Company who performed a matinee performance of *A Winter's Tale*. Unfortunately, despite a reasonable attendance, the counter-attraction of an F.A. Cup 3rd Qualifying Round tie between Crewe and Wigan County prevented the theatre from being sold out, but £8 1s was still raised. At night the Railway Volunteers held their annual dinner at the Royal Hotel. Around 100 N.C.O.'s attended, including several retired veterans of the Corps. Among the many speeches on the night was a rousing one by Quarter Master Sergeant George Riddle Gibson.

Those in the town predicting an easy victory in the war would have hopes dashed somewhat when British casualty figures started to appear in local newspapers, especially after the hard fought victories at Talana Hill and Elandslaagte, fought during the opening engagements. The figures made grim reading and a reality check for those hoping to see loved ones home for Christmas.

Members of the Railway Volunteers left at home and eager to be part of the war honed their shooting skills in a match with the Wolverton Volunteers at Holmes Chapel, winning the contest by 947-939. Among the high scorers on the Crewe side were Sergeant Johnson, Musician T. Doig and Sergeant Turner. After the match, dinner was enjoyed by both sides in the Swan Hotel in Holmes Chapel.

Further to the fund raising activities in the town, it was brought to the attention of the committee that in the event of death in service, the fund would struggle to maintain payment to dependants of the fallen. At least 64 of the 126 members of the Railway Reserve so far called to arms were married, along with 16 from the Army Reserve. By early November, QMS Gibson, secretary of the fund, reported the total amount raised was around £300, with £175 promised. Among the latest subscribers were the Crewe Co-operative Society who donated £23 12s 2d and Henry Tollemache M.P. who pledged £10. Weekly penny collections were started in the local railway workshops and offices, and in the first week £28 was collected.

Letters began to be received in town from men on the journey to South Africa. Sapper W. H. Evans, of the 10th Railway Company, wrote from their ship (S.S. *Goorkha*) to his comrade at home, Company Sergeant Major Stapeley.

> *'We left Southampton on Saturday (21st) at 5.00pm and we have had a very pleasant sail. The sea has been very calm all the way. It was grand going through the Bay of Biscay and we have stood the voyage very well. I have not been sea-sick yet. We have physical drills on deck every day. It would do you good to see us with our sea-clothes on. We have a sea-cap, a blue jersey and our trousers rolled up to our knees. We look more like sailors than soldiers. We had a grand view of the coast of Portugal and Spain and several lighthouses on our sail since we left England. It is quite a treat. I don't care how soon we land in Africa and get our work done. The sooner we finish "Old Kruger" the better.'*

Sapper Alfred Joseph Coleman also of the 10th Railway Company wrote:

> *'....they have provided us with good food including porridge, fish, meat and vegetables, with coffee for breakfast and tea for tea-time.'*

On November 1, activity at Crewe Station saw troop trains heading for Liverpool en-route to South Africa. Among them were four trains carrying men, horses and equipment of the Army Service Corps.

Next day news reached Crewe that British forces had suffered reversals at the hands of the Boers. On October 30 (later christened

'Mournful Monday'), a British force under Lieutenant General Sir George White was badly mauled during the Battle of Ladysmith and on the same day, a British column commanded by Lieutenant Colonel Carleton surrendered at Nicholson's Nek, which resulted in the siege of Ladysmith.

Men of the 8th Railway Company also penned a few lines home while aboard S.S. *Malta*. Sapper J. Swinwood wrote to QMS Gibson about the early part of the voyage.

> 'I am very pleased to tell you that up to now we are having a splendid voyage. The water is more like a large lake than an ocean. We sighted Cape Finisterre last night and we passed Cape St. Vincent this morning (Friday) at 7.30. We expect to arrive at Gibraltar on Saturday. Our lads are enjoying it grand and all seem in high spirits going out, excepting young Thompson who went into the hospital this morning with sea-sickness. We pick up the Guards at Gibraltar and put down the Camerons. There are about 1,600 on board, very nearly all Reserve men.'

Twenty-year-old Crewe Works fitter, No.2558 Sapper Arthur Henry Foy, who joined the Reserve on February 28, 1899, wrote a series of letters to his parents, John and Selina (nee Wainwright) of 10, Beech Street, Crewe (originally of 20, St. Paul's Street, Crewe), throughout the early period of the war. He was also in the 8th Railway Company and his first letter was written while still on home shores at Chatham.

> <u>October 21, 1899</u> - 'Dear Mother and Father, Just a line to let you know I am still quite well and getting ready for parade in the morning at 7.40. Leave Waterloo (London) 12.40 for Southampton, sail tomorrow (Sunday) 9.00am.'

> <u>October 28, 1899, S.S. Malta</u> - 'Arrived at Gibraltar last night, Friday midnight, quite well. Give my respects to Charlie Fletcher and friends. P.S. Send us about 6 Beecham pills and let us know how they are all getting on at Crewe.'

> <u>October 31, 1899, Las Palmas, Canary Islands</u> - 'Dear Mother and Father, I write these few lines hoping they find you all quite well and hoping you had a good Bonfire. Tell Jack to set some rip raps off for me.....got some coal on the ship at Las Palmas at a coaling station....the last place we stopped at (Gibraltar) was a beautiful place especially at night when the town was all lit up with lights of different colours. I thought it a sight of a lifetime and so did the rest who had never seen it. We stayed there all Saturday and a lot of little boats came up to the side of the ship selling fruit, tobacco etc. You could get a basket of figs (about 7 or 8 lbs in it) for 6d, grapes large bunches for 2d and 3d, apples 1½d, oranges ½d, cigars less than ½d each, 25 for 1s and tobacco about 2d per oz.

We set sail at night once more....the farther we got out to sea, the hotter the climate is. In fact we are going to parade in bare feet tomorrow on deck and the officers of the ship are commencing to wear white slops and overalls for trousers. We shall pass the equator shortly.'

<u>November 10, 1899</u> - *'Have had a little sea-sickness which is only to be expected. They allow us flour and raisins on Wednesdays and Sundays for a pudding which we have to make ourselves. They then cook it for us. We have rice pudding on Saturday and one half holiday to see the football match as usual. That reminds me that the Alex was playing Stockport yesterday, November 11, ask Jack how they went on as we cannot get a Sentinel now very well. We have a short church parade every Sunday morning. We generally sing "Onward Christian Soldiers" and a few other hymns that are well known out of the hymn books that they lend us.'*

<u>November 13, 1899</u> - *'We are encountering what we call the "Eastern Gales." The wind is very rough and the ship gets tossed about like a bit of cork, the waves even dashing through the port holes, which are small windows in the side of the ship to let the light and fresh air in down below. The gales get worse the nearer we get to Cape Town. According to what I hear, we have two days sail yet before we land, having up till now been on the water 22 days and the most we have been without seeing land is 14 days so far. We get up at 5.45 in the morning, take our beds in at 6.00 and get a wash then breakfast. Parade at 10.00 for inspection, 11.00 for physical drill, dinner at 12.00, parade at 3.00 for drill again, tea at 4.00, parade for beds at 5.00 and go to bed at 9.00, lights out at 9.15. All are going on very well from Crewe under the circumstances, except one fellow with a touch of fever (in the hospital).'*

<u>Wednesday, November 15, 1899</u> - *'We are nearing Cape Town. Expect to land tomorrow, Thursday 16th November about dinnertime. A fellow had just commenced to shave when a big wave came crashing through the port-hole and fairly drenched us and my sea-cap got washed from one end of the table to the other.'*

<u>Thursday, November 16, 1899</u> - *'We have just arrived here at Cape Town about 4.00am this Thursday morning, November 16. Quite safe and well, we are all happy and busy preparing to land and it will be a treat to be on land again. I wish you a Merry Christmas and a Happy New Year when it comes.'*

In a diary sent to a comrade, Sapper W. Cunningham of the 10th Railway Company wrote several pages about the voyage to South Africa. He mentioned that the men were not allowed alcohol while on the troopship, although this was not so for the officers. Concert parties proved to be an important way of passing the time, and one such party on November 6 (a grand smoking concert) saw the Crewe brothers A. and F. Ellis and G. and S. Harvey among the artistes. An amusing line in the concert programme asked the audience to refrain from throwing rotten eggs during the performances! Sapper Cunningham also reported on the excellent food they were receiving while on board. For breakfast the troops received coffee, bread and herrings or bloaters, or Irish stew and porridge. Dinner consisted of beef, mutton or pork with two potatoes per man and supper was a cup of tea, with bread and butter or marmalade. Comradeship was also mentioned in the diary. All the Crewe men on board seemed to get on well, although fights had broken out between members of the Guards. Several items of equipment had gone missing or had been stolen and a number of the Crewe men had been victims, including Cunningham himself, who lost a pair of boots, which had to be replaced at his own expense.

Not all Crewe men currently on their way, or in South Africa were of military stock. One such person was Mr G. Waine, son of the late Mr E. Waine of Henry Street, Crewe, who had been chosen for his experience and good judgement, to drive an armoured train from Mafeking to Dundee - a journey described in *The Crewe Guardian* as '*a perilous journey.*' Sworn in as a special constable, Waine undertook the trip with his engine protected by steel plates, pulling four trucks fitted with the latest machine guns.

By November 13, quite a number of First Class Reservists from Crewe had received warrants from their respective regimental headquarters, summoning them to active service. The majority of the men called up were from Crewe Works and it was estimated that the total called from the town was now around 200.

When in South Africa, many of the Railway Reserve would, at some time, man the armoured trains travelling across the country, in often isolated areas. On November 15 (the same day as the S.S. *Goorkha* arrived at Cape Town), the vulnerability of this mode of transport was highlighted when the Boers derailed one between Frere and Chieveley. Among the 58 British prisoners taken in the incident was *The Morning Post* war correspondent (and future British Prime Minister) Winston Churchill.

Upon arrival on South African soil, the primary role for the Crewe Engineers would be line maintenance, with them stationed at two different locations. The 8th Railway Company and 31st Fortress Company would be under Captain W. R. Stewart, who was in charge of the Western Section at

De Aar. The rest of the Crewe men (10th Railway Company) would find themselves at Naauwpoort Juntion (Midland Section) under Captain J. H. Twiss, along with the 20th and 42nd Fortress Companies. Both sections would be augmented by the newly formed Railway Pioneer Regiment.

Sapper Arthur Henry Foy wrote his usual letters home a few days after landing on foreign soil. The first was written at De Aar railway station:

November 18, 1899 - *'Left Cape Town, Thursday night, November 16, by train bound for a place called Orange River, a distance of about 660 miles from Cape Town. I thought they would have packed us in like herrings but I find myself in a first class saloon with plenty of ease and comfort….we got out for lunch at a small station. Of course they would call it a large one out here, there being a coffee bar on the station, coffee 3d a cup and sandwiches. Tell Jack no bun and coffee for a penny out here. Things are filthy dear out here, a lemonade is 6d, but I shall not go short while I have money. I weighed myself at the station and was surprised to find I was about 7lb heavier than I was at Crewe and only thin (khaki) clothes on. The scenery we have seen is beautiful. Anyone would give a fortune almost to come out here, it is quite a treat…..I may say we (Royal) Engineers will be alright, all the other soldiers envy us and class us as gentlemen soldiers of the British Army. We have arrived at a place called De Aar, quite safe. We change here for our destination.'*

November 20, 1899, Orange River - *'Expecting to advance very shortly, we follow the troops up with the railway. As we came through one of the stations on our way here, we heard a tale of a Boer being shot in the act of cutting wires and one of the principal British station masters was caught just about to send a telegram to the Boers with information. They shot him also. Was rather hot yesterday (Sunday). We worked till dinner time. About 3pm they marched us down to the river to bathe and we did enjoy it. We have not received any letters from Crewe and are eager for one. I believe the 10th Company have gone on to Natal, a part of the Crewe lot are with them you know. At several stations we stopped at, people would give almost anything for a badge off our coats. One fellow happened to have the engines off his old tunic and a lady gave him 1lb of butter and 1lb of cheese for one and was very pleased with it. Tell Jack to send me a paper, they would think a lot of a Sentinel out here. Them South Wales Lancers are here from Australia. So have to close now, weather clearing up now. Remember me to Dick Chesters and others, tell them I am quite well.'*

On November 23, the men of the 8th Railway Company and 31st Fortress Company were involved in their first action when caught up in engagements at Belmont, and two days later at Graspan. They were part of a Royal Engineers force in Lord Methuen's column which included the 7th and 11th Field Companies and a Telegraph Section.

The Battles of Belmont and Graspan
November 23 & 25

The First Division, under the command of Lieutenant General Lord Methuen, were faced with the task of forcing their way north, following the railway lines, to relieve the besieged town of Kimberley. The base for his flying column had been established at De Aar, where thousands of tons of food and supplies had been accumulated in readiness of his advance. In the early hours of November 21, the column began its march. It consisted of a Naval Brigade, the Guards Brigade, the 9th Brigade, the 9th Lancers and two batteries of artillery (18th and 75th) - a force totalling around 8,500 men. When they arrived at Belmont Station, the Boers (around 2,000) were waiting for them on the range of Belmont Kopje. The Guards and the 9th Brigade launched an attack under heavy fire from the open ground up towards the Boers positioned on the hills, entrenched on the crest. When faced with the bayonet, the Boers fled and fell back to the next station on the line - Graspan. While the column advanced, the Royal Engineers, supported by an armoured train, followed closely behind, repairing the line. On November 24, this train was attacked, with three Sappers suffering wounds.

At Graspan on November 25, the fighting was of a similar pattern with the Boers again occupying the higher ground. This time the Naval Brigade and the 9th Brigade attacked the Boers' hilltop positions and again, the Boers fled. The British suffered around 300 casualties at Belmont (53 officers and men killed) and 250 at Graspan, with Boer casualty figures reported as 'light.' This however, opened the route for Methuen to reach the Modder River and be within striking range of Kimberley.

Letters appeared in the local newspapers from Crewe men involved in the battles, describing their thrilling but dangerous involvement. In many of these, sizes of the clashing forces and casualty figures were vastly exaggerated, and involvement in the action also varied. Sapper G. H. Wearne of the 8th Railway Company wrote to his mother on November 25:

> 'We got to Orange River last Monday and encamped there for two days and then proceeded up the country. We have had a great battle at Belmont. There were about 4,000 Boers and 3,000 of the English. We were about one mile off the battle which was a terrible slaughter. All the Boers were at the top of a hill and our men at the bottom. The Guards charged them with fixed bayonets to get them off the rocks....Afterwards there was an awful sight as they brought in

> the killed and wounded. Some were shot through the head and others through the legs and arms. It was something terrible......They seem to be old men who are fighting (for the Boers). The Boers hoisted the white flag as a signal to surrender and after our troops had ceased firing, the Boers started firing again. There were about 260 killed and wounded on our side but we cannot tell how many Boers were killed. We had to lay down under cover all the while, so I can say that I have seen action for the very first time in my life. We were that hungry while the battle lasted that we caught a goat, killed it and ate it.'

Corporal S. Wolfe, also of the 8th Railway Company, wrote to a comrade about his involvement in the action at Belmont and Graspan.

> 'During the battle we got out and lay each side of the train in skirmishing order.....Yesterday we had another fierce engagement at Graspan. The naval gunners lost very heavily; not many of them escaped being wounded. The armoured train had many narrow escapes of being hit. Bill Burns and five or six more Crewe men are on it.....Many shells flew directly over our heads and some of the Crewe lads were told to take ammunition to the naval gunners, several having narrow escapes, but fortunately most of the shells did not burst.'

Sapper Foy continued to inform everybody at home of the goings-on in the war zone. Here he writes on Sunday, November 26, from Graspan, about the action at Belmont.

> 'I take the opportunity of writing a few more lines to you (railway lines I mean of course) as we are never far from them.....Our troops won a grand victory on Thursday, there was supposed to be about 4,000 Boers killed. The Boers lifted some of the rails, so that we should have to stop and repair it and the wires were cut all over the place.....We are just beginning to get used to the weather out here which is very hot in the day and very cold at night. We Engineers are the same as the song goes "Hiding In The Ammunition Van" only we are in the railway carriages all the while the other troops are marching. We simply keep the lines in good order as we travel up the country and we sleep in the railway carriages at night. The other day some of the men caught three goats, and as we happened to have a butcher with us, they soon had them killed and cooked.....Ike Attwood is out here with the Engineers and Charlie Brocklehurst (Alf Crooks' old mate). I think we are going on to Kimberley as soon as possible. Don't think this war will last much longer now, they the Boers keep putting the white flag up now for our troops to stop firing all the while.....I conclude with sending my best love to you all and wishing you all a Merry Christmas. I remain your affectionate son, Arthur Henry.'

Sapper James Brookes of the 31st Fortress Company wrote from Honey Nest Kloof on November 27, to his comrade at home, Corporal Brereton.

> *'We arrived at Orange River on November 14 after 48 hours ride in the train. We were joined there by the 8th Company of Royal Engineers (Swinwood's lot) and after staying 4 days, we proceeded to Belmont. We were ordered out of the train as there was a fierce battle raging…..After the battle, they brought in the dead and wounded of the British troops and Boers alike. I helped lift a great many of the killed and wounded out of the ambulance wagon. One fellow had half his head blown clean away and another was shot in the face…..We have had a very narrow escape. We were out repairing the line with the armoured train and luckily for us a mounted trooper who was out skirmishing rode up and told us there were about 3,000 Boers up the line. The minute they saw us they opened fire on us and we had to retreat smartly.'*

Three days after the action at Graspan, the men of the 8th and 31st Companies were again heavily involved, when Lord Methuen's column clashed with a larger Boer force at Modder River.

The Battle of Modder River
November 28, 1899

The Boers decided to make their next stand where the Modder and Riet rivers met, utilising the steeped riverbanks as natural defences. Methuen and his column, continuing up the railway line to Kimberley, approached the Boer position, unaware that the enemy were there in force (around 3,500 men), with the majority hidden from view in their entrenched positions. Without warning the Boers opened fire, sending the British troops diving for what cover they could find on the sparse plain. Here the main part of the column lay, pinned down for hours under a baking sun. Anyone who moved or rose from the ground (and some did, searching for water) were shot by Boer marksmen. However, the British artillery continued to pour fire into the enemy lines and a collapse of the Boer right flank saw stalemate ensue as darkness fell. When dawn broke, the Boers had fled their positions, leaving Methuen in control of the battlefield and the Modder River crossing points. Again British losses were heavier with 75 killed and 413 wounded. Boer casualties were estimated between 80-150 killed and wounded.

A few days later Sapper J. Brookes wrote home to Crewe regarding his involvement in the battle.

> 'It was a terrible affair, we were right in among the fire line, both the 8th and 31st Companies. We started in the rear of the line, but were soon in amongst it…..Shells and bullets were flying all around us and we had to go through a river which took us up to our waists…..Our troops lost heavily but only one engineer was wounded – Corporal Wilkinson. He dropped just by me but I hear he is only slightly wounded.'

Sapper Brocklehurst of the 31st Fortress Company wrote to his parents (of Rose Villas, Hungerford Road, Crewe) on December 2, 1899 from Modder River about life in South Africa and action at Graspan.

> 'I am starting this letter this morning as I am on the sick list with an injured eye. I hurt it while catching a goat for supper. I had just collared her when my foot slipped on a stone and I fell with my eye on the goat's horn…..We finished up at Orange River having made two trestles for the bridge at Modder River which is blown up. We then entrained in the construction train which is an ordinary pass train with materials attached for repairing the Permanent Way where the Boers have pulled it up. It is not much work as the Boers simply knock off the nuts from the fish plate bolts and draw the rails, sleepers and all complete to the sides of the line…..Our train is preceded by the armoured train and followed by other luggage and provision trains…..At Graspan I was with the Naval Brigade. You see our company helped them to get their big guns out of the wagons then pulled them with ropes into action. A party of us, in fact the section to which I belong, took a trolley of ammunition up to the guns. I stayed with the guns and worked like a Trojan carrying shot and shell from the line to the guns and also fusing shrapnel shells. I had many narrow escapes but was not hit. One chap with me was shot in the foot and has since had it amputated. Another near me was shot in the arm.'

After the battle, Sapper Brocklehurst, bivouacking near a cottage, came across a dead Boer, who had been shot through the head.

> 'The dead Boer that we found in the yard was becoming a nuisance so I dug a grave and having bound his head in a waistcoat, buried him…..We expect this will be the last battle before Kimberley. I heard a rumour that the 10th Company with S & A Harvey and E. Broach came up this way today.'

Sapper J. Evans, of the 8th Railway Company, described events during the Battle of Modder River and life in general, when writing to his brother, who resided in Market Square, Crewe.

> 'They started firing at 6am on Tuesday morning and were at it until dark. One poor fellow belonging to the Coldstream Guards, which came on the S.S. Malta

with us was standing close against the line reading a letter which he got from his wife, when a bullet struck him in the head and he fell dead, the letter in his hand…..I have seen all three battles so far and there are scores of dead horses all over the place and they don't half smell with the hot sun. It was lucky I got 6d worth of camphor and a bottle of chlorodyne before we left Chatham, for they are both good things for keeping the fever away…..Prisoners keep getting captured daily and they say it won't last much longer, for they get the worst of everything and they are getting tired of it. They have found us plenty of work, for since we left Orange River, we had to repair every bridge that the line goes over as they have tried to blow them up and yards of the line they have broken up and dragged away in the fields…..After the battle I was on guard all night and the next day over the water tanks, so you can tell how scarce water is here. Plenty of our soldiers sneak up to you in the night and will offer 2, 3 and 5s for a small tin full. One night a man offered the guard 8s 6d – all the money he had – for a drink of water and this guard took the money off him and gave him a drink. I gave them all a little drop and told them to sneak off again for they are strict on water…..They have dragged all the horses that have been killed in a heap and they number 95. I have been out twice for a row on the river; we are enjoying it grand.'

Sapper J. Swinwood of the 8th Railway Company was in the thick of the action during the Battle of Modder River. He describes briefly their involvement when writing to QMS Gibson:

'We were in skirmishing order at 4.00am but they were not satisfied with that and ordered us to support the left flank which was over two miles away. We had to cross the river waist deep and we just got across when a volley came onto us and Wilkinson* of the Deviation got shot in the leg, but not serious…..The engagement lasted 14 hours and we were out all that time without food…..We have lived in a railway carriage since we left Cape Town with only a break for two days at Orange River. They say the Engineers do not fight, but don't they? We know better. Champion, Wolfe, Godkin and Williams are in our compartment. Our men are fairly well in health considering the weather.'

*Probably the first man from Crewe to be wounded in action during the war, ironically from friendly fire. Sapper A. Wilkinson of "D" Company (Railway Volunteers) and the 8th Railway Company, a carpenter at home in the Deviation shop, received a wound to the thigh. In a letter home to a friend in Crewe, written from a Winburg hospital on December 5, he wrote:

'I got wounded in the Battle of Modder River, but happily it is only a flesh wound right through the thigh. I was wounded in a simple way. We had waded through the river which was about knee deep and when we got to the other side it was the position the enemy had held but they retreated and our artillery, not knowing *us, accidentally fired on us. A shell burst in our midst and I was the unlucky man to catch it. The only one in our company.'*

After the action at Modder River, Methuen and his column rested after three engagements in five days, which gave an opportunity to bring up reinforcements and more field guns. This also allowed the Royal Engineers to start the repair of the dynamited railway bridge that spanned the river and begin construction of a temporary timber structure - no mean task - as the river could rise without warning by up to eight feet. By December 8, this was completed with a combination of timber and piles, which had been built beside the twisted and blasted steel girders of the original bridge. However, the lull in the fighting would be brief, and the men of the 8th and 31st Companies would soon see action again.

The Battle of Magersfontein
December 11, 1899

After the brief respite, the column now numbered 15,000 after the arrival of the rest of the Highland Division under the command of Major General Andrew Wauchope. On December 10, Methuen was ready to progress his march to Kimberley. In their way stood a Boer force of 8,500 men at Magersfontein, situated six miles north east of the Modder River. Here Methuen began an evening artillery bombardment of the hilltops, which only gave notice of an imminent attack. Among his artillery was the naval gun 'Joe Chamberlain,' a 4.7 inch calibre weapon, and the British answer to the Boers' 'Long Tom.' This bombardment however, achieved nothing, for unbeknown to the British, the Boers had entrenched at the foot of the hills to protect themselves from British artillery fire. Just after midnight on December 11, the Highland Brigade began their advance, completely unaware of what was about to happen. They advanced in close formation, approximately 3,500 strong, compressed into a column only 45 yards wide and 160 yards long. At 4.00am, just as Wauchope was about to deploy the men, and at a range of only 400 yards, the Boers opened fire. The Highlanders, caught out in the open, didn't stand a chance. Just like at Modder River, they were pinned to the ground, not daring to move for fear of being shot. At around 11.00am, the Gordons charged the Boer line, but they too were forced to ground. After nine hours exposed to constant rifle fire, the British troops attempted a retreat, but as they rose, sustained substantial losses. Methuen had taken a terrible beating and 205 British troops lay dead on the battlefield, including Major Wauchope, with 690 wounded, missing or taken prisoner. Boer casualties were estimated at no more than 250. The carnage in the British ranks was best expressed by one Black Watch soldier who stated that his comrades had been:

'Led into a butcher's shop and bloody well left there.'

Another expressed his feelings in a poem, later published in the main London newspapers:

'Such was the day for our regiment
Dread the revenge we will take.
Dearly we paid for the blunder -
A drawing-room General's mistake.
Why weren't we told of the trenches?
Why weren't we told of the wire?
Why were we marched up in column?
May Tommy Atkins enquire.'

The Battle of Magersfontein ended any hope of Methuen relieving Kimberley, and he retreated back to his Modder River base, where he remained until Lord Roberts arrived in February 1900. The defeat became part of 'black week' for the British Army, with further reversals at Stormberg Junction and Colenso - all in the space of five days, which spelled the end for General Sir Redvers Buller, Commander-in-Chief of British forces in South Africa. He was superseded by Roberts who was to be accompanied by Lord Kitchener as his Chief of Staff. Buller remained in South Africa in charge of the Natal force.

Sapper T. Brett of "E" Company of the Railway Volunteers (Sergeant in the Volunteers) and of the 8th Railway Company, wrote to his brother, E. J. Brett (who would later serve) on December 14, about the Magersfontein engagement and experiences in the war-zone. Again the number of enemy casualties were wildly exaggerated.

'I am still alive but I think I am lucky, for our lot have had a very hard time of it. The heat is very great and the water is awful bad to drink. I am sorry to tell you I am on the sick list myself today, but I hope to be at my work again tomorrow (Friday).....We have been fighting since Sunday afternoon. This makes the fourth battle. Last Monday was a dreadful battle (Magersfontein) - our worst yet. I believe it was worse than the one at Modder River and that was a sight I hope I shall never see again, for the river had a great many

dead Boers in it.....The water is very bad to drink – well you can guess what it is like when you find dead men in it. Of course the water is very scarce here. The doctor told me my illness was on account of the water. The last battle has been a hard struggle for us. There are over 700 of our chaps killed and wounded but our loss is nothing towards the Boers. We gave them beans in their trenches. Our shells dropped in splendid but the beggars would not come out. Their loss was over 2,000. Of course we cannot tell just the numbers, for they take their dead away as fast as ever they can, so that our side will not know how many they have lost. But those trenches caught it hot. Where this battle is, the Boers have the best of us because it is all hills and we can't get at them.....I am glad to tell you I am not on the armoured train now, nor I want to go on it again. It has had some narrow escapes. The Boers nearly had it the other day. They fired three shells at it, one shell breaking one of the engine wheels.....Remember me to all friends and shopmates and members of "E" Company; Ted Earp, Dale, Holland, Billington, Turner, Spencer, Ardern etc. The Highland Regiment buried their poor brave General on the 13th along with 50 or 60 by his side. If you would have only seen this regiment, the Black Watch, before the battle, and seen what was left after, well – it would have made your blood run cold. They went into a proper hell-hole. How those brave Scotties did suffer – something terrible. They were fairly cut up. I did not see them bury the brave fellows, but I believe it was awfully sad.'

First Class Reservists and regulars of the town figured in the action at Colenso, including Gunner E. B. Palmer of the Royal Field Artillery. He wrote about the battle in a letter sent to Mr W. H. Howells of Ramsbottom Street.

'Chieveley Camp, December 28, 1899. We had a big battle here (Colenso) on December 15. We were at it from one o'clock in the morning till four o'clock in the afternoon and we had to retire. It was disheartening. The Boers had a strong position and we could not see one of them, they were hid in trenches. Two batteries on the right of us were cut up and lost 10 guns and 10 ammunition wagons and nearly all their men and horses. I never saw sights in my life – it was awful......It is chronic here. We can't get a wash, only about twice a week – if you get any more you are lucky......I have had many a narrow shave of being hit the other day.....There are German and French with them in their thousands.....Some reckon if we drive the Boers from here – which is their strongest point – it will pretty well be all over.'

The Crewe men in the 10th Railway Company were also working hard and had seen action. A letter home, dated December 17, from Sapper Alfred Joseph Coleman at Naauwpoort, Cape Colony, read:

'We are with General French's force. We were at a small fort at Cape Town (Fort Knokki) for nearly a fortnight and were then moved 507 miles up the country to this place. It took us from 1.30 on Monday afternoon until about 2pm on the Wednesday to reach here (Naauwpoort) and I can assure you it was a very unpleasant ride. We were found plenty of work when we arrived here. We set about building a large quartermaster's store, a smithy and two large railway sidings for the A.S.C. After that around 50 of us went up to a place called Arundel, about 18 miles from here, with General French's force and routed the Boers. We took their position and repaired the line and one bridge. The force is now encamped in the Boers' old position and the Royal Engineers go from Naauwpoort to Arundel every morning to work, returning here at night. We travel in open trucks and are under arms going and coming back. There is fighting every day at Arundel and the work on the line is covered by the Berkshire Regiment.....An officer was killed yesterday as we were unloading ballast. He was shot in the back just as he was returning with the patrol and the alarm was sounded and all stood to arms.....Now a word or two as to the work. Well it is very hard: pick and shovel almost all day long. We leave here at 4.30 in the morning and then return at 8pm and by the time the tools are returned to the store, it is 8.30. Then we march to the camp from the station and reach there at 8.45 and lights out at 9.15. There are some Crewe men in the platelaying section who know quite as much as the R.E. N.C.O.'s. Sapper Egerton can give any of them a bit of advice on platelaying and the officer often asks him to go along with the corporal. The section left camp yesterday while we were at Arundel for the Orange River to put a siding down for the A.S.C. and will be away for four days.....We have never heard a word of our men in the 8th and 31st Companies. The work is very trying to many of the Crewe lads who have not been used to so long a spell with pick and shovel. All are agreed on one point and that is, that the Royal Engineers have been wrongly named. They ought to have been called "Regularly Employed." '

The rising amount of casualties during the early exchanges prompted the War Office to call up more medical staff and this saw local men also receiving the call to South Africa. In the early weeks of December, Superintendent Oldham of the Crewe Ambulance Corps received a telegram from the St. John Ambulance Association HQ in London asking for suitable candidates to be part of an Ambulance Brigade to be sent to the front as soon as possible. Qualifications for service included men who were not married and of a certain age. Three names were forwarded and Private Charles Henry Powell was contacted almost immediately and told to prepare at once to commence to South Africa. He was employed in the general office as a clerk in the Central Stores of the Crewe Co-operative Society and was a prominent member of the Crewe Equalised District of the Order of Druids, as well as holding a position in the Cross

Green Lodge at Coppenhall. This lodge presented Private Powell with a fountain pen and pocket wallet on December 6, in the lodge room at the Horse Shoe Hotel and next day, he received gifts from his Co-op workmates, which included a travelling bag and small dressing case.

In December, the fund for the Crewe Reservists was swelled considerably with a concert in the Mechanics Institute and a football match between Crewe Wednesday Cycling Club and Crewe Co-operative F.C.

More First Class Reserves from the town were called up, and among them was Sapper John George Wickham, a Crewe postal worker who left on December 11 for Shorncliffe to join his unit in the Royal Engineers. As was the custom, he received gifts from fellow workers, which included a silver mounted briar pipe, a silver matchbox and a large packet of tobacco.

During the final month of the year, local newspaper headlines regarding the progress of the war made for grim reading after several crushing defeats in the space of a few days. The reversals and casualty reports did little to ease the worry of local families and friends of men currently in, or en-route to South Africa.

On Sunday, December 17, an old Railway Volunteer, Musician Noah Betts, originally of "A" Company, was laid to rest in the town cemetery. He had served in the Cheshire Regiment during the Indian Frontier campaign, and the whole Corps turned out for the funeral. On the same day, a strong rumour was circulated that the remainder of the Railway Reserve were to be called up, but despite the excitement among the 100 or so men, no official news had yet been received, although another 30 First Class Reserves received their papers to join their respective units by December 27. In one department alone in Crewe Works, this latest call-up accounted for ten men. On Thursday, December 21, some of these men received gifts from their workmates. In the Millwright's Shop, Private F. Thorley and J. Adnitt both of the 2nd Cheshire's were presented with mementoes as well as Privates G. W. Bentley, J. Hodson, C. Hodson and T. Heath of the 2nd North Staffordshire Regiment. Workmates in the Fitting Shop also afforded gifts on their departing men and Sergeant Major Stapeley of the Railway Volunteers did the honours for Corporal A. J. Topham (Cheshire Regiment) and Private Arthur Hesketh (East Lancashire Regiment). Due to the seriousness of the war and the latest British reversals, it was decided to cancel the Railway Volunteers' annual Christmas ball.

As the end of the 19th century beckoned, local traders did their best to ensure local families of men serving would enjoy the festivities as much as possible. As a prime example, Mr Barlow, a butcher in Exchange Street, supplied 70 joints of beef for their Christmas dinner tables.

Fund raising collections continued right up to the Christmas holiday with weekly subscriptions in Crewe Works raising between £20 and £30 and by December 23, the fund had so far raised £999 10s 7d, with £302 4s 5½d expended. Up until now, 97 adults and 144 children had benefited, and as a Christmas bonus, all dependant families received an extra 5s.

On December 21, Corporal Sam Wolfe wrote home to Captain Stones, regarding the skills of the Crewe men busy re-building the bridge at Modder River.

> *'Our Sgt. Major said it was the finest piece of work ever accomplished on active service. The bridge itself is 100 yards across with half a mile of railway each side. There is also a cutting on either side, 200 yards long and 17 feet deep.'*

News that members of the Railway Reserve had been longing for, finally arrived on December 22 in the form of a telegram, delivered to the Crewe Corps HQ, informing the men, numbering 104, to proceed to Chatham by December 31. After arriving at the barracks, the men were to undertake a medical and be measured for uniforms, before returning home and back to their jobs until their services were required. While back at Crewe, the men would receive regimental pay. Among the new draft were Sergeants T. Riley and H. Wadkins.

In December, Sapper Foy wrote three letters home from his base at Modder River.

> *<u>December 13</u> - 'It was great pleasure that I received your letters this morning, one dated November 11th, the other November 16th. You may tell Jack he may keep his eyes on the shop windows for photographs of the work we have done. I think one of the reporters is from a paper called "Black and White." You know the way that we have travelled by the letters I have sent from the different stations, such as De Aar, Orange River, Belmont, Graspan, Modder River. Spytfontein will be the next place and then Kimberley. Yesterday a few of our company including myself camped upon a splendid island, down the river. There was a large hotel, club rooms and boats along the riverside. It seemed just like a fairground as there was swing boats, roundabouts and things just the same at home. There was a fine many pigeons in a loft and there was only two men that had stopped on the island, so we had it all to ourselves. At night we went in some houses and found some splendid bedding, mattresses, quilts, pillows etc. This morning a fellow gave me a stick, piece of string and a hook made out of a bent piece of wire, so I made some paste and commenced fishing. I got a bite, but it slipped off the hook, the hook being no good, so I went back for breakfast of roast mutton chops instead.'*

December 22 - 'We are doing alright here, it is almost the same as Blackpool as regards camping. We have been here now at the river about three weeks and there is a rumour about making a move to Kimberley in about six weeks time. I expect last night was a show night in Crewe, so we were all fancying which shops were dressed up best. I may say there are no shops here except an old stores.....Me and several others went fishing after tea, we leave off work at five now and still have three hours for dinner. Me and another fellow caught some fish so we had them fried for supper, then I made a large tin of Quaker oats. I eat just as if I was at home so it does not matter how long we remain out here. You can rest assured about me being alright and looking after myself, and as regards the weather, it is quite midsummer here, in fact, it does not look much like Christmas. I hear the Queen has sent some chocolate for us all and they intend us having a good do. I may say Captain Stones sent me and the remainder of his Company a very nice card with different views on. I'll bet Charley and a good many others wish they had come with us and I expect they will almost envy us when we return - why you will feel quite proud, when you see our Arthur return with his medals and bars.....We shall not be all that long when our column starts going again, so cheer up and I will let you know in time to get me some cakes and pies ready.'

December 28 - 'We have just got Christmas over having had a pleasant time of it. They gave us two days holiday and on Christmas Day we all formed up while a telegram was read from the Queen, wishing us all the compliments of the season etc. They then gave three cheers for her, after which all the soldiers were served out with beer and cheese for lunch, although we missed our plum puddings.....One young fellow in our tent had a nice parcel, including a large cake, and another mince pies, so we had a nice tea amongst us.....The officers have made arrangements for a day's holiday on New Year's Day and are getting some sports up – football matches, cricket, boxing, swimming, horse races etc. General Methuen is giving two cups for football and cricket. The natives or kaffirs as you might call them have all sorts of games, just as the same in England. They play cricket and intend to pick an eleven to play against the Engineers on Monday, the losers to pay five shillings. They play football also and it is very amusing to see them boxing. I was talking to some of them last night. They say they hate the Boers very much and the Boers hate them. Should they speak to a Boer in the street, they have to take off their hat and call him "My Lord." They also tell us the Boers call us "Rhoinecks" meaning sore necks, because of the sun browning our necks.'

Not all from Crewe however, were enjoying the festivities. Sapper R. H. Galliard of the 10th Railway Company, wrote to friends in Crewe on December 30, 1899 about his Christmas Day lunch.

*Some of the men called to active service in October 1899. (**ABOVE**) 26611 Sapper William Cunningham (kneeling far left) of the 10th Railway Company, pictured with the Crewe Alexandra football team in 1898. (**BELOW LEFT**) 2nd Cheshire Regiment regular Private Robert J. Steele, who would also serve during the Great War. (**BELOW RIGHT**) Another regular called up on the outbreak of war. Frederick Nixon Walker of the 2nd Royal Warwickshire Regiment - a machinist from Crewe Works.*

Sergeant Thomas William Brett (in uniform) poses with his brothers and sister, just prior to leaving the town in October 1899. His brother Edward James Brett (also standing), would serve in the Volunteer Service Sections, and would depart for war in April 1901.

Sapper Charles Ralphs of the 10th Railway Company. He joined the Reserve on December 19, 1896 and resided with his wife Emily (nee Brookes) at 395, West Street, Crewe. After leaving with the first draft, he would not see loved ones again for nearly three years.

*(**ABOVE**) Mayhem at the bottom of High Street on October 16, 1899, as the crowd wait for the Railway Reserve. (**BELOW**) Order finally restored.*

*(**ABOVE**) The Railway Reserve, headed by their Regimental Band, march under Mill Street bridge and past the George and Dragon Hotel, on the way to the railway station for embarkation. (**BELOW**) Mayor John Jones (1898-99) of Heathfield Avenue.*

(ABOVE) The first sight of South Africa for many of the Crewe men - Cape Town harbour, with Table Mountain dominating the skyline. (BELOW) Members of the 10th Railway Company from Crewe, just after their embarkation. On the photo, taken by former Crewe resident Mr C. Bennion Brown, are A. E. Ankers, E. M. Barker, W. Biggs, W. S. Brereton, E. Broach, H. W. Butt, R. P. Calderbank, W. Capper, A. J. Coleman, W. Cunningham, A. Egerton, A. Ellis, F. Ellis, W. Etheridge, W. H. Evans, J. T. Evanson, R. Fairbrother, W. D. J. Froome, R. Galliard, W. Goodwin, J. T. Guest, E. Hallows, G. A. Harvey, S. Harvey, A. Hollinshead, H. Hubbard, J. Jones, W. Latham, W. Manning, A. Mason, C. E. Mason, W. Madeley, W. K. Mcilwraith, T. Osborn, W. Pugh, C. Ralphs, J. Reeves, S. Robinson, W. P. Roscoe, A. Sanders, W. H. Saunders, D. Scoffin, T. Steele, W. Spilsbury, W. Sumner, G. W. Surridge, A. Taylor, A. Towers, B. Walker and J. Walley.

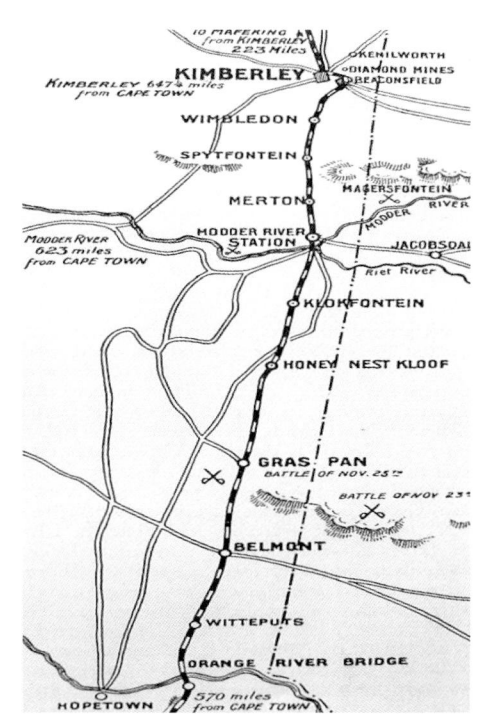

*(**ABOVE LEFT**) Lieutenant-General Lord Methuen, K.C.V.O., C.B., C.M.G., Commander of the 1st Infantry Division during the Boer War. (**ABOVE RIGHT**) His proposed route to Kimberley, following the line from De Aar. (**BELOW**) An armoured train, which many Railway Volunteers would travel on during the war. The engine was typically placed in the centre, to prevent damage from dynamited lines. The holes in the side of the carriage are rifle slots.*

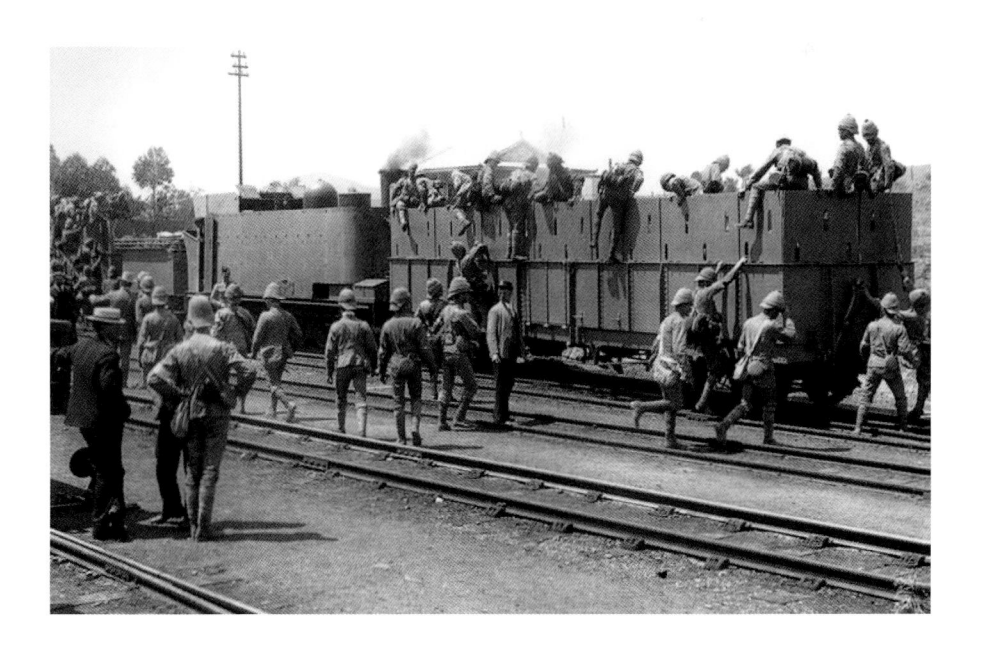

THE ENGINEERS OF CREWE.
(BY REQUEST).

Hats off, gentlemen, everyone,
   And may your hearts be filled with pride
For the men who've fought in this war,
   And for those who have nobly died.
Songs have been sung, and verses written
   About our soldiers brave and true,
But the men who deserve some praise
   Are the Engineers of Crewe.

The British Army wanted men
   Who could work as well as fight,
Men who understood railway work,
   And could soon put wrong to right.
So at last it was decided
   The best thing they could do
Was to have men with practice,
   As the Engineers of Crewe.

The Government had watched some time
   Our fine body of Engineers,
And saw they were as fine a lot
   As any of our Volunteers.
The Boer war was raging hot,
   And skilled men were very few,
At last, one day, a call was made
   On the Engineers of Crewe.

The excitement was intense
   When the news was known in the town
That men of Crewe had got the chance
   To go and win fame and renown.
The news o'er the country spread,
   And very soon all England knew—
That they'd got men of skill and pluck
   In the Engineers of Crewe.

Shall we ever forget the scene
   Of that ever memorable day
When they met on the Market Square
   Ready for Africa far away?
Thousands of people thronged the streets
   All eager to get a good view
Of our men who were ordered south —
   The brave Engineers of Crewe.

The sun was shining brightly
   As the men stood on parade,
And the scene of wild enthusiasm
   From our memories will never fade.
The Mayor addressed the men,
   Bidding them be staunch and true,
And many cheering words he spoke
   To the Engineers of Crewe.

Pathetic scenes were many
   Which brought tears to many an eye,
Husbands, wives, and children felt it
   As the time for parting was nigh,
But the men all stood it bravely,
   As brave men at parting do;
And many were the good wishes
   To the Engineers of Crewe.

The men marched off the square
   'Midst tremendous cheers from the crowd,
And as they wended their way
   The cheering rang long and loud.
Men loosed their pent up feelings,
   Their spirits more elated grew
As they gave a hearty send off
   To the Engineers of Crewe.

"Soldiers of the Queen" was played
   And "The Girl I Left Behind Me,"
When as they arrived in Mill Street
   It looked like a mighty sea.
Each available space was thronged,
   And it seemed they'd never get through,
For eighty thousand people watched
   The brave Engineers of Crewe.

At last the station was reached,
   And great excitement prevailed,
To keep the crowd off the platform
   The barriers utterly failed;
The scene baffles all description
   As the people bade them adieu,
And cheer after cheer re-echoed
   For the Engineers of Crewe.

Many farewells were spoken,
   And many a shake of the hand,
As we wished them all God speed
   And good luck in a foreign land.
Amidst wild outbursts of cheering,
   Slowly from the platform drew
The train, carrying its precious load—
   The brave Engineers of Crewe.

Weeks passed by, at last we heard
   They'd arrived on Afric's shore,
And all were fit and willing
   To go and face the wary Boer.
They have seen a few engagements,
   And great praise to them is due,
For they've been "all there" when wanted
   Have the Engineers of Crewe.

The men from Crewe have shown their worth
   Whatever their duty has been,
They are a credit to our town,
   To the Empire and our Queen;
They have been working under fire,
   When the bullets around them flew,
And yeoman service has been done
   By the Engineers of Crewe.

May the people of Crewe feel proud
   Of what our Engineers have done,
They've proved they're men of skill and pluck,
   And our Country's praise they've won.
We often think about them,
   And we hope they'll all pull through,
And give a hearty welcome back
   To the Engineers of Crewe.

Composed by Joseph Barker, 55, Vincent Street, Crewe.

(**ABOVE**) Boers, armed with the latest Mauser rifle. (**BELOW**) Typical work for the Railway Companies. Here the main bridge has been blown, so a temporary one has been quickly constructed alongside to allow continuation of traffic, while the old bridge is repaired.

'Breakfast - dry bread and coffee. Dinner - mutton bones and what bread we had spare. Tea - the same as breakfast. The fare was complimented by a "two inch square" piece of cake and four thimblefuls of rum.'

On December 30, P.C. Moreton, one of Crewe's most respected police constables, along with John Latham, left town to join their regiment, the Grenadier Guards (2nd Company, 3rd Battalion) at Wellington barracks. They were driven from the police station to the railway station in a waggonette drawn by four horses, courtesy of Mr Mellor of Earle Street, and were accompanied by twenty of P.C. Moreton's fellow constables and the Temperance Band. The young constable was following the family tradition of serving with the Colours, as his father had fought during the Crimean War and five other relations were already in South Africa. On the same day in nearby Nantwich, the Colonel of the 9th Lancers was busy purchasing 24 horses for service, taking the total to 54 from the area in three weeks. Prices ranged from £32 to £50 and the animals had been earmarked for artillery purposes and for the mounted infantry.

On New Year's Eve, the remainder of the Railway Reserve were at Chatham having departed the town from December 28 onwards. On arriving, a small number failed their medical examinations and were sent home early.

Chapter Two - 1900
-Relief But No Victory-

Life in Crewe at the turn of the new century was fairly prosperous, with the Railway Company providing the main employment for the male population in the town and a number of clothing factories providing work for unmarried females. Crewe now boasted a population of over 40,000 - an incredible rise for a town only sixty years old. Of these, around 8,000 were employed in the Railway Company Works, building and repairing rolling stock. Weekly wages for the average tradesman in the Works was around £2 for a 54 hour week (6.00am to 5.30pm, Monday to Friday and 6.00am to 12.00 noon on Saturday) although non-tradesmen earned less. In comparison, a doctor earned around £6 a week, a police constable £1 10s and a farm worker 17s 6d. At the other end of the pay scale was Francis William Webb, whose annual salary was £8,000 (about £150 a week). One of the biggest local employers in the clothing industry was John Compton's factory in Bridle Road. Compton's made cheap railway uniforms in their range, which entitled the owner to a 25% discount on his carriage rates.

Local shops were numerous, with the Crewe Co-operative movement the biggest retailer. Bargains were the order of the day and the Jackson Stores could provide couples about to marry, all furniture they would need for their new abode, delivered on the first payment of 5s down and 2/6d a week, with the total payment amounting to £6 19s 6d. Included was a square table, four strong kitchen chairs, an armchair, rocking chair, steel fender with two bars, a set of steel fire irons, a strong list rug, alarm clock, a strong iron bedstead, spring mattress, bed, bolster and pillows, dressing table and wash stand, toilet service, bedroom rug, two bedroom chairs and a swing toilet mirror.

The main entertainment in the town was the Lyceum Theatre and on January 8, the attraction was Miss Cissie Moxon's pantomime *Blue Beard*. Prices for the performance ranged between 3d and 3s. Elsewhere in the town, the police station in Edleston Road was enlarged on the opposite corner of Chapel Street to the Imperial public house. Also in this year the Council established a Municipal Electricity Works on land at the bottom of Edleston Road (which would later become Electricity Street). A new chancel and vestry were consecrated at Christ Church and a bowling green and pavilion were built at the Earle Street Sports Ground. In December the Liberal Club was opened in Gatefield Street and the Railway Company in this year opened their new hospital in Mill Street. Also in 1900, the 'khaki' election saw the Conservatives and Liberal Unionists keep power, but in Crewe J. Tomkinson of the Liberal Party defeated his Conservative opponent (J. E. Reiss) by 6,120 votes to 4,921.

The townsfolk of Crewe awoke on January 1 with hopes high that this year would see the end of the war and the men back home with their families. At around midday the town was shaken by a gas explosion at Crewe Works, which caused the partial collapse of a chimney stack in the Brass Foundry and damage to the nearby time office. Thankfully, due to the holidays, nobody was injured, but if the incident had happened during a normal working day, then many men would have been killed. Next day, the men of the Railway Reserve returned to Crewe from Chatham on a month long furlough. Estimations for their departure were for the end of the month and indications were that they would join their colleagues in the 8th Railway Company. Among the men to go were Crewe Corporation Fire Brigade members Dunn and Edwards. Two men - T. Riley and H. Wadkins while at Chatham received certificates entitling them to the rank of Sergeant.

In South Africa, Sapper Foy, enjoying a respite in the fighting, wrote home to his parents on January 2, from his base at Modder River.

> 'Things are quiet here at present. We get fresh meat almost every day and cheese and jam. They boil the meat one day and roast it another, just the same as at camp. At present we are repairing the railway bridge that the Boers destroyed which crosses the river.'

Further bad news reached the townsfolk of Crewe in the first few days of the New Year, when it was reported that local men had been captured during the Modder River engagement. But an interesting letter published in *The Crewe Guardian* on January 6, 1900 saw the story take an almost unbelievable twist. Bugler Brunt of the Shropshire Light Infantry, writing home on December 7, stated:

> 'We have got three prisoners here that come from Crewe. They have been fighting for the Boers.'

In another letter in the same edition, it was claimed that upwards of twenty prisoners captured during the Battle of Modder River hailed from the town and two more originated from nearby Stoke (during the conflict many local Liberal members remained pro-Boer and were standoffish towards the Railway Volunteers).

An epidemic of measles in Crewe during the first days of January saw schools at New Street, Christ Church and Earle Street closed, to prevent further infections. Around 300 cases had been diagnosed in the town (with six deaths reported in December 1899).

In January, the total strength of the Railway Volunteers was 754, which included all currently away on active service. A total of 300 men of the Corps assembled at the Armoury on January 6, in response to a special regimental order. They had been called there by Colonel Cotton-Jodrell with the intention of volunteering for active service. This figure (which rose to 330) was then forwarded to the War Office.

In a letter written on January 12, to his father in Market Street, Staff Sergeant T. Cooke gave an insight into ruthless British tactics.

> 'On January 10, we made a raid in Orange Free State. We came across 300 Boers but they cleared off. We burned about a dozen farms, taking everything

we wanted – horses, sheep, pigs, in fact our fellows took things such as a pianoforte and an organ, besides ducks, chickens and as much fruit as they could carry.'

More First Class Reservists attached to the Cheshire Yeomanry left Crewe in the early weeks of January, further relieving twenty more staff from the railway workshops and offices.

In the second week of January, the 10th Railway Company joined the 8th and 31st Companies at Modder River, to help in the reconstruction of the main railway bridge. This reunion brought together the majority of Crewe men who had left town on October 16, 1899. Sapper C. Ralphs wrote home on January 12 about their work in the region, which included the laying of a new line from their base to Douglas - a stretch of 24 miles. Sapper Arthur Foy confirmed the re-union in a letter home, written on the same day.

> 'The remainder of the 10th Company have joined us this week, so that nearly all the Crewe fellows are stationed here now. We may stay here a little while as we are re-constructing the bridge and they intend to run a train over it before we move from here.....The weather here is rather warm, a little rainy at times. The other morning it rained from breakfast to dinner time, so we did not go to work (more rain, more rest). Sometimes the monsoons come on and the tents and everything in them gets covered in two or three inches of sand.....I often wonder what kind of winter you are having. I often laugh when I think I am getting out of it. It is pleasant to hear the birds singing. We are being well-looked after, they are even giving us all them Buffalo Bill hats to wear because they are a bit lighter.'

One man who didn't make the original re-union with his Crewe colleagues was Sapper Alfred Coleman. An accident prevented his move to Modder River. In a letter to Lieutenant Godson from a field hospital at Orange River, he wrote about the incident.

> 'Just a few lines to inform you I met with an accident on New Year's Day at my work. It occurred during shunting operations on the loop line that we were working on. There had been a platform of sleepers erected for the purpose of unloading stores and the engine had passed the stores platform on its way down to fetch up some empty wagons. On returning, the engine collided with one of the sleepers and knocked it off the platform. The sleeper struck me in the back and I was knocked some distance away from where I was working at the time. I fell head foremost, the result being that I sustained a wound in the head and my bottom lip was cut open. I had to have four stitches put in my lip and one stitch in my

head.....I was very disappointed at being so unfortunate, for two days later my detachment were ordered to join the 8th Company at Modder River.....I was looking forward to meeting the remainder of the Crewe Engineers at that place.....There is only one man of the 10th Company in hospital besides myself and there is also one from the 8th Company who was wounded at Modder River.'

On January 13, an Army order was issued regarding the new men who had volunteered for active service. This was received at the Crewe Engineers HQ next day, for two carefully selected sections to be formed, consisting of one Lieutenant, one Sergeant, one Corporal, one Lance Corporal and twenty-two Sappers per section. The trades required were principally engine drivers, engine fitters, platelayers, boilermakers, blacksmiths, carpenters and firemen. It was also stipulated that one section would be attached to the 8th Railway Company and one to the 10th. Conditions for service consisted of no men accepted under the age of twenty or over thirty-five, with preference given to unmarried men or widowers without children. Height restrictions recorded that no man less than five foot six inches would be accepted. Unfortunately these strict guidelines saw only 22 of the 330 men qualify, so the idea of raising the new sections, was temporarily put on hold.

There was also a setback regarding the second draft of the Railway Reserve waiting to go to South Africa. Originally on a month's furlough from Chatham, this was extended for a further month, much to the disappointment of those eager to go.

Sapper Swinwood and Sapper Foy both wrote home from Modder River on January 19. Sapper Swinwood wrote:

'We are sleeping to arms every night, shoes, puttees on (so our sleep is not very comfortable) and rifles by our side. I am proud that Crewe has sent its share of men to one of the greatest wars of our time and I am pleased to be able to say that not one Crewe man in my company (the 8th R.E.) has a blot on his character. I am pleased to tell you that we are now getting a drop of ale. It is quite a treat for we have had hardly seen any since we left England. We have to pay dearly for it - 5d a pint.....We are allowed rum twice a week - Tuesday's and Saturday's. When we get rum the beer is stopped, but a drop of rum in our early morning coffee is very nice. They don't give you much; it is dished out like doctor's medicine in tablespoonfuls.'

Sapper Foy wrote to his parents, hopeful of an early return home.

'We have just received a stocking cap each which were made by the children of St. Paul's School.....I believe Buller did meet it a bit rough, but he will make up for

it shortly, and I think we shall be easily home by the 28th of February. There is not much news to send you from here except that our column is gradually getting the best of the Dutchmen. You see they have a great advantage over our men, as they get almost everywhere, even underneath the ground.'

Tragic news reached Crewe towards the end of the month after 7019 Private S. Davies died of wounds on January 23 at Chieveley, following the Battle of Colenso on December 15, 1899. He served in the 3rd King's Royal Rifles and was buried in Chieveley Cemetery. He was the first known local man to lose his life during the war. He would not be the last.

Crowds on Crewe Station gathered every day to watch the trains laden with war materials and troops pass through. On January 23, four carrying guns, ammunition and gun carriages passed slowly through bound for the Alexandra Dock in Liverpool, and next day five troop trains were spotted on their way to South Africa via the Canada Dock, Liverpool.

On January 27, the headlines in the local newspapers indicated a great British victory during the Battle of Spion Kop (January 24), but unfortunately were incorrect, and once again, the British had suffered another reversal, with heavy loss of life. Among the dead were three men with associations with the town. No.3586 Private L. Bamford of 81, Ridgway Street, and of the 2nd. King's Own Royal Lancasters, was killed in action. No.2843 Private John Lee (2nd Lancashire Fusiliers) had also been killed, along with former resident Sergeant A. E. Foster of "E" Company of the 2nd Middlesex Regiment, who had worked as a detective officer in the service of the LNWR, and for some time had been stationed in Crewe.

The Battle of Spion Kop
January 24, 1900

As well as the struggle for Kimberley and Mafeking, the British were also attempting to relieve the garrison at Ladysmith, so a two-pronged attack was instigated by General Sir Charles Warren and Major General Neville Lyttelton. The awaiting Boers were cleverly entrenched on the line of the Tugela River, and dominating the skyline around this area was a hill called Spion Kop, which was over 1,400 feet in height and formed a major bastion of the Boers' defensive line. The hill was critical for the British, for its capture, just 20 miles from Ladysmith, would mean they would hold and overlook the ground leading to the besieged town. However, poor British tactics and leadership saw another reversal, despite the British holding a numerical advantage of more than two to one (20,000 to 8,000). A total of 243 British troops were killed with many buried in the trenches where they fell in an area later christened 'the acre of massacre.' A further 1,250 were wounded or captured, compared to Boer losses of 68 dead and around 270 wounded.

Lance Corporal George Edward Guest of "G" Company, 2nd Bn. Lancashire Fusiliers, who was also a member of the Railway Volunteers and resided in Albert Street, took part in the battle and wrote home about the engagement:

> *'When the first shot was fired we all fell flat on our stomachs thus allowing the shots to pass over us, and then arose a mighty British cheer and bayonets flashed in all directions and the hill fell into our hands, the sentry being bayoneted by one of our officers. The greater part of them cleared away under cover of the dense mist and then we awaited the coming of the morning of the fatal 24th. We lined the crest of the hill and as the mist began to clear away, the enemy opened fire gradually from their strongly entrenched positions and then we began to reply. It seemed at first as though the honours of the day completely belonged to us, but we soon found out our mistake, for the enemy turned up in such great numbers and directed such a murderous fire upon us (our forces of the time being comparatively small) that for a time we completely staggered, but we soon rallied ourselves and began to show the wily Boer that when once roused, we had the spirit of the British bulldog…..Meanwhile the enemy being reinforced with artillery began to pound away at us from right and left, the Nordenfelt gun and Long Tom nicknamed "Buck Up" doing terrible execution. They mowed down the defenders of Spion Kop, the sight being horrible to all. As the day wore on and the fire became so terrific, we were compelled to retire from the crest of the hill, but not before the bravest of the brave had been killed or wounded in defence of their Queen and country. Our General fell early in the day being severely wounded along with our Colonel and the greater part of our officers who fell gallantly fighting around their General and Colonel. Thrice did the enemy gain the crest and as many times they were repulsed. The enemy were again pressing us hard when we caught sight of the gallant lads coming to reinforce us. Then up went a manly cheer and once more out flashed the bayonets for we knew we were saved, for very conspicuous among them were seen the slouched hats of the Imperial Light Infantry, many Lancashire lads among them, who rushed at once to our rescue to avenge themselves for past insults received at the hands of the Boers. It was awful to see the brave lads mowed down as they advanced without being able to fire a shot in return…..The sights were something awful, men being utterly blown to pieces. Our stretcher bearers worked manfully in the carrying away of the killed and wounded. They were constantly fired upon by a "generous foe." Even the Red Cross flag was shelled. It was a miracle how I escaped as where*

I lay I saw twenty killed and fifty wounded. It was now growing dark and after bravely contesting our own for 14 hours under a burning sun with no water and all thoughts of food forgotten, we received the word to retire, but even then, though completely worn out, we were loath to leave the place where our comrades lay and the place we had defended so well against fearful odds. Our casualties numbered 321 of my regiment alone.....And when the Roll was called at night, to hear no response from those we loved as comrades and brothers who went forth that day in all the pride of manhood to do battle for their loved Queen and country and to uphold the honour of the British flag. Kindly thank my fellow workers and the townspeople of Crewe for their kindly endeavour to support the loved ones we have left behind.'

On January 25, Sapper W. P. Roscoe and 91 members of the 10th Railway Company were dispatched to Thebus to repair a blown-up bridge. A few days later, their work took them to Stormberg.

In the first week of February, Sapper A. Wilkinson, wounded by friendly fire at Modder River, was back on British shores, following his journey home from South Africa. He was taken from the docks at Southampton to continue his recuperation at Netley Hospital.

The month of February saw further Crewe men leave the town for the war-zone. One such man was Private E. Burgoyne; a member of the Crewe Alexandra football team, who worked in the Joiner's Shop in Crewe Works and was a First Class Reservist attached to the Lancashire Fusiliers. He was ordered to join his regiment by February 11 at Bury, but when the directors at the Alex knew of his departure, they promoted him from the reserves into the first team to play Middleton on February 10. The veteran forward more than played his part in a 10-1 victory. After the game, he was presented with a number of gifts by the centre-half of the club F. Thompson. A collection among the crowd was given to him that night in The Anchor Inn, while his team mates in the reserves presented him with a gold ring. He departed on Sunday, February 11, taken to the station in a horse drawn carriage, supplied by Mr Welsh of The Royal Hotel. At the station, a large gathering of players, officials and supporters were there to see him off, along with friends and family.

The exodus of men from the town was not however, confined just to the railwaymen, and when postal worker Levi Hughes left to join the 2nd Cameronians at Hamilton on Sunday, February 11, he became the sixth man from the Crewe Post Office to go to the front. Private William Tipler of Goddard Street and of the Shropshire Light Infantry was another man to leave the town in February, as was Alton Street resident John Holland who joined Lord Loch's Scouts on February 22 at

Camberwell. Sergeant Holland had extensive knowledge of South Africa, having served in the Cape Mounted Police for eight years, and had also taken part in the ill-fated Jameson Raid in 1896.

During the war, many gifts from the town were sent to the serving soldiers. In February, knitted socks were the order of the day, when Mrs Swinton of High Street sent 33 pairs and Miss Hibbert and Miss Sumner of 94, Victoria Street, 130 pairs.

In South Africa, the tide of war, currently flowing in favour of the Boers, would start to turn with the arrival of Lord Roberts and Lord Kitchener. On February 6, they left Cape Town, arriving at Lord Methuen's camp at Modder River two days later. A letter home from Sapper Foy, confirmed the arrival.

> *'Lord Roberts and Lord Kitchener arrived here yesterday (February 8). I was able to have the pleasure of seeing two of England's great men.'*

On February 8, many of the Crewe men received a tin of chocolate, sent over from England courtesy of Queen Victoria. The tin box was designed by J. S. Fry & Sons of Bristol and carried an embossed portrait of the Queen (also later produced by Cadbury and Rowntree) and was bound with red, white and blue ribbon. Every soldier in South Africa received the gift and all recipients had to sign a receipt on delivery. The boxes were highly valued both in South Africa and at home and regularly fetched £5 when sold. Sapper Foy wrote home to his parents telling of his gift.

> *'.....I have sent my chocolate box home along with some more friends, as one by itself may have got lost, so we have chanced them all together and I have sent you half the chocolate, as it is not every day you can have a present from the Queen. It is not necessary to tell you to take great care of the box for me. It has gone to Mrs Bowyer, 94, Mill Street, with the same mail as this letter.'*

The tin belonging to Sapper T. Coops of the 31st Fortress Company, was put on show in Mr W. Hamilton's shop in Market Street, Crewe and drew great crowds.

Lord Roberts planned to capture the Orange Free State capital of Bloemfontein, while relieving Kimberley on the way. On February 11, his column, consisting of 18,000 infantry and nearly 8,000 cavalry and mounted infantry, rode out of camp to begin 'the great flank march,' leaving Methuen and 5,000 men at Modder River fronting the entrenched Boers at Magersfontein. The idea devised by Roberts was not to confront the enemy at Magersfontein, but simply swing around the eastern end of their positions, thus leaving the railway line route and launching his formidable column onto the dry barren veldt, where their movements were much less predictable. Just four days into the march, Major General John French's cavalry division rode unopposed into Kimberley. The siege here was over. Britain rejoiced. The first train to enter the town was driven by a member of the Railway Volunteers, with another acting as his guard.

On February 13, 1900, another serving Crewe man lost his life. No.5272 Private William Maude of the 3rd Grenadier Guards died of dysentery at the Orange River Station. He had sailed to war on the S.S. *Goorkha*, along with the 10th Railway Company and had previously worked in the Copper Shop, Crewe Works. On February 24, it was reported that another local man had died in South Africa. Private G. Charlton of the 9th Lancers, who at home was a carter in the employment of Mr Wallace Lumb (wine and spirit merchant), had 'died' of enteric fever in a Winburg hospital, but thankfully for his wife and two children, it turned out to be another War Office error, and a man with the same name and in the same regiment had died instead.

As the end of February approached, there was still no sign of the second draft of the Railway Reserve going to war. However, in the final few days of their month's furlough, Crewe Engineers HQ reported that it had been extended to the end of March.

Sickness and fever in South Africa was sweeping through the British ranks and Crewe men were among the victims. One such man was Corporal Sam Wolfe of the 8th Railway Company, who contracted enteric fever and was in a poor state in a Winburg hospital. Thankfully, a few weeks after his condition was reported, his health improved sufficiently for him to be transferred to a hospital at Cape Town.

A day after the relief of Kimberley, the British made steps to capture a large Boer force commanded by General Cronjé, who had now moved from their position at Magersfontein and were entrenched along the banks of the River Modder at Paardeberg Drift. Early British attempts to storm the enemy lines met with heavy casualties; however, a sustained artillery bombardment slowly eroded Boer defences and the will of the defenders. In the early hours of February 27, Cronjé surrendered along with 4,000 of his force. British troops entered the Boer laager (a camp defended by a circular formation of wagons) and were horrified to see the results of their artillery fire. Shrapnel had cut to pieces many of the oxen and horses used to pull the wagons and the smell of this slaughter-house proved unbearable. Dead animals were also floating in the river, which was the only source of water for the thirsty troops, and not all filled their canteens upstream away from the carcasses, and soon many were prone with enteric fever. The British had won their first major victory of the war, made even sweeter due to the fact that it had occurred on the nineteenth anniversary of the Battle of Majuba Hill (the resounding Boer victory against the British in 1881). This victory would mark the turning point of the war.

Among the victorious troops was Sergeant G. Jones of Crewe, who was a member of the Railway Volunteers and a First Class Reservist in the Shropshire Light Infantry. He wrote home about his part in the battle.

> *'My baptism of fire was at Paardeberg and I have no doubt that you have read of our great success there......After a night's march of 20 miles, we arrived at Paardeberg and we only had time to drink a cup of coffee, when the order came to fall in.....We soon found ourselves in front of about 6,000 Boers who were strongly entrenched in the bed of the river and were pouring terrible rifle fire at us. We advanced in line like one man until we got within 300 yards of the enemy's position. We then lay down and commenced our day's work, which lasted from 7.00am until 7.30pm, under a blazing sun with no water and no food.....During our advance we had about a dozen men knocked over. Either the Boers could not shoot that day, or else it was our luck, for had we been where they were, I do not think there would have been many of them left. When night came, we retired about 600 yards for a night's rest, but I can assure you that there was not much rest, for we were put on outpost duty. On the roll being called, we found we had 9 killed and 38 wounded. The next morning at daybreak we found ourselves advancing in the trenches which the day before the Boers had held. We remained there till Wednesday the 21st of February, when we were relieved by the Gordon Highlanders.....On the night of the 26th, my regiment (the Shropshire's) were ordered to form up in single line in front of the Boer position. We marched down at night and about 2.00am we opened fire - volleys by sections and kept it up for almost an hour. The enemy returned the salute, but their bullets went whizzing over our heads and we had only one officer shot. We marched back to camp before daybreak and at breakfast the next morning (February 27th) our brave Colonel read us a telegram to say Cronjé had surrendered. We were all glad to hear this, because things had begun to look rather serious, so much so that we had been expecting orders to take the position by the point of the bayonet, which would have meant the loss of hundreds of England's brave sons.....We afterwards proceeded to the laager and the sight was one which I will never forget. The trenches were about 8 feet deep and well-protected from shot and shell, but dead horses, cattle etc. and also wounded Boers were lying all about the place and the smell was simply dreadful. I did not see any dead Boers as they had either been thrown in the river or buried, because the enemy do not like us to get any ideas as to the extent of their losses.'*

Meanwhile in back in Cheshire, Nantwich Brine Baths were commissioned by the directors to be used by ten wounded British officers, in their recuperation programme.

The fever epidemic in South Africa warranted a further call at home for men with medical experience. Superintendent T. Oldham of the Crewe Ambulance Volunteer Corps, who was also a Crewe postal worker, was one such man who accepted the call, as a Sergeant in the Royal Army Medical Corps. He was to leave for the front by March 6.

On March 2, Sapper Foy wrote home stating that the majority of the Crewe men were still at Modder River and the bridge they had been working on, was nearly finished. Then on March 9, he wrote:

> *'We are doing very well here having had another grand open air concert last Saturday night. The following night we did not come off so fortunate as it rained rather heavily. The next day being Monday we had rather a heavy hailstorm, the smallest being as large as a pigeon's egg.'*

This would be the last letter sent home by Sapper Foy.

After the fall of Kimberley, the next town on the British agenda was Ladysmith, where Sir George White and his garrison remained encircled and constantly bombarded by the famous Boer 'Long Tom' guns. General Buller was given the task and after severe fighting around the outskirts of the town and losses of around 1,200 men, Ladysmith was relieved just before sunset on February 28, when Major Hubert Gough of the 16th Lancers at the head of his men, rode unopposed into the town. Civilians and soldiers rushed to greet them and thus ended the 118-day siege. On March 3, Buller's column made its formal entrance, which was witnessed by Winston Churchill:

> *'The scene was solemn and stirring. The streets were lined with the brave defenders, looking very smart and clean in their best clothes, but pale, thin and wasp-waisted – their belts several holes tighter than was satisfactory.....All through the morning and on in the afternoon the long stream of men and guns flowed through the streets of Ladysmith and all marvelled to see what manner of men these were – dirty, war-torn, travel-stained, tanned, their uniforms in tatters, their boots falling to pieces, their helmets dinted and broken, but nevertheless magnificent soldiers, striding along, deep-chested and broad shouldered, with the light of triumph in their eyes and the blood of fighting ancestors in their veins. It was a procession of lions.....I waved my feathered hat and cheered and cheered until I could cheer no longer for joy, that I had lived to see the day.'*

Among the wounded during the attempt to relieve the town was Private G. Faulkner of the King's Own Royal Lancaster Regiment, who resided in Coppenhall.

News of the relief filtered through to Crewe folk just after 10.00am on Thursday, March 1, and the townsfolk reacted with much greater enthusiasm than all previous successes. By 11.00am all principal buildings in the town were adorned with Union flags. Men, women and children waved small versions in the streets and buses and cabs went about their business decorated in red, white and blue ribbons. Shop windows were also dressed accordingly and carried posters with the words *'Bravo Buller,'* or *'Bravo Tommy Atkins.'* When the men of Crewe Works heard the news, there were wild scenes of patriotic enthusiasm and in the General Offices, *Rule Britannia* was sung with much gusto. Schools in the area shut at noon, so the children could join in the celebrations and during the day, the bells at Christ Church rang out to add to the party atmosphere. In Nantwich the scenes were just as wild and *Rule Britannia* and *Soldiers of the Queen* were sung over and over again by the large crowd assembled on the square.

Further men left Crewe to proceed to the war zone. Dr. James Reginald Atkinson (son of Dr. James Atkinson), who held a commission in the Railway Volunteers (Surgeon Lieutenant), presented himself at Aldershot on March 8 and on Saturday, March 10, Privates J. Scragg, A. Marsh and G. Tagg of the 2nd Shropshire Light Infantry, left Crewe on the 8.05pm train to Shrewsbury, among enthusiastic scenes. Private Scragg, who was a musician in the Engineers Band and his two comrades were accompanied to the railway station by a large crowd of well-wishers and his band, who played *The Absent Minded Beggar* and *Soldiers Of The Queen* en-route.

Fund raising and gifts donated for the front continued at apace in the town, fuelled by British successes, and by early March, QMS Gibson released a new statement for the Crewe Reservists Fund, which amounted to £1,724 0s 10d. Payments to dependants left £1,137 17s 10½d. Schoolchildren in the town played their part, and pupils at Edleston Road held penny concerts every Friday, which raised £10. Four pounds was donated to the fund, with the rest used to buy khaki coloured wool, which the girls knitted into 150 helmets and 40 pairs of socks. These were then filled with tobacco, pipes, scented soap, cigars and stationery. The pupils of the Hightown Wesleyan School also donated 49 pairs of socks.

Back in South Africa, enteric fever continued to affect many in the British ranks. Contaminated water and poor sanitary conditions in the overcrowded camps were the major causes of the disease. Even when the men received water which was pure or had been boiled, there was a risk of contamination from the water bottle the soldier was carrying. There was also no known cure for the disease. Men were offered a vaccine on the outward voyage to the Cape, but because of adverse side-effects, very few took up the inoculation. Naive British views on the handling of water only added to the problems. Dr. Conan Doyle (creator of Sherlock Holmes), who was a practising doctor in South Africa (and would later be among the worse cases during the epidemic at Bloemfontein) wrote on the matter:

> 'It is heartrending for a medical man who has emerged from a hospital full of water-borne pestilence to see a regimental water-cart being filled, without protest, at some polluted wayside pool.'

On March 11, another Crewe man lost his life to the fever when No.2744 Sapper C. Parker of the 8th Railway Company succumbed to his condition in a De Aar hospital. Formerly a member of the Railway Volunteers, he later joined the Royal Engineers and ended up in the same company as his Crewe comrades (Sapper Parker's name is not commemorated on the Boer War memorial in Queens Park). He was buried in De Aar Cemetery (Grave 160).

On March 13, Charles Henry Powell of the St. John Ambulance Brigade, who had left town in December 1899, wrote home about his experiences. He was stationed at No.5 General Hospital, Orange River.

> 'After a fortnight mobilising in London, we proceeded to the Royal Military Hospital at Netley and spent a week in practical hospital training. Early on the morning of Januray 3rd, we left for Southampton and embarked directly on arrival on the Kildonan Castle and at 5.00pm, amid great enthusiasm, we set sail for the shores of Africa......On Sunday morning, the 21st, we disembarked. We camped at Green Point Camp, Cape Town until February 1st when we were surprised to receive urgent orders to proceed to Orange River......This is a journey which a good number, if not all our "active" Crewe Engineers have experienced and in itself it is an experience never to be forgotten.....I am now acting as a clerk in this hospital.....We work from 6am to 6pm and then do 6 hours night duty every other night in the hospital wards.....We have now over 300 cases in hospital including a great number of enteric cases and a lot of dysentery and all description of wounds.....We have two Crewe boys in hospital at present, so I am of some little service to my own townsmen.'

On March 13, Lord Roberts and his all-conquering column entered the Orange Free State capital of Bloemfontein.

Stores, supplies and men continued to pour into South Africa and to many; the war was in its final stages. Upwards of 30,000 fresh troops were landing every month, but the railway network, needed to supply this vast army was hardly up to the task. Without the railways, the British could not supply their garrisons, so the work of the Royal Engineers, in particular, the Railway and Fortress Companies, was crucial if Britain was to bring a swift end to the war.

At Bloemfontein, enteric fever swept through the ranks. When Roberts entered the town, he had with him only ten small hospital units and these were soon swamped with men struck down by the fever. Public buildings in the town were converted into hospitals, but many lay on the bare ground in their tents and also on the floor of the makeshift hospitals. A shortage of bedpans and chamber pots only worsened the situation. Many men suffering with dysentery simply relieved themselves between the tents, further contaminating the ground. In March 1900, there were around 207,000 British troops in South Africa, but only 800 doctors and an equal number of nurses. A *Times* reporter wrote about conditions at Bloemfontein. His report shocked the nation.

> *'Men were dying like flies for want of adequate attention. Hundreds of men to my knowledge were lying in the worst stages of typhoid, with only a blanket and a thin waterproof sheet (not even the latter for many of them) between their aching bodies and the hard ground, with no milk and hardly any medicines, without beds, stretchers or mattresses, without pillows, without linen of any kind, without a single nurse amongst them, with only a few ordinary private soldiers to act as "orderlies" rough and utterly untrained to nursing and with only three doctors to attend 350 patients. The tents were bell tents, affording accommodation for from 6 to 8 men when working and in sound health. In many of these tents there were 10 typhoid cases lying closely packed together, the dying against the convalescent, the man in his "crisis" pressed against the man hastening to it. There was not room to step between them. The ground is as hard as stone and at night the temperature falls to freezing point. The heat of those tents in the midday sun was overpowering, their odours sickening. Men lay with their faces covered with flies in black clusters, too weak to raise a hand to brush them off, trying in vain to dislodge them by painful twitching of the features. There was no one to do it for them.'*

In *The Cape Times*, a reporter wrote a piece on the conditions in the hospitals that could not be read while having breakfast.

> *'The medicine glass was a broken measure glass and I am sure it has not been washed for weeks, for all around the outside edge, there was a thick rim of*

dried saliva and discharge from sore lips etc. making it a disgusting thing to take in one's hand, let alone one's lips. All sorts of medicines were administered out of the same glass, and even the thought of it made me sick.'

At the end of March, further Crewe men from the St. John Ambulance Brigade were summoned to report for active service. First Grade Orderlies H. W. Allen, I. Dickson and William Martin Measures left Crewe, again to enthusiastic scenes.

On March 29, Sergeant P. Huson of the Cheshire Regiment (and also a member of the Railway Volunteers), was wounded at Karee Siding, but fortunately his injuries were not life threatening.

On April 3, the bridge at Modder River was completed, with many Crewe men involved in the reconstruction. On April 15, two more Crewe men died of enteric fever. No.2558 Sapper Arthur Henry Foy of the 8th Railway Company and a member for four years of "B" Company of the Railway Volunteers, died at the Orange River Station. Also No.27830 Sapper F. J. Evans of the 31st Fortress Company and of Herbert Street, Sydney (Crewe) died at Modder River. Ironically, his wife received the telegram notifying her of his death at the very time she was reading her mother a letter from Sapper Evans, stating he was in perfect health. Five days later No.57 Sapper W. Madeley of the 10th Railway Company died of enteric fever at Bloemfontein, becoming another statistic of the disease infested town. He had resided at 148, Henry Street, and was married with three children. Another Crewe man, Sapper J. Swinwood of the 8th Railway Company was also suffering with enteric at the Orange River Station, but his condition slowly improved to warrant a transfer to a Cape Town hospital for recuperation.

As the numbers of the Railway Reserve depleted in the war-zone, hopes were high in Crewe among the second draft, that they would soon get the call, but their furlough was further extended until the end of May. Many of them now believed that their services were no longer required, although the consolation was the regimental pay they continued to draw while on stand-by.

On May 3, Lord Roberts marched out of Bloemfontein and began the trek north to Pretoria. He had with him, 38,000 men and 100 guns. The column stopped at Kroonstad for ten days as Roberts addressed his supply situation. The Boers continued to disrupt the rail network as best they could, and on a stretch between Bloemfontein and Kroonstad, they had cut the line in seventeen places, blown up bridges and culverts and tore up track in 1,000 yard stretches.

Meanwhile on May 4, Colonel Bryan Mahon set out with his relief column to Mafeking. The besieged town had become an obsession with the home public following the relief of Kimberley and Ladysmith and on May 17, prayers were answered when the main body of the relief force marched into the town, following the withdrawal of Boer forces. The 217 day siege was over and Colonel Baden-Powell (who later formed the scout movement) immediately became a national hero. When news of the relief reached London, the capital went crazy. Church bells rang out and squares and streets throughout the Empire rapidly filled with men, women and children, singing, dancing and embracing, in scenes rarely ever witnessed. 'Mafeking Night' officially began on May 18 and carried on until daybreak next day, although sporadically, it continued for a further five days (the celebrations were so remembered that a new verb appeared in the English dictionary. 'Maffick' for many years would be recorded in several ways, including *'to celebrate with boisterous rejoicing and hilarious behaviour'* and *'to celebrate in an exuberant unrestrained manner'*).

In Crewe, celebrations were every bit as wild as the rest of the country. Just after 10.00pm on Friday, May 18, the news broke in Crewe when a telephone call was received at *The Crewe Guardian* offices. Despite the lateness, Crewe streets were soon thronged with excited crowds. Many had sung themselves hoarse long before midnight, saluting Baden-Powell, 'the gallant defender of Mafeking.' Shortly after 11.00pm, a large crowd came from the direction of the fairground in Edleston Road singing *Soldiers of the Queen* and several delivered impromptu speeches. Now formed in marching order, the ever-increasing crowd, headed by a young lad carrying a Union flag and another playing a bugle (very badly!) marched in the direction of the West End. On arrival at the big lamp (the three lamps) in Hightown, the crowd formed a circle and after more singing, speeches and shouting, proceeded down West Street before returning to the Market Square, a few minutes before midnight. Then the crowd made their way into Earle Street where they stopped for a moment at Mirion House, the residence of Dr. James Atkinson, who was a Surgeon Lieutenant Colonel in the Railway Volunteers and had two sons currently serving. As he appeared at his bedroom window, he enquired:

"Men of Crewe, is the news that you bring true?"

He then delivered a stirring speech that lasted for several minutes. Next day the rejoicing of the previous night was soon renewed, when at 5.00am the bells at Christ Church rang out. By 8.00am the town was alive, and almost every shopkeeper displayed a Union flag, and streamers hung across every street, although strangely no flag flew on the Municipal offices or Market Hall. In Crewe Works, the Saturday morning shift arrived for work, but 'work' was not on the agenda, as the first part of the morning was used to decorate respective departments. Throughout this period, patriotic songs were sung and the old works tradition of 'banging hammers' on workbenches only added to the fun of the morning. In the General Offices, clerks proved equal to their shop floor mates, and their workplace was soon bedecked in flags and streamers. Military airs were sung throughout the shift with much enthusiasm. After breakfast in the Boiler Shop, the men formed a procession and after marching around their own department, moved on to the Steel Works and then other shops, until the procession numbered around 500. The attending foreman gave up trying to get the men back to their benches and many left long before the midday dinner buzzer, to carry on celebrations on the Crewe streets. All roads led to the Market Square and carried shoulder high among the railwaymen was Charles Crewe, one of the oldest workmen in the factory. Here the massed crowd sang songs, embraced and drank in the atmosphere. In the afternoon several of the local bands got in on the act including the Engineers, Carriage Works and the Temperance Mission. At 2.00pm, led by the Engineers Band, a large crowd made a tour of all nearby streets. Several band members wore khaki hats, while at the front of the band, a young boy held aloft a portrait of Baden-Powell, decorated with red, white and blue paper. These celebrations continued all afternoon and at 9.00pm some 50 young boys paraded around the town carrying lighted Chinese lanterns. The Mafeking celebrations had surpassed anything seen in the town for many a year. Incredibly, a few weeks later, celebrations would surpass even this day.

The saga concerning the second draft of the Railway Reserve took another negative turn when their furlough was extended until the end of June. With many predicting the end of the war when Pretoria fell, it seemed unlikely that these men would set foot on South African soil.

On Friday, May 25, Crewe Works representatives met at the Euston Coffee Tavern to make arrangements for celebrations, in anticipation of the fall of Pretoria - the capital of the Transvaal. On the following Wednesday, all Crewe Works delegates from every department met in the Commercial Room of the Euston Coffee Tavern, with other local bodies and organisations. It was decided to hold a patriotic demonstration on the Saturday after the fall, and two processions would take place - one in the afternoon and an illuminated one at night, concluding with the lighting of a large bonfire. The whole event was to be called 'The Crewe Works Carnival & Patriotic Demonstration.'

On May 27, another Crewe man died of enteric fever. No.1803 Sapper Septimus Robinson of the 10th Railway Company died at Bloemfontein. Born on March 9, 1875 at Arrad Foot, near Ulverston, he had moved to Crewe seeking work, while his parents, William and Agnes, stayed on the family farm at Nannerch, Mold, Flintshire. He had resided at 31, Rigg Street, Crewe and was laid to rest in the President Brand Garden of Remembrance in Bloemfontein. In the space of three days, two more Crewe men lost their lives to disease. On May 29 at Bloemfontein, No.1443 Sapper F. Ankers, 10th Railway Company, of 87, Cemetery Road, died and next day at Kimberley, No.78083 Driver J. Bebbington of the Ammunition Column, Royal Horse Artillery, died of enteric fever. Also on May 31, the town of Nantwich would grieve a lost son when No.10108 Private C. H. Ankers of the 15th Company, Imperial Yeomanry and of 22, Hospital Street, died of dysentery in McKenzie Farm Hospital, Cape Town. He had sailed with his company to South Africa on April 14.

At this stage of the war, information from South Africa concerning the men of the Railway Reserve was sparse and very few letters appeared in the local newspapers, regarding their work or location. In early June however, it was learned that upwards of 100 men of the 10th Railway Company were suffering from enteric fever, including several from Crewe. It is likely during this period that the majority of Crewe men in their respective units were following behind Lord Roberts and his column, repairing the lines and bridges.

On June 3, Lord Roberts marched from Johannesburg, and two days later, the news all of Britain had been waiting for finally arrived, when he marched triumphantly into Pretoria with 25,531 officers and men, 6,971 horses and 116 guns. Surely now, with both Boer capitals in British hands, the war was at an end. Unfortunately nobody had told the Boers and on June 6, Christiaan De Wet divided his forces into three and attacked and severed the railway line 30 miles northeast of Kroonstad, at Vredefort, and also at Rhenoster River and Roodewal Station. De Wet himself led the attack on Roodewal Station, where £100,000 worth of stores were stockpiled. The area was poorly defended and the Boers soon had their hands on an immense stock of provisions, stores and equipment. They also looted 1,500 mail bags and stole anything that was worth carrying. A total of 486 prisoners were captured during the actions and continued sweep, and among them were ten members of the 10th Railway Company. Two were from Crewe, captured at Leeuw Spruit on June 14, when De Wet attacked their railway construction train. The Sappers had been busily repairing a railway bridge that had been burned down, when they were set upon by around 2,000 of the enemy. The Royal Engineers had only 20 rounds of ammunition between them, but returned fire until their bullets were exhausted, whereupon they surrendered. The prisoners were forced to march for days on end, although many attempts were made to escape despite their exhausted state. Eventually all were set free. One of the men involved in the ordeal was Sapper W. Goodwin, who after his release on July 5 (at Oliver's Nook), complained bitterly in a letter to a friend, about their treatment, which had included starvation and being forced to drink dirty infected water (the other Crewe man was Sapper B. Walker).

Saturday, June 9 was the day chosen in Crewe for the Pretoria celebrations. Every part of the town was bedecked in red, white and blue and it was stated that the decorations even surpassed the 1887 Jubilee party. Tradesmen in the town tried to outdo each other in decorating their shops. Streets were strewn with streamers and flags and everywhere hung portraits of Queen Victoria, Lord Roberts, Baden-Powell and General Buller. Special attention was drawn to the efforts of the residents of Newdigate Street, Stafford Street and Sandbach Street, who had gone that little bit further with their decorations. Even dogs and horses were dressed up in the colours, whether willing or not! In the early morning, the heavens opened and threatened to spoil the afternoon procession, but almost at the same time as the midday buzzer sounded over the Works, the rain stopped and the sun attempted to break through grey clouds.

Although the procession was not due to start until 3.30pm, organisation of the cavalcade took place many hours before. A total of 58 different sections, representing all departments of Crewe Works (plus other non-railway parties and organisations) lined up with the leading section stationed over Merrill's Bridge in West Street, and the last opposite the Gas Works in Victoria Avenue. However, not even this stretch could accomodate all participants, and a number of sections had to 'fall-in' around Queens Park.

The whole parade, which was to be headed by a body of Crewe policemen, was a blaze of colour, with many in extravagant fancy dress. The North Steam Sheds section, for example, were attired as African warriors, and 40 members of the Fitting Shop, as a Naval Brigade, pulled a 'Long Tom' gun on a carriage, supplied by Mr J. H. Cooke of Winsford. The continual firing of the gun, at regular periods, had a great effect on the watching masses. The Fitting Shop also formed a tin whistle band which was preceded by a banner declaring 'Ex-President Kruger's State Band' a dig at the leader of the Boer nation. No.5 & 6 Erecting Shops provided a mouth organ band, but the most impressive part of the procession were the colourful fancy dress costumes produced over a number of weeks with obvious care and attention to detail. Not all were railway sections, and one of the biggest was Compton's factory who had 200 lady workers dressed in khaki, naval and Red Cross uniforms, as well as flower girls and fairies. The town dignitaries in open carriages, including the Mayor, Councillor J. H. Moore, took their place in the procession, behind the Boys Brigade. At the head of the parade were a number of mounted men dressed as famous British soldiers. Mr George Morgan proved most popular representing 'Lord Roberts' as was Mr F. Wooldridge as 'Lord Kitchener.' There was also a place in the procession for six soldiers invalided home - four from Crewe and two from Northwich. The local bands were also well represented and included the Engineers, Steam Shed, Carriage Works, Temperance, St. Barnabas and Borough bands.

When all parties were assembled, the procession numbered 4,000 and extended over 1½ miles. Dr. James Atkinson, the president of the procession and one of the most respected citizens of Crewe, rode in a carriage and took his place at the front, with the mounted 'Lords' as his escort. At 3.40pm the procession started on its long journey. Many thousands were lining the route, with some in the crowd travelling from as far afield as Manchester, Liverpool and Chester.

Without doubt, the incredible scenes and fervour easily put the previous rejoicings firmly in the shade, and every vantage point had been taken long before the commencement of the parade. It didn't take a mathematician to calculate that on no occassion in Crewe's history, had there been so many people in the town. At any one point on the route, it took 40 minutes to see all the sections. To ensure as many people as possible could witness the event, the route was 6½ miles. Along the way, young girls and members of the local Harriers club (80 in all) collected donations for the Indian Famine Relief Fund. The route taken in the afternoon was West Street, Hightown, Victoria Street, Market Street, Henry Street, Richmond Road, Surrey Street, Vincent Street, Earle Street, Market Street, High Street, Mill Street, Nantwich Road, Walthall Street,

Alton Street, Stewart Street, Wistaston Road and finally into Edleston Road to a field adjoining Valley Brook known as Lunt's field. When all had assembled at the field, they formed a circle and Dr. Atkinson drove into the middle with the 'Naval Brigade' as his guard of honour. The sounding of the 'Long Tom' was the signal for him to deliver a long and patriotic speech, which was met with much applause. Afterwards *God Save The Queen* was sung, followed by three cheers for the Queen, Lord Roberts and General Buller.

At night, even more people, encouraged by the fine evening weather, joined the throngs already lining the route and gathered for the finale - the lighting of the large bonfire on Lunt's field. Such were the crowds, for a time, the principal streets in the town became impassable, with no thoroughfare for vehicles. Many carried Chinese lanterns and torches comprising of lighted tarred rope, which had been soaked in paraffin, which more than complimented the shops bedecked in their own illuminations, with many spelling out the words 'V. R.,' 'Victory' or 'Bobs' (nickname of Lord Roberts). A large star also shone down from the steeple at Christ Church, and of the many illuminated buildings, the General Post Office in Market Square, presented a magnificent sight.

The evening procession started just after 9.00pm over a shorter route comprising of West Street, Hightown, Victoria Street, Market Street, High Street, Mill Street, Nantwich Road, Edleston Road, before again arriving at Lunt's field. The procession was headed by the Carriage Works Band and 'Lord Roberts' (Mr G. E. Morgan), and again featured many of the more popular sections from the afternoon show. If it was possible, the evening crowd were even more enthusiastic, with the majority dressed in national colours, draped in the Union flag, or sporting Baden-Powell hats and khaki jackets. What also added to the fun of the night was that many of the party-goers possessed either a drum, toy trumpet or tin whistle and these were banged and blown throughout the procession.

It was nearly 10.45pm before the last sections reached Lunt's field. The crowning glory of the day was the burning of the bonfire constructed on the field. It consisted of 30 tons of material, with the majority donated from Crewe Works - the rest by local tradesmen. On the top was a life-size seated effigy of President Kruger. The bonfire had been built by members of the Joiners Department of the Deviation Works on the previous evening and consisted of wooden sleepers, shavings, straw and mattresses. Fourteen barrels of tar placed in the middle ensured it would burn long into the night. At around 11.00pm the bonfire fuse was lit by

Miss Mirion Atkinson (daughter of Dr. Atkinson) and at that point, the band struck up the National Anthem. The biggest cheer of the night came when 'President Kruger' caught alight, then fell off his chair and disappeared into the flames. The formalities were finally concluded by rockets fired into the dark skies and the booming of the 'Long Tom.'

The whole day passed off without incident, apart from one small boy who fell from a truck in the procession, knocking himself cold. The collection for the Indian Relief Fund (instigated by the Lord Mayor of London) had also gone well. A total of £197 0s 7d was collected, and by the time costs were deducted, £162 7s 9d was forwarded to fund managers.

The momentous day was summed up in a poem composed by Crewe North Steam Sheds worker E. Mullin:

'The Procession'
Ho! Bands strike up war tunes!
Ho! Bobbies clear the way!
For lad and lass by scores will pass
Along the streets today.
Today the doors and windows
Are hung with banners all,
From Nantwich Road and Mill Street
To distant Coppenhall.

While flows the Valley brooklet,
While blows the buzzer loud,
Never again shall Crewe behold
So glorious a crowd.
Gay was the Cottage Hospital fete,
Opening the park was gay;
But Pretoria's fete and procession great,
Shall be Crewe's brightest day.

First marched the stalwart Bobbies,
With solemn, stately mien,
Each proud to share in this pageant fair,
Each loyal to his Queen.
Next Marshals in full war paint,
Booted and spurred are found;
A gallant war horse under each,
Paws haughtily the ground.

Then followed many a horseman,
Garbed all in colours bright;

Red, white and blue and khaki hue,
Truly a brilliant sight!
But now with noise like thunder,
Rise cheers and shouting loud,
And wilder wave the banners,
And closer press the crowd.

For in his chariot seated,
The President draws near!
The bands may play till close of day,
They cannot drown that cheer!
His daughters round him seated,
His kindly face aglow,
He bows to right and to left,
Honoured of high and low.

We read of war and bloodshed,
Of noble deeds and brave;
But the Fire Brigade still lend their aid,
Their fellow men to save.
All honour to the Fire Brigade,
Heroes of peace are they;
Steady of nerve, they as bravely serve,
As in the fiercest fray.

God Bless St. John's brave Ambulance!
God bless the Nurses too!
Through shot and shell in the mouth of hell,
Nobly the work they do.
And now a cheer for the men returned
From fighting the wily Boer;
We clasp the hand of that gallant band -
Bid them welcome home once more.

But of the Steam Shed Kaffirs,
Who shall portray the might?
Each grasps a shield - their spears they wield,
All spoiling for a fight.
And what of the gentle Pierrots,
Who play the bigotphone?
The people stare at sounds so rare
Enchanted by their tone.

Now by St. George of England,
It was a goodly show,

To see the Mayor and Alderman,
Pass in their chariots slow.
And with them rode the tradesmen,
With top hats shining bright,
Till West Street maidens marvelled much,
At such a gorgeous sight.

Next in the long procession,
The Morris Dancers came,
With sashes bright and footsteps light,
They play their merry game.
Then tableaux of the Empire,
And Cyclist maids and men,
And bands galore, about a score;
Their numbers passed by ken.

Our gallant Tars from Ladysmith,
'Long Joe' they hauled amain;
Three cheers for the brave who on land and wave,
Old England's flag maintain.
'Long live our Queen Victoria,'
With loyal voice we sing -
'Long live our Bobs and brave B.P.
Hero of Mafeking!'

Back at the war zone, Lord Roberts became concerned about a strong enemy presence about 16 miles east of Pretoria and decided to do something about it. On June 11, he marched on the position with 14,000 men and 70 guns, determined to drive them beyond striking distance of the capital. A force of 6,000 was waiting and a two day battle ensued around Diamond Hill and would prove to be one of the final large confrontations of the war. By nightfall on June 12, the two armies were at stalemate, but the following day, the British again attacked, only to find that the Boers had packed up and disappeared during the night.

On June 16, just a week after the grand procession, another landmark occasion was celebrated in Crewe when the 4,000th locomotive ('La France') rolled off the production line at Crewe Works. The workforce of nearly 8,000 were given a paid holiday on the Friday and at night a banquet to honour the occasion was held by the directors at the Crewe Arms Hotel for the officials and foremen of the Works, who numbered around 100. The chair on the evening was held by the Works manager, Mr H. D. Earl who was supported by Dr. Atkinson. Francis William Webb was on important business at Euston and missed the celebration.

Letters from South Africa, especially from the Railway Reserve, were absent from the local papers during this period of the war (many would have been destroyed in De Wet's attacks at Roodewal Station or delayed due to the constant break in communication lines) with many of them either working in remote parts of South Africa or sick in hospital. Local medical men afforded a few letters telling of life in the many hospitals in the war zone. Superintendent T. Oldham wrote from No.11 General Hospital, Kimberley, where conditions seemed much better than at Bloemfontein.

'We have been here three weeks and opened the hospital very hurriedly – 390 patients before we had hardly a marquee erected…..We send a good many to Cape Town as soon as they are sufficiently recovered to travel…..It is winter here. The days are very hot and the nights particularly cold…..At present I occupy a large marquee which is the stores for the whole hospital. A sentry is "on go" round the tent 6pm to 7am. I sleep in the marquee surrounded by over £1,000 worth of spirits, besides three days provisions for over 1,000 persons. This is my particular line as I act as steward for the whole of No.11 General Hospital……The hospital staff is 236; officers 34; nursing sisters 13; 3 female servants and at present there are 832 patients…..Our camp is over a mile square and to walk from one corner right round to the same place would take a good half hour. We have over 100 marquees, 100 bell-tents, 20 horses, 25 mules and 13 natives. The hospital is two miles from town and we have every sickness and wounds. Corporal Nurse (now Sgt.) the man who, along with Lord Roberts's son tried to save the guns at Colenso, and won the V.C. is now in hospital here. We have several Boer prisoners sick. There are no houses within half a mile of our camp which is near to the De Beers Mine. The electric light has been laid on in each marquee and it is nearly all complete. A railway has also been cut into the centre of camp and a platform made. The ambulance train runs in here and tonight it left here with 70 for Cape Town…..I issue about 1,500 pints of milk per day, 500 of this being Irish (cow) milk. My issue of brandy is about 80 bottles a day, whisky 80 and port 90…..Every man in hospital is in a blue flannel suit and has a wire mattress, bedstead, hair mattress, pillow, bolster, two rugs and a nice white counterpane.'

Charles Henry Powell also wrote two letters home that appeared in the local press in June, 1900. His first was from No.5 General Hospital, Orange River.

'Enteric fever and dysentery account for the greater portion of our medical cases and you will at once judge the amount of work, when I say that about 4,000 patients have been treated in this hospital since our arrival on February 3…..I have agreed to serve another period of six months if necessary…..I am

sorry to say that we (the St. John) have lost three men by death, three are being invalided home to England and two more are lying in hospital now, all from enteric fever. I attended the funeral of Sapper Foy of Crewe.'

His next letter, written on June 12, was from No.3 General Hospital, Kroonstad. Here he tells of the final days of Sapper Arthur Foy.

'.....I think the event which caused greatest excitement and the greatest display of patriotism was the Relief of Mafeking. When the news was confirmed, everybody (except the Boers) appeared overcome with joy. But we who are engaged in hospital work are often bearers of news which is not joyous and in many cases, as in the present, most sad. I refer to the illness and death of one of our Crewe Engineers, Sapper Foy at Orange River. Although not actually under my care, I often visited him and endeavoured to cheer him up by retailing scraps of "home news" and as a last token of respect for him, as the only Crewe person at Orange River, followed him to his last resting place.....We left Orange River at 6.00pm on May 31st (to Kroonstad) and proceeded direct to Naauwpoort. Here we changed after waiting two hours in a biting frost, we continued our journey en route to Bloemfontein.....I ascertained that a lot of Crewe men were encamped in Bloemfontein, but was not fortunate enough to see any of them. At Springfontein I met Arthur Dunn of the Crewe Engineers who is now employed as a shunter. About 9.00am we loaded into open trucks and resumed our journey to Kroonstad and saw plenty of evidence of the recent fights and marches of the troops – dead animals, newly dug graves, rifled stores, broken railway lines etc. We arrived at Kroonstad about noon.....Our hospital consists of 30 large marquees and 50 bell-tents and our patients number 500. There is a large force of Boers in this vicinity and we are daily expecting an attack. The town has been entrenched and fortified during the last few days.'

On June 30, the Railway Volunteers still at home, left town under the command of Colonel Cotton-Jodrell during the Crewe Works summer holiday for their encampment at Chatham which was to last four weeks. A total of 618 men (22 Officers, 39 Sergeants and 557 other rank; "A" Company - 95 men, "B" Company - 79 men, "C" Company - 116 men, "D" Company - 113 men, "E" Company 97 men, "F" Company - 107 men, Staff - 11 men) assembled on the Market Square at 8.00am and again the route to the station was lined with spectators. When at camp, the men took part in several shooting competitions and again, the opposition were no match for the Crewe Corps. The Sergeants of the Royal Engineers mess were beaten 536-528, with Sgt. Johnson (64pts.) and Sgt. Latham (63pts.) top scorers for the Crewe team. Then they beat the Lanark Engineers 608-510, with notable scores from Sgt. Latham (65pts.), Sgt. Johnson (62pts.), Sapper Capper (62pts.), and Corporal Crumble (62pts.). They returned to Crewe on July 26, and once again a large crowd turned out to see them march from the station to Market Square.

After De Wet's triple attack on June 6, which cut the British supply route to Bloemfontein, Roberts dispatched Kitchener to protect the lines and also Kroonstad, which De Wet now threatened. These were dangerous times for the men of the Royal Engineers, especially the Railway Companies, who were often working on lines in isolated parts of the country and prone to attack at any time. Lord Roberts, fed up with continual attacks on the railway network, decided to employ ruthless punishments to help protect his supply route and ordered farms to be burnt anywhere near the railway, where the line had been cut or attacked, with the occupants taken into custody.

In July of this year, the British began to build blockhouses to protect railway bridges and important stretches of track. These were substantial stone structures which offered considerable protection against attack, but elsewhere a more simplified and cost-effective blockhouse was constructed, out of corrugated iron sheets. Eventually Lord Kitchener, in his drive to trap the Boer commandos, would supervise the building of up to 8,000 of these structures, which would be manned by around 50,000 troops and 16,000 natives. They were sited with interlocking fields of fire, surrounded by trip wires and joined together by barbed wire and trenches spread across the veldt (the longest continuous line of these blockhouses was from east of Pretoria to Komati Poort, a stretch of 175 miles). The men of the 8th and 10th Railway Companies would help in the construction and later in the war would help man them.

Enteric fever claimed two more Crewe men in July. On July 21, No.3251 Private A. Burgess of the 1st King's Royal Rifles died at Newcastle and thirteen days previous No.1221 Trooper Arthur Cecil Morris of the 5th Company, Imperial Yeomanry, succumbed at Kroonstad. A letter home from Trooper R. Oakley of Crewe, from the Imperial Yeomanry Branch Hospital in Cape Town, told of Trooper Morris's final battle with the enemy.

'The last day we were together was the 31st of May when we went under Lord Methuen to try to relieve the Duke of Cambridge's Own and the Irish Yeomanry and we fought one of the hardest fights that have taken place in the Orange

River Colony. The fight lasted from daylight to dark and although "Ciss" Morris was a long way from well, he fought like a Briton and we were close together all day. He had been gradually weakening for some time and that day completely knocked him up. The column took three days rest, but he was unable to come on with us when we moved away in pursuit of De Wet. I shall never forget him saying "Good-bye" to me that morning. He was fairly broken down and tears stood in his eyes as we shook hands. The next news I got was from home, asking me if it was true he was dead.....I failed to learn anything definite until, by chance, I met the very fellow who nursed him right through his sickness. He had fallen victim to that terrible scourge enteric.'

On Saturday, July 28, a brass memorial plaque was mounted on the south wall of the Parish Church in Nannerch, Flintshire, in honour of Sapper Septimus Robinson, who had died on May 27 of enteric fever. He had been a choir member of the church for ten years. The next day, a special service was held and twenty members of the Crewe Wheelers Cycling Club,* with whom the deceased had been associated, rode from Crewe to attend. After the service, they visited Sapper Robinson's mother at the farm at Plas Yw, then spent the afternoon making an ascent of Moel Arthur. They later had tea at the home of Captain H. W. Buddicom, viewing his collection of curios and 'machinery room.'

*Other sources stated the party attending were Crewe Engineers. This could well have been true as several of the Railway Volunteers were also members of the Crewe Wheelers Cycling Club.

On July 30, the British rounded up many Free State Boers in the Brandwater Basin area and by August 9, some 4,500 were prisoners. Many Boer fighters had simply lost the stomach for a fight. After all, they had lost both capitals, all towns of any importance, and most of the railway network was now in British hands.

Roberts then launched his vast column towards Komati Poort to capture the last stretch of railway, while General Buller moved along the line that ran from Durban to Ladysmith and into the Transvaal. On September 1, Roberts proclaimed the annexation of the Transvaal and on September 24, an advanced British column entered the almost deserted town of Komati Poort. For the British there was nothing else to capture, and Roberts had achieved all of this in less than a year, and many in the ranks believed they would be home for Christmas. General Buller left for England on October 24 and Lord Roberts on December 11, after Lord Kitchener was made C-in-C in South Africa on November

29 (Lord Roberts would be promoted to C-in-C of the British Army). Many troops were indeed sent home. The reduced man-power was re-organised and the British started to dismantle their supply structure. This delay however, gave the Boers some much needed time to regroup, and begin what would be a third phase of the war. Their plans were to take the fight to the British with a number of small-scale skirmishes over a large area, by attacking minor garrisons, destroying railway lines and bridges and causing as much disruption as possible. This period of 'guerilla war' would signal more British losses than in all previous battles and engagements.

Letters from the front continued to be published in Crewe newspapers, although now, with no major battles being fought, they appeared only sporadically. Writing from Christiana on October 1, was Dr. Atkinson's son, James, better known in Crewe as 'Doctor Jim.' He was serving in General Settle's column as second in command of the medical staff and had worked at the 11th Base Hospital at Durban and then at Kimberley, where he had treated several Crewe men suffering with enteric fever, dysentery and wounds. Here he tells of the hardships endured on a column march and the burning of Boer farms.

> 'We started from Vryburg with about 1,000 mounted men, 2,000 infantry and 500 natives, about 1,000 mules and 90 ox wagons each with a span of 16 oxens. General Settle was in command of the column. We set out for a place called Schweizer Reneke where there was a garrison of 300 odd men besieged by the Boers and they had been shut up in this place for about seven weeks. We set out purposely to relieve these people. On our way we passed a large farm belonging to Pretorious, the renowned field cornet who had signed the oath of neutrality, but having broken it, all the stock was looted or sent back to Vryburg and the farm was afterwards burnt. It was a first class place in every way – a library, bedroom, drawing room, kitchen, and of all things a grand piano. All were burnt and two adjacent farms, from which we were fired at, were also burnt, because the owners of them had signed the oath of neutrality and consequently we did not consider them, as by the treachery of those within these farmhouses, lots of our poor fellows were sent to their last resting place. We first looted the farms and then burnt them, but in those cases where the occupants were loyal and gave us assistance, they were all respected and any necessaries that we took from them were paid for. On arriving at Schweizer Reneke we discovered the Boers had all fled. We remained there for three days and jolly glad I was to have the rest. The only things in the way of food obtainable at the stores or their so-called hotels in this place were tea and pickles and we regaled ourselves sumptuously at the Byger Hotel with a cup of tea without milk or sugar. The place is on the Hartz River, which is now a series of puddles, but which in the rainy season, is, I

believe, a raging torrent. Lord Methuen's column arrived a day after us, but he did not come into the place but trekked north. During the time that we were there, we had nothing but sandstorms which are something dreadful and you in England can form no idea of what they are like. We left the place none too soon as a lot of our men were falling sick. We trekked to Tolly de Bere's farm at Vierfontein. I got in well with the advance party and managed to collar an egg and a goose. With the arrival of the main column everything eatable was looted. There were about 16 women and children in the farmhouse. We camped there the night and the next morning the farm was burnt in consequence of the treacherous conduct of the occupants. I was with the rear guard that day, so I went up to a farm and had a long chat with the people. They had got some bedding and odds and ends on the veldt and were seated round a fire. When the column had passed the rear guard we fired the house. The women all wept copiously and I myself was very upset. This however, is one of the things of war, and as these people had behaved very un-Christian like after all, perhaps they were served right. I got them greatly into my favour by giving them some little attention and prescribing for them and giving them a huge bottle of physic. You are probably aware that the Dutch people are very fond of physic. It was a very distressing scene. At another farm which we passed, I went investigating on my own account and in an outhouse I found some cartridges, one of which I have kept, called the Clip. The Cape Police were rather annoyed at me because I would not report this, because had I done so, the farm would have probably been burnt to the ground. We struck the Vaal River between Bloemhof and Christiana and then came alongside the river at Christiana. Before we reached the Vaal, I caught a fat goose and killed him by hitting him over the head with my riding whip. This was on the morning of the 29th of September, so that night we had a Michaelmas goose for tea. We have now come into Christiana without stores and we are to wait here for a few days until the stores come up from Warrenton, which is on the railway, and then on the move again. I don't know where we shall go next, because this, as you know, is a flying column and may be sent anywhere. The place we are at present is the prettiest I have seen in South Africa, but the country we have come through is simply awful. You can have no conception of it. It is perfect desert, a total wilderness. Often we cannot water our horses for more than 24 hours at a stretch and then the water was more like thick pea soup than anything else. The troops mostly had well water and I have seen men fighting for water at a well as I have never saw men fight in my life before. In fact I was so taken up with it that I got a snap shot of one scene, which I hope to send home. I have seen men drinking water that horses have trampled through and defiled and made it appear like slimy mud and on this account we have had lots of cases of dysentery. It is not possible to boil water at all times and we get tea or coffee where it is possible, but often, through the want of wood or time, or a great excess of wind, this is impossible. Another "nice" thing is getting up in the middle of the night, generally about 3.30am to start at 4 o'clock, and then being in the saddle until 7pm, by which hour it is perfectly dark. We generally stop at 10.00am for half an hour for breakfast and at one or two o'clock have another halt for dinner in order to give the horses a rest and to out span the oxen. When the day's work is done you are dead tired and after trying to get what you can to eat, you endeavour to obtain a few hours sleep. You are not allowed to take your boots off when you sleep for fear of a night attack. We do not exactly dread these night attacks because we have got somewhat used to them and we can take precautions, but it is the constant sniping where the great danger lies and not in open battle. We have had very few casualties, the worst case being that of a native scout, who was shot through the elbow and the hand. I operated upon him and took off his arm, the arm being completely shattered and the elbow being knocked all to bits. In fact without amputation there was no prospect of the man making a recovery. The Boers have not made a stand against us at any place. They only sniped at us especially at night time. It was a bit "jumpy" at first being in the midst of the fighting line, and when you are tired you pay little or no attention to it. There are 3 doctors in the field hospital and 4 regimental doctors and I am second in command. The P.M.O. has gone on a visit to Warrenton since we have been here, so that I am left in charge of the whole column for the time being. There is great difficulty in getting any fresh vegetables or eggs and we cannot get any condensed milk, because of the transport, our first considerations being munitions of war and the second our sick. I have however, done the best as a makeshift with Nestle's and Mellin's food and give this in all bad cases in place of milk. We have about 15 dysenteries and one of them is really bad. I have visited several farms in search of milk or eggs for our poor fellows, and today have found a little milk and 12 eggs after much exertion. Our food consists daily of one pound of tinned meat, one pound of "hard tack," one sixth of an ounce of tea, some sugar and some jam, the latter being greatly prized by "Tommy." I suppose they give us jam to get plenty of sugar inside, because it is very sustaining and I can assure you the men like it. Bread and potatoes I miss most, and I shall have a good tuck in when I meet them again. I forgot to mention that when in Vryburg, we got 40 natives to act as stretcher bearers; they are great cowards at all times. They sent me to their head boy yesterday to say that they wanted to go home to their wives and other relatives, but I explained to them that I should have them flogged if any of them attempted to desert, so that settled the matter. Everybody I need hardly say, is tired of this war and anxious to get home, but still the men endure great hardships and discharge their duties cheerfully, knowing that it is for the well-being of the dear old country.'

Superintendent T. Oldham also wrote home, from the 11th General Hospital in Kimberley. His letter was addressed to Mr W. Eardley:

'Everything is expensive, hardly anything is less than 3d and coppers are almost unknown. A glass of beer costs 6d, whisky 9d and that for the common whisky. Food is also expensive. On September 30, in company with 7 civilian gentlemen, we visited Magersfontein and thoroughly enjoyed the day. We picked up pieces of shell, shrapnel and some bullets. We also saw the

> *graves of the Highlanders. It was very fortunate that we went then for all persons are now kept away from the battlefields of Belmont, Graspan, Modder River and Magersfontein owing to the Boers being about there.'*

By November, the British, due to their farm burning policies, faced a refugee problem. Boer families who had men fighting simply had their homes burnt to the ground and this saw numbers of the homeless rise at an alarming rate. The British had to act fast or see them starve to death. Therefore refugee or 'concentration camps' were hastily set up. The majority of the refugees were women and children, but the camps lacked the fundamental basics to sustain even a standard existence, and with so many (mostly under canvas) crowded together in all weathers and with inadequate sanitary conditions, this was a recipe for disaster on a massive scale.

In the early hours (around 4.00am) on Wednesday, November 7, the Royal train, carrying Queen Victoria passed through Crewe Station, although due to the time of day, only a handful of people witnessed the event. Mr Philip Howman of Crewe drove the pilot engine *Prince of Wales*, arriving fifteen minutes prior to the Royal train, which had attached two engines, with the first driven by Mr W. J. Phillips and the second by Mr Ben Robinson, who were both well-known Crewe drivers.

On November 10, it was reported in *The Crewe Chronicle* that upwards of 30 men of the original draft of the Railway Reserve had now been invalided home and with the 5 who had died, around 90 men remained, although a percentage of these men were also suffering from disease. The rest were operating in many different parts of the war zone. No date was fixed for their return, but what was certain was the fact that they would not return as one body. This of course ruled out a formal homecoming, so it was suggested that when all had returned, a day would be arranged in their honour. Many of the serving men, now back in town had recovered sufficiently to go back to their civilian employment, but remained in a state to return to South Africa if the need arose.

In December, a scarlet fever epidemic hit Crewe. Especially affected was the south ward. This month also saw the introduction of electricity in the shops and larger houses in the area.

As men returned from South Africa due to the scaling down of British forces, First Class Reservists of the town also came home. On December 14, a party was held at 36, Beech Street (the home of Mr G. Hurst), to welcome home Private George Tonks of the 23rd Bn. Royal Welsh Fusiliers.

Towards the end of the year Chief Officer Gawthorne of the Crewe Division of the St. John Ambulance Corps, received a further request from the HQ of the Brigade in London, for additional volunteers for active service. As a result, Private W. Thornton left Crewe for Aldershot on Christmas Eve. Being a medical man in South Africa was a perilous job and it would be inevitable that some of the staff would contract the diseases they were trying to cure. This would happen to Charles Henry Powell, a prominent and much-respected member of the Crewe Ambulance Corps, who had left for South Africa on January 3, 1900. On the homeward voyage to England after completing his first term of service, he was struck down with enteric fever and transferred to Netley Hospital on arriving at Southampton on December 21. Whether he contracted the disease on the ship, or in hospital at Kroonstad is unknown, but in a letter dated November 21, to Mr J. Derbyshire (Manager of the Crewe Co-operative Society), it gives a clue to his condition when he left for home.

> 'Today I commence my homeward journey hoping to arrive not later than December 26. I am thankful to say that my health is fair, but I am feeling rather run down, probably the sea voyage will bring me back to my usual health and strength.'

Other Crewe men lay dangerously ill as the year came to an end. Crewe Alexandra veteran Private E. Burgoyne of the Lancashire Fusiliers, was very poorly in a South African hospital suffering with enteric fever and Mr A. Lewis of Ivy House, Crewe received news that his son, Lieutenant J. A. Lewis of the 13th Hussars, was still on the danger list after being badly wounded on November 29. Fortunately both men would make a full recovery.

For the Railway Volunteers, the year concluded on Friday, December 28, with their annual ball in the Mechanics Institute after the postponement the previous year. Around 400 members and their lady friends attended, as well as a number of regular soldiers on furlough.

Chapter Three - 1901
-More Railwaymen Required!-

A distinguished visitor was the cause of great excitement in Crewe on January 2, 1901, when General Sir Redvers Buller, who had recently returned from South Africa, arrived in town, as a guest of Lord Crewe. When rumour of his visit circulated, a large crowd soon gathered at the station top, eagerly awaiting his arrival. The General and his wife, Lady Audrey, arrived at 6.15pm, having travelled up from Exeter, and were mobbed and cheered by the enthusiastic crowd, with many pushing

Two buildings built in the town in 1900. **(ABOVE)** *The Crewe Corporation established an Electricity Works on the banks of the River Waldron on land just off the bottom of Edleston Road.* **(BELOW)** *The LNWR Company Hospital in Mill Street.*

(**ABOVE**) British dead after the Battle of Spion Kop. (**BELOW**) The burial ground today. The majority of the fallen were interred where they lay. Roughly translated Spion Kop (Spioenkop) means (spioen) 'spy or look-out' and (kop) 'hill or outcropping.' In 1906 Liverpool F.C. renamed their banked stand 'Spion Kop' in honour of the many Lancashire men who lost their lives during the engagement, and many other football clubs replicated the idea. The village of Spion Kop near Mansfield is also named after the battle.

(**ABOVE LEFT**) Lord 'Bobs' Roberts and (**ABOVE RIGHT**) Lord Kitchener. Their arrival in the war-zone marked the turning point in the war.

(**ABOVE**) A much-prized Queen Victoria chocolate tin. This one belonged to Sergeant Thomas William Brett of the 8th Railway Company.

*The Modder River bridge. (**ABOVE**) The north span after being dynamited by the Boers.*

*(**ABOVE**) The reconstructed 'Crewe built' bridge, completed on April 3.*

FROM CREWE TO THE CAPE

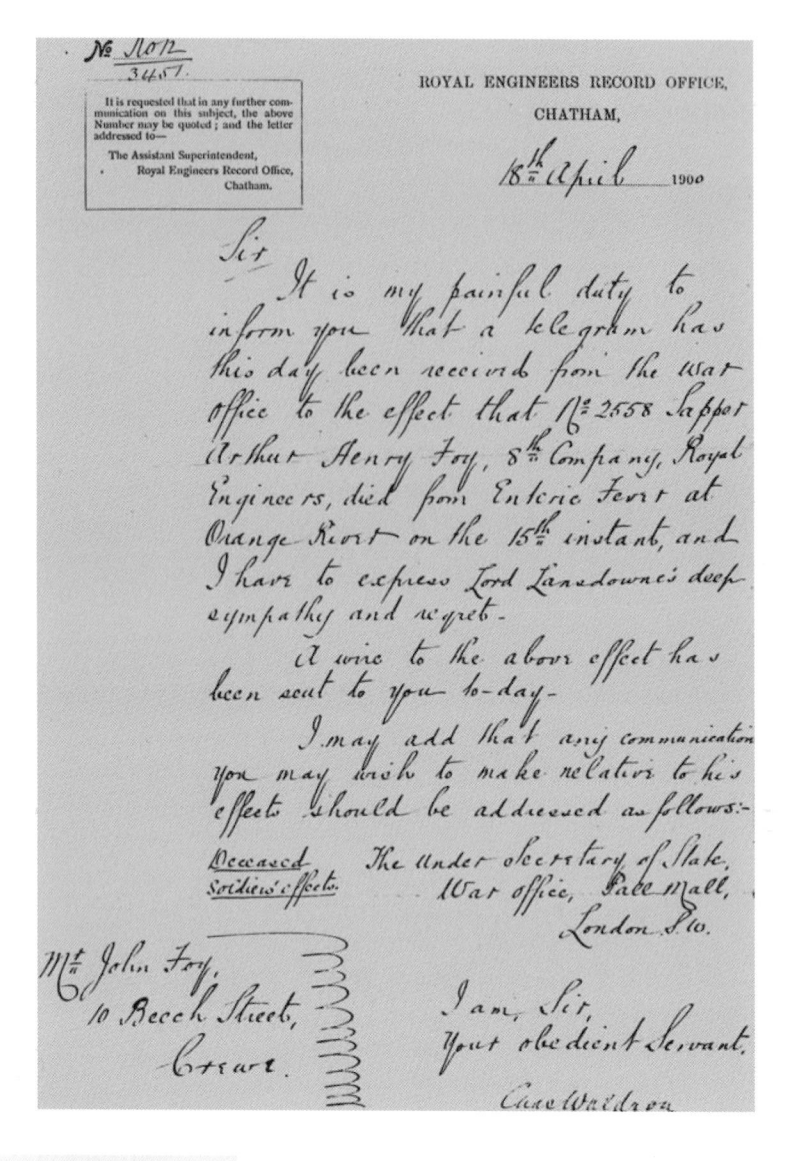

> No. ЛОЛ / 3451
>
> It is requested that in any further communication on this subject, the above Number may be quoted; and the letter addressed to:—
> The Assistant Superintendent,
> Royal Engineers Record Office,
> Chatham.
>
> ROYAL ENGINEERS RECORD OFFICE,
> CHATHAM,
>
> 18th April 1900
>
> Sir,
>
> It is my painful duty to inform you that a telegram has this day been received from the War Office to the effect that No. 2558 Sapper Arthur Henry Foy, 8th Company, Royal Engineers, died from Enteric Fever at Orange River on the 15th instant, and I have to express Lord Lansdowne's deep sympathy and regret.
>
> A wire to the above effect has been sent to you to-day.
>
> I may add that any communication you may wish to make relative to his effects should be addressed as follows:—
>
> Deceased Soldiers' effects.
>
> The Under Secretary of State,
> War Office, Pall Mall,
> London S.W.
>
> Mr. John Foy,
> 10 Beech Street,
> Crewe.
>
> I am, Sir,
> Your obedient Servant,
> Cae Waldron

(**LEFT**) A faded photograph of Sapper Arthur Henry Foy. (**ABOVE**) The casualty letter sent to his parents.

*(**ABOVE LEFT**) Colonel Baden-Powell. (**ABOVE RIGHT**) Sapper Henry Beckett of the 45th Fortress Company, who left his home at 7, Clifton Street, with the first draft of the Railway Reserve. The photo was taken in Mafeking. (**BELOW LEFT**) A newspaper boy in London announces the end of the siege. (**BELOW RIGHT**) Mafeking celebrations took place all over the Empire. Here two young boys from North Shields take part. The small boy standing is Arthur Stanley Jefferson - later to become Stan Laurel of Laurel and Hardy fame.*

(**ABOVE LEFT**) *The grave of Sapper Septimus Robinson.* (**ABOVE RIGHT**) *The plaque erected in Nannerch Church.* (**BELOW**) *British troops march triumphantly into Pretoria - capital of the Transvaal.*

(ABOVE) *The Fitting Shop as 'The Naval Brigade' on June 9, 1900 - 'Pretoria Day.' The 'Long Tom' gun is just behind them.* *(BELOW)* *Sergeant Thomas William Brett of the 8th Railway Company.*

(ABOVE) The 4,000th loco to roll off the Crewe Works production line - 'La France.' It was a four-cylinder compound 4-4-0 type, shown at the Paris Exhibition in 1900.

(ABOVE) More work for the Railway Companies at Norvals Pont, after the bridge over the Orange River was blown on March 7, 1900. (BELOW) QMS George Gibson enjoys a cat nap during the Chatham encampment, July 1900.

forward in an attempt to shake the General's hand. After his warm welcome, he departed to Crewe Hall in one of Lord Crewe's carriages. Next morning, the Lord, his wife and guests paid a visit to the Railway Works. The party arrived at the General Offices and were warmly greeted by Francis William Webb, who then proceeded to escort them on a tour of the principal departments. As General Buller passed through the relevant workshops, he was given a rousing cheer. The party then visited the newly opened Electricity Works, before they retired back to Crewe Hall for refreshments, much to the disappointment of a large crowd that had gathered at Coppenhall Terrace, who had hoped that the party would return to the General Offices. Lady Buller and Lord Crewe's sister, Lady Fitzgerald, visited the Cottage Hospital on January 5, and spent 90 minutes talking to patients, especially in the children's ward. On Sunday, January 6, General and Lady Buller attended a church service at Crewe Green, again accompanied by Lord and Lady Crewe. The church was packed to capacity, with many more congregating outside, hoping to get a glimpse of the Victoria Cross winner (won during the Zulu campaign). Next day, General Buller and his wife left for home although only a small crowd gathered at the station to see them off on the 10.51am express to London. Few had anticipated the departure, but as the train left the station, they were given a rousing send-off from passengers on nearby platforms.

The excitement had barely calmed down, when another dark cloud descended, after news reached Crewe that another brave son had lost his life. No.118 1st Grade Orderly Charles Henry Powell of the St. John Ambulance Brigade had recovered from his enteric fever somewhat in Netley Hospital to warrant his colleagues and friends to plan a welcome home party, but a week after his initial recovery, things took a turn for the worst, when he contracted pneumonia. He died in the afternoon of January 4, aged just 22. His body arrived in Crewe around 10.20am on Monday, January 7, and was met by his father and undertaker, Mr T. Smith, as well as a party of St. John Ambulance men under the supervision of Chief Officer Gawthorne. The body was taken to his home at Walnut Villa, 186, Bradfield Road in Coppenhall, until the funeral, which took place two days later. All along the funeral route to Coppenhall Church, crowds gathered to pay their last respects, standing in silence as the snow fell throughout the afternoon. House blinds remained closed as the cortege passed, which included upwards of 150 employees from the Crewe Co-operative Society, a large number of scholars from the Wesleyan Sunday School in Coppenhall and members of the Crewe Wednesday Cycling Club, Ambulance Brigade and the 'Cross Green' Lodge of the Order of Druids.

The gloom and despair continued into the month, when on January 22, after being on the throne since 1837, Queen Victoria died after a long illness. The news in the local area was conveyed by an official notice posted in *The Crewe Guardian* office window shortly after 7.00pm. Most tradesmen in the town who were still open, immediately shut up shop, and later that evening the minute bell began to toll at Christ Church and continued for over half an hour. Flags flew at half-mast at Christ Church, the Market Hall and throughout the town, and next day the bells again rang out a sorrowful peal from the afternoon until early evening. Smoking parties and balls planned for the next couple of weeks were cancelled as a mark of respect and on Sunday, January 27, special services were held throughout Crewe. Saturday, February 2, was the date of the funeral and all over the Empire, people prepared to pay their respects. In Crewe the railway works were closed, along with all shops, public houses and other business establishments. No sporting events took place and the theatre was also closed. Flags flew at half-mast throughout the town and the weather added to the sombre occasion, as it was wet and cold, with the occasional flurry of snow. Of the few who walked the streets, many were dressed in black, although the majority of the townsfolk stayed at home for private mourning. Only a Sunday service ran on the trains and all public buses were cancelled. Next day special church services were held throughout the town with the Mayor, members of the council, and corporation officials attending Christ Church. The Crewe Engineers took part in the service at St. Paul's, marching there from the Market Square, with both officers and men in full dress uniform and the officers donning crepe armlets. For a short time, the war in South Africa was forgotten.

Back at the war zone, Lord Kitchener, in January 1901, began to expand the blockhouse line. With the lines in place and his continued 'scorched earth' policy, the Boers would, eventually have nowhere to hide or obtain food stocks. Kitchener also planned extensive sweeps between the blockhouses and barbed wire, using mounted troops. Back in Britain, Kitchener's strong arm tactics were not viewed by all as being 'exactly fair' and anti-war opposition grew, fuelled by the tedium of the neverending guerrilla war and the atrocious state of the concentration camps, where the deaths of Boer women and children were regularly reported on. Emily Hobhouse, a forty-one year old spinster from Cornwall visited a number of these camps and reported back to all who would listen, at meetings held all over the country.

Confusion reigned in Crewe at the HQ of the Crewe Railway Engineers, when on Wednesday, February 6, a notice was received from the War Office to provide two Volunteer sections of 25 men, to be accepted for service, in readiness to travel to South Africa, with the new contingent of Yeomanry and Volunteers. Had the War Office overlooked the fact that 100 men of the second draft had now been waiting for over thirteen months, on Army pay while on furlough? On the same day, another Crewe man lost his life in South Africa. No.1984 Private J. Thomason of the 2nd King's Shropshire Light Infantry died of disease in Pretoria.

A week after the funeral of Queen Victoria, the Mayor of Crewe announced the proclamation of King Edward VII from the balcony of the Post Office on the Market Square, to a crowd of around 3,500.

Superintendent Oldham meanwhile, at No.2 General Hospital, Kimberley, had a narrow escape on February 11/12, when a cyclone hit the hospital and destroyed large parts of the camp. Luckily no one was seriously injured, although upwards of 30 marquees (from a total of 100) were ripped to pieces with only 7 left standing.

On Thursday, February 21, another order was received by the Crewe Engineers at their HQ, for the two Volunteer Service Sections to be in readiness for their call up. The second draft of the Railway Volunteers had, at very short notice, now received orders to proceed to Chatham, on Monday, February 25. On the Saturday before departure, they were entertained at the Crewe Arms Hotel, by Colonel Cotton-Jodrell and the remaining Railway Volunteer officers. Most gratifying for this draft was the fact that they were to be originally attached to "E" and "G" Companies of the Royal Engineers under their own officers, namely Lieutenants Charles Sidgwick, N. H. Brierley and A. C. Tweedy. Lieutenant Tweedy was an assistant foreman at the Longsight Locomotive Department and before his departure to Chatham, his workmates presented him with a six-chambered revolver. He was also a popular member of the Crewe Alexandra Cricket Club and excelled as a batsman.

When the day arrived for departure, the scenes on the Market Square were just as enthusiastic as the first 'send off' in October 1899. This time Crewe Works was not closed, but around three-quarters of the workforce were absent after breakfast, so they too could witness the event. Traffic was diverted from the march route and every vantage point, no matter how precarious, was utilised to the full. Again the balconies over the Birmingham Bank, the Post Office and other places of business at the far end of the Square had been converted into temporary grandstands. By 9.00am the streets were already crowded as the sun shone brilliantly. At the sound of the bugle just after 10.00am, the men formed up in their respective detachments ("E" and "G") to face Mayor Dr. Wilson, who then delivered a stirring speech:

"Colonel Cotton-Jodrell, officers, non-commissioned officers and men of the South African contingent. I am here today in the name of your townsmen to wish you God speed in the heroic mission on which today at your country's call you go forth. I congratulate your Colonel that under his command he has such a splendid set of men. I congratulate the railway company that in a spirit of self-sacrifice they are ready to send you in response to your nation's call, and I am proud as one of your townsmen to know that you are all men of Crewe. For the second time in a comparatively few months, Crewe has been called upon to send a large contingent to South Africa, men specially trained for a particular purpose. We thus hold, I think, a unique position amongst the towns of England. Already your comrades beyond the sea have gained a high reputation and have won the praise and appreciation of all their officers. We know full well that you will maintain that reputation, that you will do your best to equal it, if not excel it, and we know too that the honour of the Engineers, the reputation of your splendid Battalion and the credit of Crewe is safe in your hands. We trust that your presence and work in South Africa will equally help on the peace which we so much long for. We promise you that in your absence we shall not forget those you leave behind and we hope that very soon you will return again and that when the roll is called, every man, hale and hearty, will be here to receive that welcome we long to give him. I wish you once more in the name of the town goodbye and may God be with you."

After some encouraging words from Colonel Cotton-Jodrell and the playing of the National Anthem, the Colonel handed over command of the men to Captain Jackson, who along with Lieutenant Collins, were to accompany the men to Chatham (Sapper T. Thompson, fireman of 102, Ruskin Road, "E" Company, and Sapper J. Miller, fireman of 10, Vincent Street, "G" Company, originally down to travel did not make the journey).

The second draft, to a thunderous cheer, which echoed from the Square to Chester Bridge, then proceeded to march to the station after Captain Jackson gave the order *"Form fours, right turn and quick march."* They were headed by a force of around 30 policemen under the command of Superintendent Meredith, the Crewe Carriage Works Band, the Bugle Band of the Corps and then the Regimental Band, who struck up *The Girl I Left Behind Me*. Walking closely behind were Colonel Cotton-Jodrell, Colonel Kennedy and several members of the Corps who had served in South Africa. Like the previous 'send off' the men had great difficulty in fighting their way through the vast crowds of well-wishers. Again spectators climbed on roofs, garden walls and up trees on the route to the station.

At the station top, a force of policemen stood by the doors to prevent the crowd from entering the premises, but the tide of humanity soon pushed them aside and once again, the doors buckled under the pressure, as a crowd of around 7,000 poured onto the platforms. It was a miracle that nobody was killed in the crush. Women and children were caught up in the confusion and several fainted and were in danger of being trampled underfoot. The special train taking the men to London was waiting in a bay opposite the North Stafford line, and a row of nearby carriages afforded a great viewing platform for the most athletic of the crowd. The arriving Volunteers had great difficulty in boarding their carriages as the crowd seemed intent on hugging and shaking the hand of every departing soldier. At exactly 11.30am, the special train, adorned with a huge Union flag hung on its helm, slowly moved away to deafening cheers, which were punctuated by the firing of fog signals placed on the line. After the train had moved out of view, it pulled into a quiet siding, where the men were each handed delicacies kindly donated by Mr F. Colclough of the Hop Pole Hotel. After this short stop, the green flag was waved and the train steamed out of Crewe at 11.45am on its journey to London. They eventually arrived at Chatham at approximately 7.00pm and were met by the band of the Royal Engineers. At Brompton Barracks, the new draft enjoyed a hot supper and were then informed that over the next few days, they were to partake in musketry training at Gravesend. The three officers in charge of the Crewe men left for Chatham on Friday, March 1, following a night with fellow officers at the Crewe Arms Hotel.

On the same day another medical man from Crewe died in South Africa. No.1702 Private W. Thornton of the St. John Ambulance Brigade, who left Crewe for Aldershot on Christmas Eve, 1900, succumbed to enteric fever at Elandsfontein. He was buried in Primrose Cemetery, Germiston. Aged just 20, he had been employed in Button's Iron Foundry. His parents resided at 44, Farrington Street.

By March, the townsfolk had not exactly clamoured to have electricity supplied to their homes and business premises and only 72 consumers had been connected. Medical statistics for 1900, released in March stated that the population of Crewe was around 44,000 and there had been 1,420 births (710 male and 710 female), of which 56 were illegitimate. A total of 677 deaths were registered for the year (363 males and 314 females).

On Thursday morning, March 14, the second draft of the Crewe Railway Reserve set sail for Cape Town on the S.S. *Saint Andrew* from the Royal Albert Docks at Woolwich. Unfortunately Sapper Gater of 60, Peel Street, and of "G" Company, did not accompany his comrades as he was suffering from severe pneumonia and confined to the hospital. At first he was so poorly that the medical officer held out little hope of his recovery. However, a week later, his condition had improved. Around a dozen Crewe men, invalided home from South Africa, who had been part of the original first draft, were also on board with their Crewe colleagues. Meanwhile, the two Volunteer Service Sections had now been formed. The majority of the men, in what effectively was the third draft of Railway Volunteers, were single and aged between nineteen and twenty-five. They had been medically examined on March 11, by Surgeon Lieutenant Gray. The officers in charge of the two sections had also been chosen. Lieutenant E. Davenport would be in charge of No.1 Section, with Lieutenant Charles Maitland Forbes Trotter in command of the other.

On Saturday, March 23, the new draft paraded at the Armoury and were formally sworn in by Mr W. Eardley J.P. On Monday, March 25, the men received their uniforms from the Army Clothing Stores. Only three sizes were sent, so Compton's factory assisted in the alterations. On Monday, April 1, the men were inspected at the Drill Hall in Wistaston Road, by Colonel Cotton-Jodrell and Captain Stones, and next day, they were inspected on behalf of the War Office, by Colonel Ross of the Royal Engineers. Before being dismissed, they were photographed outside the Drill Hall, looking resplendent in their new uniforms. They then enjoyed supper at the Crewe Arms Hotel and after all formalities had concluded, Sapper Edward James Brett was presented a handsome marble clock by QMS Gibson, donated by the men of the Iron Moulders Department. Mention was also made of his brother, Sergeant Thomas Williams Brett, who had gone to South Africa with the first draft, been invalided home but had recently returned.

Two days later, on Wednesday, April 3, the two Volunteer Service Sections gathered on the Market Square to take part in their own 'send off.' Again, this now familiar scene would be witnessed by a sizeable crowd of 'well-wishers' who numbered around 12,000, gathered on the Market Square and all along the route to the station. The men had earlier enjoyed breakfast at 9.00am with Mayor Wilson at his residence at 'Coila' who was unable to attend the farewell due to a prior engagement. The men marched to the station again among chaotic scenes and reached the station top at 11.45am, ably accompanied on their march by the Regimental Band. At the entrance of the double doors were upwards of 40 police officers, who were monitoring a gangway which allowed a number of privileged guests onto the station. The marching men did not however, enter the station this time through the main entrance, and proceeded over the bridge, before turning by the station-masters house, to enter via the horse siding. Unfortunately the following throngs also followed and despite the attempts of railway officials and policemen, the crowd gained entrance to the platforms. The men then, with some difficulty, formed up in front of their awaiting carriages, before the order was given to entrain, which was done despite incredible scenes of enthusiasm around them. Shortly after noon, the carriages were shunted on to the 12.10pm London express. The train then slowly pulled away as the band played *Auld Lang Syne*. The vast crowd waved hats and handkerchiefs until the train disappeared out of sight. It had been another momentous day in the short history of the railway town.

The Crewe Engineers currently serving in South Africa were so far unaware about the new drafts. A letter appeared in *The Crewe Chronicle* on April 10, from a time-expired member of the 8th Railway Company, who was clearly unhappy about his extended stay in the war-zone and the non-involvement of his comrades still in Crewe.

> *'Sir, I am desirous that the public should know exactly upon what footing the Volunteer Reserve Engineers stand. Several members like myself, both Tower Hamlets and Crewe Railway Volunteers, are time expired and have been for some little time, while many more will have concluded their time for which they agreed, within the next few days. Yet on demanding their discharge, they were informed that they would be expected to do twelve months beyond their time. There are also many married men who are on the 5th rate of working pay. Now as far as I can gather, some 106 men on the Volunteer Reserve are following their usual employment at home and at the same time receiving exactly the same pay from the Government as we are who are out here. Do you think therefore that if the Government can afford to pay these men this money without getting any material advantage, they could well afford to send them out here to relieve us who are thoroughly worn out by the war? I am sure that those now at home would be only too glad to relieve us and give us the rest we have really earned. As I dare say you are aware we landed at Cape Town on November 16, 1899 and proceeded up country immediately, joining Lord Methuen's division on the 19th of the same month, with which we remained until the Relief of Kimberley, experiencing such fighting at Graspan, Belmont and Magersfontein. From there we went on to Mafeking. After doing some very useful work up there we returned to De Aar and then we started up through the Free State and the Transvaal. Here we not only had exceedingly hard work to do, but some very severe fighting – to quote one instance, Zumkerbosch. I think therefore that no one can deny that in the 15 months, such as we have experienced out here, we have done our share and that if we have earned praise which has been*

universally given to the Engineers in this war, we have every right to expect the authorities to take some steps to relieve us. Yours "A Worn Out Sapper of the Crewe Railway Volunteers." '

With the third draft now settled in at St. Mary's Barracks in Chatham, tragic news reached Crewe just eight days later, when on April 10/11, Lieutenant Charles Maitland Forbes Trotter, in charge of No.2 Section died following an accident. On the Wednesday evening of April 10, after finishing a course on musketry practice, he had tried out a horse belonging to Lieutenant Moseley, in the hope of purchasing the animal, as all officers were required to be mounted. He proceeded with the horse to the Great Lines in the purpose of exercising the steed, when it suddenly bolted. Despite strenuous efforts to halt the horse, it crashed into fencing, flinging Lieutenant Trotter to the ground with considerable force, fracturing his skull. He managed to stumble to his feet and walked to the residence of Colonel Rideout, where medical assistance was immediately sought. Upon the arrival of Doctor Hugo, Lieutenant Trotter complained of a pain in his stomach and then suddenly fell dead. Born on June 16, 1882, he was just 18 years and ten months old. The news of his death was relayed to the men while they watched a show at Brompton Barracks. Lieutenant Trotter's association with the town of Crewe had begun a few years previous as a premium apprentice when he became a pupil in the Civil Engineers Department. He soon joined the Railway Volunteers as a Second Lieutenant (made up to Lieutenant when called up for active service) and was a member of "B" Company. He was a young man with great musical ability and had only recently performed a leading role in a Gilbert and Sullivan opera, and was also a renowned athlete. His parents resided at Polesworth, near Tamworth, with his father the incumbent of the village church.

On Saturday, April 13, Lieutenant Trotter's body was transferred from Chatham to the home of his parents at Polesworth Vicarage (158, High Street). On that morning, the men of the Volunteer Service Sections paraded at 6.30am and proceeded to the Casualty Hospital where the body was lying. A procession was formed which consisted of the Band of the Royal Engineers, around 200 men of the training battalion and all Royal Engineer officers on duty. The coffin was conveyed on a gun carriage, with the bearers drawn from the Crewe men, while the rest of the Crewe contingent formed the escort, under the command of Lieutenant Davenport and Sergeant Jones (instructor of the Crewe Corps). The mournful procession then made its way to the London, Chatham and Dover Railway Station, where the coffin, surmounted by the officer's helmet and sword plus three wreaths, was transferred to a special van. On arrival at Polesworth Vicarage, the coffin was covered in a Union flag and placed in a large ground floor room filled with floral tributes. Back at Crewe, a number of Railway Volunteers assembled next day on the Market Square, under the command of Lieutenant Lemon (accompanied by Sergeant Robb and QMS Gibson) ready to proceed to the funeral to act as bearers and a firing party. At the railway station, the men were joined by Colonel Cotton Jodrell, Lieutenant Colonel Kennedy, Captains Stones, Tandy and Jackson and Lieutenants Collins, Bowes and Godson. Here a special train was waiting and this commenced for Polesworth at around 1.00pm. At Stafford, they were joined by Lieutenant Davenport who had travelled up from Chatham. The train arrived at its destination shortly after 2.00pm and all along the approaches to the church and vicarage, thousands of people had turned out, with the arrival of the Volunteers in their scarlet uniforms, only adding to the solemnity of the occasion. The funeral cortege then proceeded to the churchyard, headed by the Regimental Band, followed by the firing party, with arms reversed, and as the coffin was carried from the vicarage by the Company Sergeant Majors and the NCO's of "B" Company, the band, under the direction of Bandmaster Coen, struck up with *The Funeral March*. Unfortunately Mrs Trotter, the mother of the deceased, could not attend due to illness. A Company of the Boys Brigade around 80 strong lined the main walk leading to the church and two troopers from the Staffordshire Yeomanry were also present. After the formalities of the church service, the coffin was lowered into the ground and the firing party fired three volleys into the grey skies. After everything was concluded, the Crewe party were provided with tea by the Trotter family, before leaving for home, where they arrived around 6.00pm. Lieutenant F. R. Collins of "C" Company of the Railway Volunteers was quickly chosen to replace Trotter as commander of No.2 Section.

On the same day as the funeral, the S.S. *St. Andrew* docked at Cape Town. The second draft had originally landed briefly on April 8, but then sailed to Port Elizabeth to assist in the embarkation of a number of troops.

The death of an old military man occurred in the town on April 19, when 75-year-old Edward Malone of 5, Castle Street, Crewe died. Retired from the railway works for five years, he had served for 24 years as a soldier - nine as a Corporal in the 5th Dragoon Guards. During this spell, he had taken part in 'The Charge of the Heavy Brigade' at Balaclava, receiving 17 individual wounds. Mr Malone was buried in Crewe Cemetery on Monday, April 22.

On Saturday, April 27, the Volunteer Service Sections paraded at 4.30am and left on the 5.10am train for Southampton. Even at this early hour, many lined the streets to see them off. They arrived at the docks shortly after 10.00am and eventually left at 4.00pm on board S.S. *Pinemore*, along with 1,200 others (Sussex Volunteers, Baden Powell's Police, Imperial Yeomanry and Scottish Rifles). Each Crewe man travelled with a silver mounted pipe, which had been presented to them by Lieutenant Trotter's father.

On Saturday night, April 27 and in the early hours of Sunday morning, a fire in Crewe erupted at the Cobden clothing factory, and was one of the biggest seen in the town for years. The factory, situated off Earle Street (at the rear of St. Peter's Iron Church) was completely gutted and £4,000 worth of damage was caused.

On May 11, another local serviceman lost his life in South Africa. No.3589 Sapper J. J. Darlington of the 45th Fortress (Steam Transport) Company, was accidentally shot dead at Bloemfontein. He had only been in the country a few weeks, after departing with the second draft of Railway Reserve (member of "A" Company). Three days later, another member of the Railway Volunteers died after a long illness, although he was not one who had travelled to South Africa. Sapper Edwin Fellows of 2, Wellington Square, Crewe died after a nineteen-week illness. His funeral on May 21 was attended by 40 fellow members of "E" Company, commanded by Lieutenant Lemon. He was buried in Crewe Cemetery with full military honours.

On the same day of the funeral the Volunteer Service Sections arrived at Cape Town. They had been at sea for twenty-four days and would disembark next day. Towards the end of the month, No.1 Section joined up with the 8th (Railway) Company, who had left Vereeniging for Avoca (near Barbeton) on May 6. Here, the Company proceeded to put up a deviation bridge to replace the one washed away, and then started the repair of the permanent bridge. This consisted of four spans of 31.6 metres, with three damaged. The pieces to repair them were either constructed by the Company on the spot, or obtained from a pair of similar girders at Kaapmuiden, where the bridge had been damaged beyond repair.

As painful as the news of death at the front was, it was now becoming news that was arriving on a regular basis. On June 3, No.2671 Private C. Hodson of the 2nd North Staffordshire Regiment died at Wakkerstroom of dysentery. He had worked in the Millwright's Department in Crewe Works. Another Crewe Works employee, Private

John Latham of the Grenadier Guards and of New Street, lay dangerously ill with enteric fever at Norvals Pont. Good news lay in short supply during the early part of 1901.

A row erupted in the town in June regarding the pay for three men currently serving in South Africa, who were employed by the Crewe Corporation Fire Brigade. Their pay of just over £1 every six months was to be stopped after June 30, saving £3 10s every half year.

On August 31, the townsfolk of Crewe planned a patriotic demonstration in regards to raising monies for the Crewe (South African) Volunteer and Reservists Memorial Fund. On June 25, at the Euston Coffee Tavern, the committee met to discuss all proposals. It would be one of the largest and greatest processions the town had ever witnessed, with over 100 different sections taking part.

On June 30, a total of 470 Railway Volunteers left Crewe for their annual encampment at Chatham. When the men returned at 5.00pm on the following Sunday, they were greeted with shocking news, which eventually had the whole town up in arms. It was learnt that No.27831 Sapper Tom Roberts of the 31st Fortress Company and formerly of "B" Company of the Railway Volunteers, had lost his life on the Pietersburg line, north of Pretoria (five miles north of Naboomspruit), on July 4. Sapper Roberts of 152, Broad Street, Coppenhall, Crewe, had been acting as the engine driver, ably assisted by Fireman T. Mitchell and Guard R. Kennedy of the Imperial Military Railways. Their locomotive had been halted by an explosion on the line, caused by a mine, but despite the men being unarmed, the trio (according to later reports and letters from the front) were marched onto the veldt and all shot in the back of the head. Sapper Roberts, who was around thirty years of age, left a widow and two children. Letters sent to local and national newspapers, told of the shocking murders, although the manner in which they were killed, differed slightly. The first letter was from an N.C.O. in the Shropshire Light Infantry.

'I am sorry to tell you the news about one of the Crewe lads. His name is Roberts. He was a fireman at Crewe and a tall young chap. He was taking a train to Pietersburg and the Boers pulled some rails up. Of course the train was derailed and the Boers pounced on it. The escort in charge consisted of one officer and 15 men of the Gordon Highlanders. They fought well for it. The officer and nine men were killed and the remainder wounded and then the Boers got the engine driver, the fireman and the guard, took them out on the veldt, strapped their arms behind them and shot them in cold blood. Is it not enough to make the troops take the law into their own hands and shoot every

man that they catch? It has caused a lot of trouble amongst the troops, for they swear vengeance and that is what it will come to. I feel very sorry for his wife and children and we ought to get our own back one way or another.'

The next letter was from a fellow Crewe Engineer Reservist.

'We have all been very much upset about poor Roberts's death this week. There are seventeen bullet holes in the side tank…..Two Boers caught hold of Roberts and held him by each arm while the other held the muzzle of a Mauser to his forehead and sent him on his long journey.'

The incident was so shocking, the story made *The Times.*

'The train left Naboomspruit at 3.15pm and was derailed when 18 inches of track was blown away. Travelling on the Pretoria/Pietersburg line, they were ambushed by a Boer force of 130-150 men. Lieutenant Best of the Gordon Highlanders was one of the killed. There were five others killed, two died of wounds and eight seriously wounded. Three other soldiers were also killed plus three natives. Guard Kennedy was thrown to the ground from the guards van and shot in the head at very close range. Engine driver Roberts and Fireman Mitchell were ordered from the train. Roberts was shot as he stepped on the ground, the latter on the engine cab steps. The Boers then sacked a supplies truck, burnt the train and fled.'

On July 18, Corporal A. Ross of No.2 Volunteer Service Sections wrote to Mayor Wilson, telling of his early experiences in South Africa. He was now attached to the 10th Railway Company and was writing from Viljoen's Drift.

'I am requested on behalf of the NCO's and Sappers of the No.2 Service Section to write you a few lines to let you know how we are going on. Up to the present, the Crewe men are all looking very well and have enjoyed the best of health. I think if we can get through the next month we shall have nothing to fear. I fancy the winter here is the worst time as it is very hot in the daytime and terribly cold at night. We have had plenty of work since we arrived here. As soon as we landed at Cape Town we were sent up country. We did not know our destination until we had been on the train three days; then we were told that No.1 Section were bound for Vereeniging and our Section (No.2) for Heidelberg. At this place we arrived after being in the train a week. Some of the men were fortunate as they had a sleeping saloon to ride in, but eight Sappers and myself were in the open truck for four days and nights. I think I was the only one that felt anything from it. I caught a severe cold, but I soon got well again. We were only at Heidelberg a week when we were marched to the hospital to see

if we had any trace of the fever or the plague. The doctor fettled one or two of us with sore throats and the rest of the time we did odd jobs about the place. We were then sent down to Vil-Joen's Drift to take charge of the construction train. We had plenty of work. The first job was to take up the deviation that was used when the Vaal River bridge was broken up. This was north of Vil-Joen's Drift, about three miles from our camp. The next job, we went to work on platelayers lurries and we made a horse landing 250 yards long for the unloading of horses. We also made a horse kraal to hold 1,000 horses. We have made a good name for all we have done. We have built several blockhouses for the garrison and have been called out twice to "blow ups." The first one was on June 28th, a place two miles past Vredesfort Road and 37 miles from here. It was our first experience of a "blow up" so you can imagine how anxious we all were to be off. We were at work at the kraal when we got word of the affair and in less than twenty minutes were on the way to put things straight. It was a rough mess with it only being a single line. We had to lay a road around the wreck. It was the mail train from Cape Town. The trains do not run at night. It was the first train in the morning. Usually they put one or two trucks in front of the engine to find the dynamite, but in this case only one truck was out in front and this turned nearly upside down. The engine fell down the bank on its side and a saloon next to the engine was badly damaged. It happened to be the same saloon that our men rode in from Cape Town. No.501 jumped off the engine to save himself; the engine fell on him and nearly crushed his head off. He formerly belonged to the 9th Lancers and had been through the whole of the campaign. He was anxiously looking forward to going home in September. The next affair ("blow up") only happened yesterday (the 18th of July). We heard the "report" and we all thought it was one of the big guns. The engine however got over quite safe but it uncoupled part of the train. We were on the scene in about half an hour and found that it was only a small charge. It had damaged two lengths of rails. Fortunately no vehicles left the rails, so we soon put some new ones in and were back to our camp in 65 minutes. Lieutenant Collins and Sgt. Hitchcock (Crewe) happened to be away at the time. They had gone over the same spot not long before with the lurry. I fancy the plot was laid for Lord Kitchener, as a goods train following his train found the charge. The dynamite was laid in the barrel of a carbine rifle and only the breach of the rifle was found. We have been very lucky up to the present as regards the Boer bullets. We had a few whistling over our heads the other day whilst we were at work, but luckily we have not met any mishap. We had the pleasure of seeing all the Free State officials as they were going down country as prisoners. They were a nice looking lot; they looked more like a lot of well-fed navvies.'

Corporal Ross continued his letter commenting on the appetite of the Crewe men and stated that their rations did not satisfy their hunger. The remedy for this was to eat Quaker Oats for breakfast and supper! He concluded by thanking the girls back home for their knitted balaclava caps which had done a sterling job in keeping out the night cold, while under canvas or on guard duty.

Sapper R. Chesters, the well-known Crewe runner, who was in No.1 Section, also wrote home on July 21, to Mr W. Jones, a telegraphist on Crewe Station. From his letter it was learnt that they were at Avoca, where disease was prevalent and several Crewe men were in hospital with enteric fever. He also told of the trip from Cape Town to Avoca which took a fortnight to complete. He ended the letter by describing the place as being *'twenty miles from anywhere.'*

In July, Britain sweltered in a heatwave. In Crewe it had serious effects in several departments of the Works, especially in the workshops which housed furnaces. Several men in the Steel Works had to be sent home suffering with heat exhaustion and temperatures were so high on July 18, that all the chainmakers were sent home. Two deaths occurred in the town during this period - both attributed to the adverse weather conditions.

On August 31, the Crewe Patriotic Carnival Demonstration and Fete, in aid of the Crewe South African Volunteers and Reservists Memorial Fund, took place in the town. Although in recent times, Crewe had excelled in putting on a 'show' for various events, nothing up to this date would compare to this magnificent day. Over 200 sections (further numbers were added after the printing of the programme, which stated 105 sections) each averaging between 20 and 25 participants, were to officially take part, and almost every public body in Crewe and the surrounding district were represented, especially the railway workshops.

Fears that rain would spoil the event were unfounded, and happily for the organising committee, the sun shone down on Crewe to provide ideal conditions. A sea of flags, streamers, bunting and portraits of all who had excelled in South Africa, decorated the town. Flower arrangements were also prominent, as residents attempted to outdo their neighbours. Many streets deserved special praise, including High Street, which was a blaze of colour and also included a suspended seven foot high star, erected in the centre of the street, containing 126 differently coloured lights, constructed by electrician Arthur Milton. Other notable efforts were made in Market Street, Earle Street, Victoria Street, Hightown, West Street, Edleston Road, Mill Street and Nantwich Road. Never had the town presented such a magnificent picture to the visiting masses (estimated at 10,000), who had arrived during the morning on the 41 special trains laid on by the LNWR, with some day-trippers travelling from as far afield as Rugby.

At 1.30pm, the sections in the procession assembled for the start at 2.00pm. The line of participants stretched from Merrill's Bridge in West Street to Wistaston Road Bridge, and when the procession was in full flow, would be over 2½ miles in length. The route for the procession took them down West Street, Hightown, Victoria Street, Market Street, Earle Street, Hall O'Shaw Street, Surrey Street, Vincent Street, Earle Street, Market Street, Exchange Street, Wistaston Road, Walthall Street, Nantwich Road, Edleston Road, Exchange Street, High Street, Mill Street, ending with a counter-march up and down Nantwich Road to the Earl of Crewe's Park (courtesy of Thomas Cliffe, Esq.), where members of the public would be charged 6d admission.

Promptly at 2.00pm the procession were given the signal to move off, headed by Mr J. A. Dutton (Chief Marshal), then Mr George E. Morgan on a grey charger, reprising his role as 'Lord Roberts,' who also acted as Chief Mounted Marshal. The first of the many bands in the procession were the 2nd Cheshire Royal Engineers (Railway Volunteers) Band, who were again under the expert conductorship of Bandmaster Coen. Many of the sections caused much hilarity as they marched along, due to their antics and amusing fancy dress costumes. 'The Darktown Fire Brigade' of the No.1 Electric Shop (Crewe Works) were responsible for a great deal of fun, and a placard on the front of their section read: *'14 Days Notice Should Be Given In Case Of Fire.'* The Nut & Bolt Shop entered themselves as the 'Works Nursery' which consisted of around 60 youths between the ages of fourteen and eighteen, marching in double file behind 'Professor Split Pin' (their father) and 'Lady Set Screw' (their nurse). The 'children' were dressed in long pinafores, baby hats and red socks and carried a baby's bottle and rattle. The North Sheds men turned out as the 'Mottle-Nosed Naval Brigade' which featured nearly 60 men dancing and singing to the hornpipe, who were under the command of 'Rear-Admiral Captain Lambton' (Mr J. Barnett), who was ably-assisted by his petty officers J. Grant, F. Davies and C. Vickers. The Carriage Works employees drew much attention to their section, which represented the capture at Paardeberg of the famous Boer leader General Cronje, who was well impersonated, as were his men, who were surrounded by 'khaki troops.' Another who provided great amusement was local newsagent and well-known athlete Mr T. Hossack, who pushed a dilapidated bassinet containing two squalling youngsters, complete with large bottles and comforters. One of the most unusual sights in the procession was provided by the Millwrights Shop, who called their ensemble 'Prince Lay Gun and his Gun Lay Bins from Mars.' Over 30 took part, attired in magnificent straw costumes, complete with towering two feet high helmets, all painstakingly produced over a six week period by Mr N. S. Mckenzie. Other interesting sections included Mr J. N. Woodbridge's lorry, which carried a solid piece of coal, weighing a ton, which was to be broken up and sold in aid of the fund. A strong contingent of men from the LNWR Sheds at Birkenhead were attired as 'Highlanders' and marched behind a placard which stated *'Kitchener Refused Us.'* A carriage carrying the oldest employee in Crewe Works also drew enthusiastic applause. Mr Foster, born in 1817, had commenced working at Crewe in 1842. Two wagonettes laden with Reservists who had returned from South Africa (for various reasons), were wildly cheered by everyone. Nearly all were dressed in khaki and the men present included Sappers W. H. Etheridge, R.Galliard, A. Ellis, F. Ellis, J. Evanson, A. Egerton, R. P. Calderbank, W. D. J. Froome, S. Harvey, J. Walley, G. W. Surridge (all of the 10th Railway Company), Sapper W. Evans (45th Fortress Company) and Sappers P. Elson, E. Atherton, G. H. Edwards and J. Greenhalgh (8th Railway Company). Non-Railway Volunteers in the procession included Privates K. Bebbington and G. Leigh (2nd Cheshire Regiment), Private G. Tonks (Royal Welsh Fusiliers), Gunners T. Hodgkinson and J. Wainwright (Royal Field Artillery), Sergeant G. Allman and Privates A. Quiggin and J. Richards (King's Shropshire Light Infantry), Privates S. Hampton and A. Mostyn (Durham Light Infantry) and Sergeant Levi Hughes (Cameronian Scotch Rifles). The whole procession ran smoothly from the off and only a few minor incidents were recorded. The section belonging to the Marmion Clothing Factory had an unfortunate mishap en-route. The framework of their section depicting 'Faith, Hope and Charity' became entangled in a streamer, as the section turned from Exchange Street into Wistaston Road, causing the whole structure to collapse. With this exception, the whole procession arrived at the Earl of Crewe's Park in good time, although during a crush at the lodge gates (the main entrance to the fete), six ladies fainted and had to be treated at the lodge. When all had arrived, Dr. Atkinson delivered a rousing speech and also thanked the demonstration committee for their efforts and arrangements. The events on the field kept the large crowd (estimated at 18,000) entertained throughout the rest of the day. Several bands, including the Over Silver Band and the Crewe Temperance Silver Band played a number of tunes in the afternoon, and the Crewe Original and Crewe Royal Morris Dancers both proved a big hit as they went through their dance routines. Another attraction was the Fitting Shop's 'Naval

Brigade,' who performed a cutlass drill and field gun exercises. The highlight for many though was the show put on by the 'Red Indians.' As dusk fell, they 'burnt' a prisoner at the stake and whilst the fire burned fiercely, danced around it, while chanting a war song. It was not surprising therefore, that they were awarded the premier honour of best fete artistes.

In the evening more local bands played, as the crowd danced the night away, with the celebrated 'Wells' lights illuminating the whole affair to great effect, until the day's events concluded around 10.00pm. During the day a large number of prizes were awarded for the various sections, which had been donated by local tradesmen. Included in the winners were the Fitting Shop, Compton's employees, the General Offices 'Pierrots' and the Crewe Bakers Association. Many other awards were also handed out and the prizes varied from a box of whisky to a set of false teeth! During the day, nearly 200 collectors, which included ladies in fancy dress and members of the Crewe & Tally-Ho Harriers collected nearly £110. In all (after expenses), £321 10s 11d was raised for the memorial. Programme sales numbered 6,600 and a prize was donated to the child who sold the most programmes. This was awarded to A. Glaves of 40, Edleston Road, who managed to sell 336. The only downside of the day had been the non-attendance of Mayor Wilson and members of the town council, who not only failed to take their place in the procession, but also refused the request to stop the traffic through the principal streets. Despite this, the whole event would be long remembered.

Part of the day was filmed by the Warwick Cinematograph and Film Company and was shown in the Co-operative Hall from September 4.

In September, the Census figures for Crewe stated that 42,074 resided in the town, of which 21,585 were male.

On September 14, it was reported that Lord Roberts had put together an official list for the Secretary of War, of all men who had rendered special and meritorious services in South Africa. Among the list was Superintendent F. H. Oldham of the Crewe Ambulance Corps, who was due home in October. September 18 saw the 8th Railway Company arrive at Kroonstad where they were put to work erecting wire fencing along the railway line to Wolvehock. Part of the fencing was electrified and was so arranged that bells rang in the nearest blockhouse if the wires were cut or disturbed. On September 21, a letter from Sergeant J. Emery, originally of "G" Company of the Royal Engineers (now attached to the 45th Fortress Company), who was among the second draft of men to leave Crewe, told of another 'meet-up' of local men in South Africa.

At Kroonstad, a section of the 8th Railway Company were greeted by members of the second draft and a detachment of the 45th Fortress (Steam Transport) Company, in which some Crewe men were serving. Lieutenant Davenport (of the Volunteer Service Sections), was approached to arrange a smoking party to welcome the newly arrived 'Crewies.' Assisted by Sergeant H. W. Hitchcock (No.2 Section), Corporal W. Worrall (No.1 Section) and two Lance Corporals, the evening was arranged for Friday, September 20, with a programme of musical acts drawn up. After Sergeant Emery (Chairman of Events) proposed a toast to the health of the King, many of the Crewe men indulged in singing and playing their favourite tunes. Among those participating was Sapper 'Dan' Morbey, who performed several tunes on his mouth organ. Sergeant Emery gave a fine rendition of *Pretty Salina*, followed by Sapper A. Jones with *Queen of the Earth*, while Corporal Parsonage was loudly encored for his rendition of *Getting Larger*. Other notable efforts were performed by Sapper J. H. Garbett (*It's Hard to Say Goodbye*), Sapper W. Talbot (*The British Navy*), Sapper W. H. Battison (*As Your Hair Grows White*), Sapper H. Hinett (*The Postman's Knock*) and Sapper Champion (*On the Benches in the Park*). After an interval, where the health of the 8th Railway Company was proposed, the evening continued with more songs from Sapper Prince (*Songs of the Sea*), and Sapper Joseph Lloyd (*Thy Face is Near in My Dreams*), before the night's entertainment was concluded with the singing of *Auld Lang Syne*.

On September 27, the names of No.1183 Sapper W. Pugh (of "F" Company, Railway Volunteers) and No.1794 Sapper J. Jones ("C" Company), were published in *The London Gazette*, having been granted the Distinguished Conduct Medal. No.1804 Sapper W. Sumner ("C" Company) was also mentioned for special and meritorious service in the field, by Lord Roberts. All three served in the 10th Railway Company.

Meanwhile at home, several officers of the Railway Volunteers had the opportunity of meeting Lord Roberts, when, along with other battalion officers in Cheshire and Lancashire, they were invited to Knowsley Hall on the Tuesday evening of October 8. Lord Derby had sent out the invitations and many of the local officers obliged.

Through October, several more members of the Railway Reserve returned home from the war, including Sergeant G. Beckett, who had gone out with the second draft and resided at 163, Edleston Road.

On October 12, the annual Railway Volunteers firing competition took place at Holmes Chapel, with eight teams competing. The participants marched from the Market Square at 9.40am, wearing their undress uniform and accompanied by a dozen drummers and buglers. In charge was Captain Beaumont (of "B" Company), ably assisted by Lieutenants Bowes and Lemon. Along the route, they stopped several times for refreshments (including one at Sandbach), with the range reached at 2.00pm, a distance of approximately twelve miles, with the actual marching time calculated at three hours and thirty-seven minutes. The competition, witnessed by Colonel Cotton-Jodrell, was won by Sergeant Shaw's section with 42 points.

As the end of October approached, more Crewe Reservists returned home. On Saturday, October 19, Chester Street was the scene of great excitement as the residents welcomed home Sergeant George Jones of the 2nd King's Shropshire Light Infantry, who joined his unit in December 1899 and had left for South Africa a few days before Christmas Day. During his service, he took part in the Battle of Paarderberg and around 50 other engagements. During the celebrations, he told of the shocking murder of Sapper Tom Roberts and of taking part in a football match in Pretoria, along with several other Railway Volunteers, where he won a medal. Next day another local, Sapper Barnes, arrived at Southampton and Sergeant W. Taylor of the King's Shropshire Light Infantry, returned to his home in Forge Street, to a hero's welcome.

Despite improved conditions in the camps and field hospitals, men dying of disease continued to be an issue, and in Cape Town, a plague epidemic claimed more military lives, including No.6593 Private J. Hayes of Crewe. He served in the 3rd King's Own Lancaster Regiment, and died on October 23.

More fund raising took part in the town on November 12, when a Patriotic Fancy Dress Ball was held in the Mechanics Institute.

Sapper Barnes, a prominent member of the Bugle Band of the Crewe Engineers, finally returned home in mid-November and was treated to a 'welcome home' dinner at the Hop Pole Hotel, by twenty members of the Railway Volunteers. The special dinner was prepared by host Mr F. Colclough. But as more men returned, there was a call for medical men to put their names forward for active service. Private Thomas Gibson of 204, Walthall Street, at once volunteered. He left for Aldershot on November 26.

There had been many heroes of the war, in the eyes of the British public, and one such man was the defender of Mafeking, Baden-Powell. So news spread like wildfire in the local area when he was sighted in Nantwich on November 1. He was making a short, but surprise visit to Stapeley House, home of Major Kearsley, and had arrived on the 3.08pm train from Shrewsbury. Only a few members of the public saw him depart the station and climb into a carriage, but that was enough for the news to spread. Next day quite a crowd had gathered at Nantwich station in the hope of catching a glimpse of the great man. At 1.12pm he climbed aboard the train for Evesham, entering the saloon from the stationmaster's house. He was given a loud cheer as the train slowly steamed away.

As a lasting tribute to the late monarch, the Queen Victoria Memorial Children's Ward was opened on the Wednesday afternoon of November 6, at the Crewe Cottage Hospital. The money for the ward (£515 plus £250 to furnish) had been raised by public subscription. It was unveiled by Lord Crewe's eldest daughter, Lady Annabel Crewe-Milnes. Around 3,000 local schoolchildren attended the ceremony, along with several dignitaries, including the Bishop of Chester, Francis William Webb and the Mayor Dr. Wilson.

To augment the Crewe Reservist and Volunteer Memorial Fund, two ordinary balls and a fancy dress ball were held on the evenings of November 13 and 14. Held in the Town Hall and Co-operative Hall, around 100 guests attended on each occasion.

A special banquet was held at the Crewe Arms Hotel on November 15, to celebrate Francis William Webb's fifty year association with the LNWR. Sixty guests took part in the celebrations, including Works manager, Mr H. D. Earl.

On November 27, Private A. Hesketh of the 1st East Lancashire Regiment, returned home from the war, where he had been wounded in the head and had also lost two fingers. He resided in Forge Street and returned to find the street covered in bunting and flags. A banner also honoured his return with the words *'God Bless You Tommy Atkins, Your Country's Love To You.'*

Not all homecomings however, were happy events. On December 4, Sapper William Thomas Lawson came home, but was met with the sad news that his young daughter had died a few weeks earlier after choking on nut shells. Little Celia Lawson, aged just 19 months, had swallowed the shells on November 20, but despite an operation performed by Dr. Liddle, she died a few days later.

As a third Christmas of the war approached, heavy snow in the local area caused major travelling problems.

On December 14, it was reported that No.1797 Sapper Frederick A. Lewis, who had been part of the second draft, was dangerously ill with enteric fever at Mafeking. Four days later Sapper A. Cookson of the 8th Railway Company, returned home to Crewe after a two year absence. However, the news of the death of another Crewe man in South Africa cast quite a gloom over the town during the Christmas festivities. No.6378 Private Charles Moses, aged 20, of the 3rd Wiltshire Regiment, had died of enteric fever at Kroonstad, on December 7. He had been well-known in the town and was the son of Samuel Moses of 53, South Street. During his time in South Africa he had several close calls and was captured by the Boers. Stripped of all his possessions and with his horse shot, he escaped by running eight miles, with only his shirt to cover his modesty.

On December 27, the Crewe Engineers Annual Ball took place at the Mechanics Institute, with 500 attending. After the meal, dancing commenced at around 9.30pm and continued until 4.00am. On the same day, ambulance man F. H. Oldham arrived at Southampton after returning from South Africa. On the Saturday evening he was greeted by friends at Crewe station, before proceeding to Stockport to visit his parents - his father being the former Inspector of Police at Crewe.

Sapper J. Rowbottom wrote home about Christmas festivities at Kroonstad, where many Crewe men were engaged in work with the Steam Road Transport. On Boxing Day the men of the garrison (around 2,000) enjoyed a meal and then took part in a series of sports events - the prizes donated by the citizens of Kroonstad. A small detachment of the 45th Fortress Company, which included 16 men from the Railway Volunteers (under the command of Lieutenant Davenport) were very successful. Sapper W. Talbot won the ½ mile scratch race and Sapper Williams was third in the obstacle race. There was also a tug-of-war competition, where two teams, mainly of Crewe men, drew each other (45th Company v 8th Company), which was won, after a titanic struggle, by the 45th Company. In the final they met the Military Police team and after a ten minute contest, emerged victorious. The winning team each received five shillings and comprised of Sappers W. Bickerton, W. Morgan, J. Rowbottom, C. Healey and W. Talbot. Over the Christmas period a cricket match also took place at Kroonstad between the 45th and 8th Companies and all bar three were Crewe men (Sergeant Ankers, Sapper Walmsley and Sapper Hogg). The scores were as follows:

8th Company (1st Innings)

Corporal Parsonage	c&b	Hogg	4
Sapper Butt	c&b	Garbett	4
Sapper Rowe	c&b	Hogg	4
Sapper Stockton	b	Garbett	0
Sapper Tirrell	b	Garbett	0
Sapper Maybury	b	Garbett	0
Sapper Lloyd	run out		4

Sapper Hewitt	b	Hogg	11
Sapper Boulton	c&b	Talbot	4
Sapper Battison	not out		6
Sapper Ganner	b	Hogg	0
		Extras	5
		Total Score	**42**

8th Company (2nd Innings)

Corporal Parsonage	c&b	Garbett	1
Sapper Butt	run out		7
Sapper Rowe	b	Talbot	7
Sapper Stockton	b	Garbett	9
Sapper Tirrell	b	Garbett	0
Sapper Maybury	b	Ankers	8
Sapper Lloyd	b	Garbett	28
Sapper Hewitt	b	Hogg	2
Sapper Boulton	b	Garbett	2
Sapper Battison	b	Garbett	1
Sapper Ganner	not out		0
		Extras	3
		Total Score	**68**

45th Company (1st Innings)

Sapper Garbett	c&b	Stockton	2
Sapper Talbot	c&b	Parsonage	2
Sapper Walmsley	b	Parsonage	10
Corporal Bickerton	b	Lloyd	7
Sapper Hogg	b	Parsonage	3
Sergeant Ankers	b	Lloyd	8
Corporal Boughey	not out		4
Sapper Rowbottom	b	Parsonage	0
Sapper Healey	b	Parsonage	0
Sapper Hinett	b	Parsonage	0
Sapper J. Heap	c&b	Lloyd	5
		Extras	3
		Total Score	**44**

45th Company (2nd Innings)

Sapper Garbett	b	Parsonage	0
Sapper Talbot	b	Parsonage	1
Sapper Walmsley	b	Lloyd	3

Corporal Bickerton	b	Lloyd	0
Sapper Hogg	b	Parsonage	0
Sergeant Ankers	b	Lloyd	0
Corporal Boughey	not out		32
Sapper Rowbottom	b	Lloyd	4
Sapper Healey	b	Parsonage	0
Sapper Hinett	b	Parsonage	0
Sapper J. Heap	c&b	Lloyd	13
		Extras	1
		Total Score	**54**

During the Christmas period, a large hamper arrived at camp, sent from home, and each man received a plum pudding, a pipe and a quantity of tobacco. One Crewe man who wasn't enjoying the Christmas fun and games was Sapper 'Dan' Morbey, who had been struck down with enteric fever, but thankfully was making a slow recovery in a nearby hospital.

Lance Corporal Tom Baystone of the Royal Welsh Fusiliers also afforded a letter home towards the end of the year, when writing to Mr H. Lynes.

> *'I am glad to tell you that my Christmas was not a bad one, thanks to the kindness of those contributing friends in Crewe Works. I received the two parcels quite safe; the one from the officers and friends yesterday. I thank one and all for their good offerings and it puts me more deeply in thanks to reflect that I am over 6,000 miles away and not forgotten. With regards work, we are still at our old job, as when I wrote before. I have not seen a Boer since last September, although I travel miles upon the veldt. They are getting scarce, I can positively say. I believe these next winter months will break their backbone. I do not care how soon it is over, but I should like to be in this country to see the finish. I believe I am the only one left of the lot that joined our regiment, they have all disappeared somewhere or other. There is nothing startling done as yet – the same routine week after week. 300 odd captured? It is just the same here in the blockhouses – the old routine, getting bunk-eyed looking for Boers and watching the float bob. We are luckier than some – we have a good river here (the Vaal). Some of the Crewe anglers should come out here. There are plenty of fish.....A Boer that was captured told me that half the Boers out fighting are now only waiting for England to get a Liberal government in. He said they would give them back their independence.'*

So ended 1901, with the war still not resolved. The British had great difficulty in hunting down the marauding Boer guerrillas and the public at home had grown tired of the war and of Kitchener's inability to serve 'that final victory blow.' In fact the year had seen somewhat of a Boer revival. They had, on several occasions, led their forces into Cape Colony, although their objectives of raising new recruits among the Cape Afrikaners, did not materialise and proved only a small irritant. It was estimated that there were only 20,000 fighting Boers left in the field and although there were still upwards of 200,000 British troops in South Africa, many of them were employed in guarding the Cape ports, railway lines and manning the blockhouse system. The sweeps had continued unabated and slowly eroded the strength of the remaining enemy forces. In May, the 'bag' contained 2,500, with 2,200 added in June and 1,800 in July, but the Boers continued to gain small victories throughout the year. On May 29, they had surprised a British force at Vlakfontein and inflicted around 180 casualties (49 killed). On September 17, Jan Smuts won a victory during the Battle of Elands River, when they attacked a contingent of men from the 17th Lancers, with many Boers dressed in khaki, which had enabled them to get within yards of the British before they were detected. When Kitchener learned of this ruse, he renewed orders that any Boers caught wearing British uniforms, were to be shot on the spot. Kitchener remained adamant that his blockhouse and 'scorched earth' policies would win the day and by the end of October, 10,000 square miles of territory in the Transvaal and Northern Orange River Colony and 4,200 square miles around Bloemfontein had been declared completely cleared of the enemy. On December 23, the Kroonstad to Lindley blockhouse line was completed to further hem in the remaining Boer marauders, but still they remained a force to be reckoned with, and to prove this point, De Wet and his men surprised a British force on Christmas Day at Groenkop (around Tweefontein) and inflicted considerable casualties. The war was still very much alive and would now enter a fourth year.

Chapter Four - 1902
·Welcome Home Tommy Atkins·

Following the Christmas Day reversal around Tweefontein, Lord Kitchener planned a series of events to finally wear down the remaining Boer forces and thus bring the war to an end. The sweeps continued but the January 'bag' brought only 1,400 'bitter-einders' into the prisoner of war camps. So in early February, Kitchener hatched an idea to employ four super columns, each 9,000 strong (roughly one man every ten yards) in a line 54 miles long, which was to form the open end of an enclosed rectangle

(TOP LEFT) The Earl of Crewe c1897. *(TOP RIGHT)* General Sir Redvers Buller - a guest at Crewe Hall in January 1900. *(BELOW)* Queen Victoria, whose death in January would mean that two campaign medals would now be awarded for the war (QSA, KSA).

Men of the second draft of the Railway Reserve to leave the town. (**LEFT**) Arthur William Maybury of 79 Middlewich Street. He was attached to "G" Company of the Royal Engineers, and would later join the 8th Railway Company. (**BELOW**) William Kent, also of "G" Company and of 18, Wesley Street (later of 17, Betley Street).

*Members of the Volunteer Service Sections. (**TOP LEFT**) Sapper Charles Henry Bennett of 159, Broughton Road, Coppenhall and No.2 Section. Prior to working in Crewe Works, was a cabinet-maker. (**TOP RIGHT**) Sapper Edward James Brett of No.1 Section. At the time of departing, he was boarding at 4, Beech Street, Coppenhall with James and Mary Ardern, and was a crane driver in Crewe Works. (**BELOW**) Sapper Richard Chesters (standing second right), of No.1 Section.*

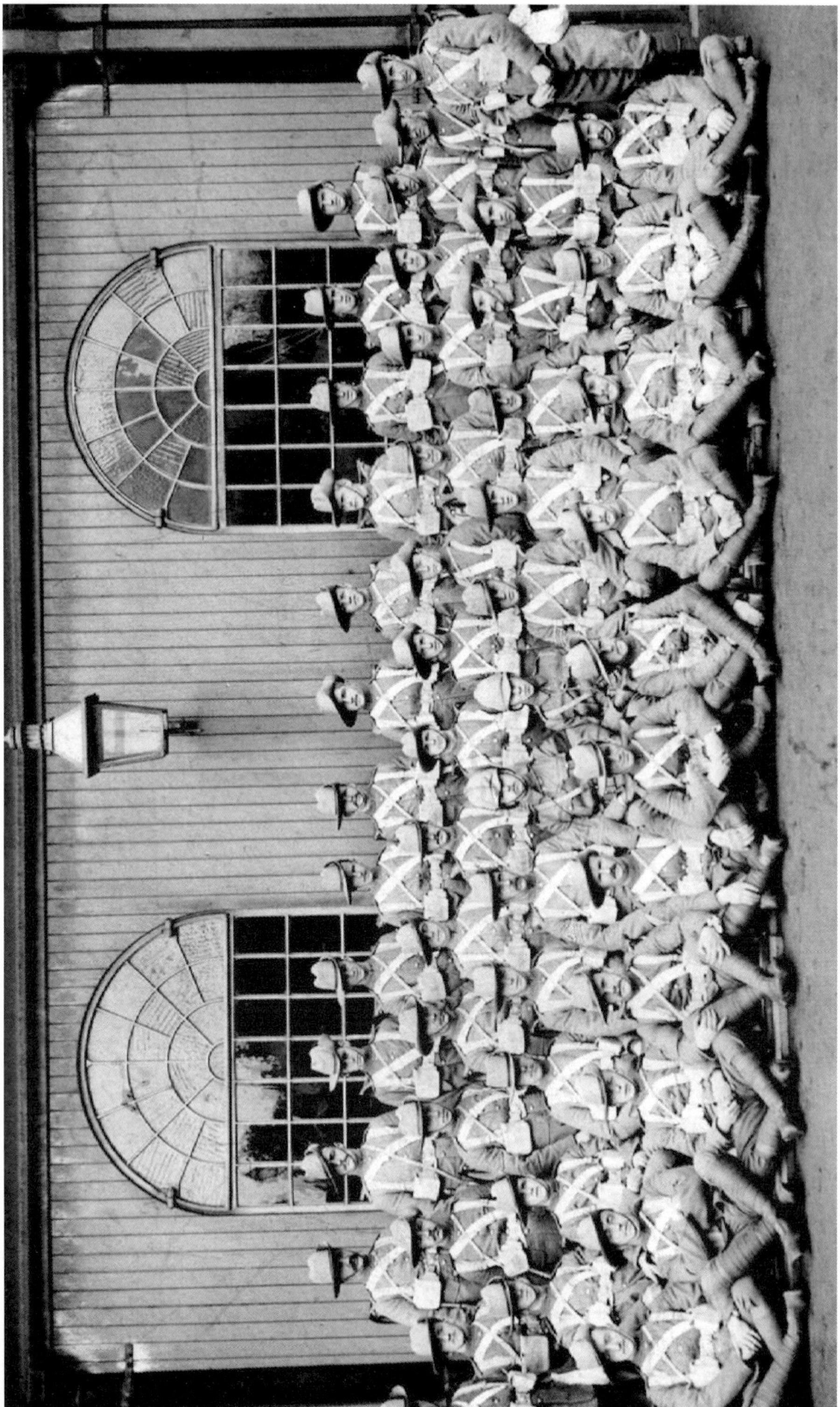

*(**OPPOSITE PAGE**) The Volunteer Service Sections. The photograph was taken on April 2, 1901, outside the Drill Hall in Wistaston Road. The officers in the centre are (left) Lieutenant E. Davenport and Lieutenant Charles Maitland Forbes Trotter. (**TOP**) 8560 Sapper Percy Powell (sitting) of 14, Herdman Street, poses with another member of No.2 Section (see also page 18). (**ABOVE**) Sapper Powell (far left) and comrades, while at Chatham, just prior to departure.*

*Two more members of the Volunteer Service Sections. (**TOP LEFT**) Sapper Jabez Wareham (No.2 Section), whose brother Thomas also served. (**TOP RIGHT**) 2nd Corporal Archibald Claud Parsonage (No.1 Section), pictured with wife Sara Elizabeth and children (from left to right) Lillian May, Doreen, Marjorie and Harold. (**BELOW**) The grave in Polesworth Church cemetery, of Lieutenant Charles Maitland Forbes Trotter.*

(ABOVE) The grave of Sapper Tom Roberts (dark cross), murdered by the Boers on July 4, 1901. He is buried next to R. Kennedy of the Imperial Military Railways, also killed in the same incident.

(ABOVE) Sapper F. M. Gibbons (arrowed) of "G" Company, Royal Engineers. He would later join the 10th Railway Company.

*(**ABOVE**) Crewe officers Lieutenant N. H. Brierley (left) and Lieutenant Charles Sidgwick (second from right). Major Schofield of the 45th Fortress Company is pictured far right. (**BELOW**) A derailed train attended by Lieutenant Sidgwick's men.*

(ABOVE) The railway built Mechanics Institute (Town Hall) in Earle Street. The building had a number of shops situated on the ground floor including the 'Euston Coffee Tavern' which was on the corner of Chapel Street. This establishment's profits went to support the Cottage Hospital in Victoria Avenue.

(LEFT) Crewe's first Mayor, Dr. James Atkinson (1877, 1877-78), and President of the Patriotic Demonstration Committee.

CREWE

Patriotic Carnival, Demonstration and Fête

IN AID OF THE

CREWE SOUTH AFRICAN VOLUNTEER & RESERVIST MEMORIAL FUND.

Saturday, 31st August, 1901.

OFFICIAL HANDBOOK, PRICE TWOPENCE.

Published by authority of the Demonstration Committee.

WILMOT EARDLEY, PRINTER, CREWE.

(*ABOVE*) Cover of the Carnival programme.

of blockhouses and barbed wire. The columns were to sweep forward and trap the Boers against the blockhouse lines which had been further reinforced with extra troops and seven armoured trains, equipped with guns and searchlights. At dawn on February 6, the sweep began, but by February 8, only 285 Boers had been captured, although large numbers of cattle and horses had been rounded up. The blockhouse lines however, did not hold, and on the Kroonstad/Lindley line, the wire was breached by simply snipping it with wire-cutters. A week after the initial sweep, the columns made an about turn, but again the results were disappointing; that was until the last day, when, on February 27 (the anniversary of Majuba Hill), Colonel Rawlinson's column captured 778 rebels, 2,000 horses, 200 wagons and 25,000 head of cattle. However, the Boers were still active in the field, and a British reversal at Yzer Spruit on February 24, saw British casualties numbering 12 officers and 369 men. Worse was to follow on March 7, when Lord Methuen's column of nearly 1,200 were virtually wiped out at Tweebosch. What made the defeat even more embarrassing was the fact that Lord Methuen (wounded in the thigh) became the one and only British General to be captured during the war.

Lord Kitchener meanwhile continued his quest for victory by introducing more controversial measures. First of all he armed the many thousands of Africans employed by the British Army and secondly ordered his column commanders to leave any stray Boer women and children on the veldt, instead of bringing them into the concentration camps, thus leaving the Boer guerillas responsible for their upkeep.

Back in Crewe, the damp New Year weather contributed to a scarlet fever and measles outbreak. On the advice of Dr. Greenwood, the medical officer of Crewe, the Edleston Road Infant School was closed. The scarlet fever wards in the Isolation Hospital were soon crowded, with 26 patients.

On Saturday, January 4, the wives and children of the men currently serving, were treated to afternoon tea in the Town Hall, thanks to the efforts of Dr. Atkinson, his wife and daughters. Men also invalided home or on furlough were also among the 1,100 who attended, with many in uniform. The party started promptly at 4.00pm, with rooms throughout the Town Hall decorated with bunting, flags and patriotic banners. The caterer, Mr E. R. Hill of Earle Street laid on a sumptuous meal, as the organisers had requested carte blanche instructions to spare 'neither trouble nor expense.' Included in the feast were 230lbs of currant bread, 220lbs of seed cake, 1,000 pork pies, 350 cheese cakes, 500 mince pies, 400 Madeira buns, 325 Victoria buns, 200 rock buns,

800 raspberry and lemon sandwiches, 15 boiled hams (cut up into sandwiches), 80lbs of beef, 60 tongues and an enormous amount of bread and celery. As the guests tucked into the mountain of food, the Crewe Engineers Band played. One of the distinguished guests was Charles Bebbington of Church Street, who had ridden at Balaclava in the Charge of the Heavy Brigade during the Crimean War. Even at eighty-five years of age, he was a picture of health and looked resplendent in a smart suit decorated by a bar of campaign medals. He had worked for many years on the Forge Street gate of Crewe Works, but had retired a few years previous.

During an interval between tea and the planned entertainment, Mrs Atkinson was presented with a bouquet of flowers (supplied by Willaston Nursery) by Miss Morgan, daughter of Lance Corporal W. W. Morgan, who was serving in South Africa. Reverend D. McVarish also took this opportunity to say a few choice words. He himself had been chaplain to the British garrison at Ladysmith during the siege and was now connected to St. Paul's Church in Crewe. This was followed with a few words by Sapper Barnes, who had recently returned from the front and the speech making was concluded by Dr. Atkinson. After the meal, the tables were cleared and at 6.00pm the entertainment started, which included a lavish lantern show in the science room, a talk on the siege of Ladysmith by Reverend McVarish, a piano recital, and a comic verse and banjo solo by Sapper S. Harvey. During a break, a thousand toys and presents were given out to the children, mostly of a military nature, before further acts, songs and dances concluded what had been a most enjoyable afternoon.

One week later, on January 11, another popular Crewe resident returned home from the war. Surgeon Captain Ernest Bailey of the Surgeons Rhodesian Field Force, received a pleasant surprise when greeted at the station by friends and family and the Crewe Steam Sheds Band. While in South Africa, he had been appointed to General Carrington's column, and also ran the affairs of No.1 Field Hospital in Northern Transvaal. He had travelled extensively with the mobile columns where he had treated the wounded on both sides.

With the joy of a homecoming there was also the heartache of more Crewe men losing their lives in South Africa, and in the space of twenty-eight days, four more were buried in the South African soil. On January 23, No.1662 Private C. G. Cole, 2nd King's Shropshire Light Infantry, and of Gladstone Street, died of disease at Middleburg, and eight days later, on January 31, No.1565 Sapper T. Coops of the 31st

Fortress Company, who had been in the first draft of Crewe Engineers, died in an armoured train crash at Burgersdorp, where three other Sappers were also killed. Sapper Coops had been a worker in the Crewe Steam Sheds. Then on February 10, another member of the Railway Reserve, No.1551 Sapper W. Talbot of the 45th Fortress Company and of 25 Charles Street, Crewe, died of multiple injuries, while working at Kroonstad. The quartet of deaths was completed on February 20, when No.3539 Private Thomas Wareham of the 1st King's Dragoon Guards, died of disease while at Kroonstad.

At Crewe Engineers HQ, the retirement of Surgeon Lieutenant Colonel James Atkinson (Dr. Atkinson) was announced. He had been associated with the Railway Volunteers since its conception and had also been connected with the old 36th Company of the Cheshire Volunteers.

February saw the continuation of the scarlet fever epidemic, and an outbreak of measles and diphtheria saw closure of more local schools. Of 407 scholars at Edleston Road, 271 were absent through sickness and of 231 pupils at Christ Church Infants, 120 had been struck down with one of the ailments. Wistaston Road Infants also reported that 60 out of 180 pupils were poorly, so all three schools were subsequently closed for one month. February figures also showed that consumers of electricity in Crewe now numbered 160.

On February 14, Sergeant T. Riley wrote to the ex-Mayor Dr. Wilson from the Steam Road Transport at Cape Town. Again the water shortage was the main topic of the letter.

> '.....We have weathered the plague safely, but the restrictions regarding it are still in force, as one or two odd cases have appeared at long intervals. Now we are threatened with a water famine as no rain has fallen for months and the authorities state that they have only about 20 days full supply in the reservoirs. They have for the past fortnight restricted the inhabitants from using it for house baths and have further cut it off every day at 3.00pm. I am however glad to say that the Tommies in the Castle will not be affected thereby, as two years ago, the Steam Road Transport bored for water in the Castle ditch and found a good supply, so we have put an engine and pump down and are prepared to pump about 5,000 gallons daily.....There are three of our men just come down country from Winburg hospital - Sergeant D. Heap and Sappers Morbey and O'Neil and are waiting for a boat for home. There are also Lance Corporal Mottram and Sapper J. Rowbottom at the Base Depot bound for home - time expired.'

On Wednesday, February 26, another Crewe Engineer, Sapper Osborn returned to his home in Brook Street, Crewe.

In March, Dr. Greenwood announced the medical report for Crewe for 1901. There had been 1,311 births in the town (682 males, 629 females), of which 55 were illegitimate and 710 deaths (386 males, 324 females).

On March 14, a brief stop at Crewe Station by the Prince and Princess of Wales caused much excitement. They arrived at 2.20pm and departed ten minutes later for London.

At the war zone, Crewe men continued to fall ill or be injured in accidents while at work. A report in *The Crewe Guardian* on March 15, told of a bad injury to a Crewe Engineer. Whilst working in a government workshop at Kroonstad, Sapper E. Collier of Brook Farm, Basford, had trapped his right hand in an engine cog-wheel. The badly mangled hand was amputated at the wrist by camp surgeons. Another mistaken report from the War Office caused much initial anguish for the Dodd family of Ludford Street, when it was stated that Sapper Dodd had died of enteric fever. Fortunately the report was yet another clerical error.

With many of the Crewe men still in South Africa, it was comforting for loved ones and friends to receive a letter. These letters also informed townsfolk of the whereabouts of those still in the war zone. On March 25, No.8551 Corporal A. Ross of the 10th Railway Company wrote from Bronkhirst Spruit, East Transvaal, to Mr J. Norman, who was chief of parcels staff at Crewe Station.

'Dear Sir – I now take the pleasure of writing you a few lines on behalf of your late servants Sappers C. W. Tandy, J. Key and myself…..We have been erecting an electric fence since last October to try and keep the Boers from crossing and to keep them from getting into the Bush Veldt, Northern Transvaal. A few have crossed in one's and two's. If they tamper with the wire it rings a bell at the blockhouses on each side. The blockhouses are at intervals of a mile or a mile and a half close to the line side. I enclose you a sketch of the electric fence eight man blockhouse. It will give you a good idea what our work is like. We have to camp outside the barbed wire fence. It is not very nice scrambling amongst the barbed wire at night when there is any sniping going on. The Boers seldom come near the line in the daytime. It is chiefly at night, but I think the Boers won't last much longer, as they keep bringing hundreds of them in nearly every week. Our twelve months is up with the colours, but I have heard that we shall have to stay out until the end of the war unless they send some more volunteers to relieve us as there is plenty of work for engineers to do. I have heard we are going to help make a new line from Harrismith to Ladysmith. I think I have told you all this time, I am pleased to say that all three of us are in the best of health. Kindly remember me to Mr Garner, Mr MacKenzie, Mr Sorton and Jim. I conclude with best wishes.'

Another letter dated April 4, was also published in the local press. It was written by Sapper A. E. Ankers of the 45th Fortress Company, who was at Sannah's Post, Steam Road Transport, Orange River Colony. It stated that, to break the tedium of blockhouse duty, the Crewe men held concerts and smoking parties.

In April, Sergeant Dan Heap came home to 96, Cemetery Road, and on April 12, was entertained at the Lion & Swan Hotel in West Street, by members of the Coppenhall Church Choir. Upwards of 35 enjoyed the evening and the meal, laid on by host Mr W. H. Coates. The previous day, Corporal W. Worrall returned home and was given a rousing reception by fellow clerks in the General Offices.

Many people in Crewe deserved special praise for their efforts during the period of the Boer War. One man who seemed to be involved in all aspects of fund raising and looking after dependents of serving men was Dr. Atkinson. On Saturday, May 3, at St. Peter's Men's Club, his tireless dedication was rewarded when presented with an illuminated address, enclosed in a dark English oak frame, by the Crewe Reservists who had returned from the war. It was also a token of thanks for organising the party on January 4, and around 50 guests enjoyed a meal at the presentation. Also in May, it was announced that Captain George Whale of the Crewe Engineers, had been promoted to Major. He had been associated with the Corps from the beginning and had held the position of Senior Captain during the whole period.

The May Day Festival held on Wednesday, May 14, was another occasion for the people of Crewe to organise a procession. The 'May Day Queen' was Miss Lily Delaney of Hungerford Road, who was transported in a carriage drawn by four grey horses, wearing an ivory satin dress, made by Miss Stubbs of Herdman Street. On the dot of 1.00pm, the procession moved off. As well as the children in the parade, there were also many local bands and dance troupes. The procession eventually reached the Crewe Alexandra football stadium at 2.30pm, where the children formed up in front of the main grandstand. Escorting the May Queen were her maids of honour, Miss Gertie Delaney (sister), Miss Annie Rigby, Miss Annie Ellis and Miss Connie Badger, and her maids in waiting, Miss May Dunne and Miss Ethel Parsonage. After the coronation of the May Queen, dances were performed by several dance troupes including the Crewe Alexandra Lady Morris Dancers. After the singing of the National Anthem, the children were marched to the luncheon room of the Crewe cattle market, where they enjoyed a fine spread. Afterwards they returned and entertained the crowd with several dance routines.

In 1902, Crewe was a town still growing and the demand for school places prompted another school to be built in the area. In May, a total of 400 applications were received for the position of headmaster and headmistress for the new Bedford Street School, which had been funded by the LNWR Company.

As the war drew to a conclusion, more Crewe men returned home and there were parties in Liverpool Terrace and Forge Street. However, on May 14, many of the Crewe Engineers who had been invalided home, were requested to appear before the medical officer of the battalion, at the Corps Armoury, in view of returning to South Africa for future duty.

On May 20, another local medical man lost his life. No.16898 Lance Corporal J. Brennan of the Royal Army Medical Corps, who had been sent to the war-zone to help quell the tide of disease, became a victim himself, after contracting enteric fever and dying in Harrismith Hospital (Orange River Colony). His father had received a letter off his son on May 2, which stated how well he was. Lance Corporal Brennan was 25 years of age and had worked, prior to war, in Market Street as a hairdresser and tobacconist.

Newspapers in Britain continued to fill column inches with the imminent ending of the war and on May 15, sixty Boer delegates gathered at Vereeniging to discuss peace proposals. By now many on the Boer side had had enough through starvation, and lack of fit horses and cattle. Another factor against a Boer continuation was the uprising of the Zulu nation. On May 6 at Holkrantz, a total of 56 Boers were killed and nearly 400 cattle taken during a confrontation with Zulu warriors. Left with little alternative, the Boer delegates, on May 31, cast their votes in a marquee at Vereeniging and voted in favour of Kitchener's peace proposals by 54 votes to 6. The parties involved were then rushed to Pretoria and by 11.05pm on the same day, the war was over.

On May 31, in the late news column of *The Crewe Chronicle*, it was reported that an official announcement of the ending of the war was 'expected at any moment.' The report proved to be accurate.

Early next day in South Africa, British troops fired off their rifles all along the blockhouse lines, and the garrison guns thundered their victory peal, and within a few days the vast majority were preparing for the voyage home. The Boers too, came out of their hiding holes, all 21,000, to lay down their arms. The war had cost the British taxpayer more than £200 million and 21,942 British and colonial troops had died during the campaign. The casualty breakdown was as follows:

	Officers	Men
Killed in action	518	5,256
Died of wounds	183	1,835
Died of disease	339	12,911
Accidental deaths	27	771
Died as POW's	5	97
Total	**1,072**	**20,870**

Nobody knew the figure for Africans who had died on the British side, but it was estimated at many thousands. The War Office also later announced that 400,346 horses, mules and donkeys had been 'expended' during the campaign. On the Boer side, there were approximately 7,000 deaths in the ranks, as well as over 2,000 foreign volunteers and 13,000 Afrikaners. No one knew the exact figure of men, women and children who had died in the concentration camps, but it was believed to be around 20,000.

News of the end of the war did not filter through to the townsfolk of Crewe until around 6.30pm on Sunday, June 1, with many informed during church services. It soon spread to every part of the local district and it didn't take long before Crewe was again a profusion of bunting, streamers and flags. Groups soon formed to cheer away the frustrations of war and a number of revellers made their way to Dr. Atkinson's home. To get his attention, a small stone was thrown at a window, which smashed the pane, but Dr. Atkinson delivered a short speech, before asking the gathering to go home and respect the Sabbath, which the majority did, after brief visits to the houses of Mayor Alderman McNeill, Francis William Webb and officers of the Crewe Engineers. Generally, due to the fear of upsetting homeward bound churchgoers, the celebrations were somewhat muted and put on hold until the next day.

Early Monday morning though, the town was ready for a party, with the younger fraternity first to emerge on the streets. Most of the apprentices in the Crewe Railway Works, unable to concentrate, came out after enjoying a morning of merriment, and they were soon joined by the women of the clothing factories, which included the employees of Compton's in Wistaston Road and Harding's in Vincent Street. The bells of Christ Church rang out as the railway workers left their workbenches, to swell the considerable numbers on the streets. School children were given a half day holiday and once again, just like the celebrations witnessed during the relief of Mafeking, the fall of Pretoria and during the Patriotic Demonstration, Crewe went wild. During the afternoon, a number of gentlemen associated with the patriotic fund conceived the idea of organising an evening procession, and by 6.00pm, several thousand people had assembled on the Market Square, many in costumes from the previous year's festivities. Mr J. A. Dutton, along with W. E. Dutton and S. Simpson perfected the arrangements and by 7.00pm, between four and five thousand people were ready to take part in the victory parade. This started from the Market Square along Market Street into High Street and then to Nantwich Road, with the whole route lined with spectators. The police and mounted marshals ensured that things didn't get out of hand and led the way, followed by a number of Crewe Army Reservists who had returned from South Africa. They included Trooper J. W. Dunning of the Cape Mounted Police, Sergeant G. Beckett, Sapper W. S. Brereton, Sapper J. H. Walley (Crewe Engineers) and Private A. Quiggin (Shropshire Light Infantry). Others in the parade included the Crewe Lady Morris Dancers, the Temperance Silver Band (under Bandmaster Stubbs), the Crewe Gaiety Girls (under Lizzie Lester), and the Crewe Steam Sheds as 'The Bottle-Nosed Navy.' The procession then continued down Nantwich Road into Edleston Road, then Exchange Street, Market Street and Earle Street, before returning up Victoria Street to Hightown and turning near the Chetwode Arms Hotel to return to the Market Square, where an immense crowd was waiting. Despite the mayhem on the streets, a total of £8.8s.7d was collected en-route for the Crewe Reservist Memorial Fund.

In Nantwich, news reached the town at around 8.00pm on the Sunday evening, and a large crowd soon gathered on the town square. The church bells rang out and a bugler sounded 'Cease Fire' at every street end. The rejoicing continued long after midnight, until the police intervened. Next day the celebrations were every bit as lively as their Crewe neighbours.

Festivities continued throughout the week, and on Sunday, June 8, congregations in the local churches were larger than normal, as thanksgiving services were held all over the country to mark the end of hostilities and the restoration of peace.

On Monday, June 9, Sergeant J. Emery of 12, Chester Street, returned home after recovering from enteric fever. He attended a welcome home party laid on by the juvenile branch of the Loyal Excelsior Lodge, Grand United Order of Oddfellows.

During June, several members of the Railway Volunteers were promoted, including Lieutenant F. R. Collins and Lieutenant J. A. Bowes who were both made Captains. On Thursday, June 19, a meeting was held in the Mechanics Institute regarding the winding up of the Crewe Reservist Fund. Up until this date, a total of £2,677.7s.3½d had been raised, with £2,561.9s.11d distributed among the families of the serving men, with twenty-four cases still in receipt of allowances.

With so many members of the Railway Volunteers still in South Africa, it was important that the Corps continued to train, just in case further men were required for active service. On Saturday, June 21, the remaining Crewe Engineers assembled on the Market Square at 2.00pm, then proceeded to the drill field off Victoria Avenue under the command of Colonel Cotton-Jodrell. During exercises it was announced that the Corps would attend their annual camp at Aldershot on July 5.

On June 23, the committee of the Reservists Memorial Fund contacted Lord Roberts in the hope that he would endorse their plans for the memorial and fountain and become a patron. Mr J. R. Dutton personally communicated with Lord Roberts's office. The request proved successful and a reply (on July 14) read:

> 'Dear Sir, I am desired by Field Marshall Lord Roberts to acknowledge the receipt of your letter of the 23rd ultimo, and to say that he will gladly give his patronage to the scheme for the erection of a public monument and drinking fountain at Crewe in commemoration of the large number of officers and men who have served in South Africa. His Lordship has every sympathy with the movement and hopes that your efforts prove eminently successful. Yours faithfully, H. Streatfield, Lieutenant Colonel, Private Secretary.'

With one celebration finished, yet another opportunity for the townsfolk of Crewe to let their hair down arose with the coronation of King Edward VII, which was set to take place on June 26. However, two days before the event, formalities were postponed due to the King developing appendicitis. Much of the town was already decorated and there had been plans to close the Railway Works from the Wednesday night until Monday morning. This therefore, had to be postponed, much to the disappointment of the workers. Not all the arrangements though could be called off, and a party for upwards of 10,000 local children and the distribution of their special coronation medals went ahead as scheduled, as the food had already been bought and prepared. This was served in their respective schools, where the medals were also presented. The following 17 schools took part; Hightown Wesleyan (1,019 pupils), Mill Street (699), Earle Street (397), Beech Street (1,139), St. Mary's (437), St. Paul's (903), Christ Church (1,119), Edleston Road (1,303), St. Barnabas (928), Wistaston Road (215), New Street (166), Pedley Street (643), Bedford Street (691), Broad Street (757), Maw Green (121), Mr Dishart's School (116) and the Oxford

Street Wesleyan (12). Most of the other planned festivities were postponed, including the lighting of a large bonfire on a site off Ruskin Road (on a piece of vacant land at the rear of Walthall Street). On the actual day, all bunting, streamers and Union flags had been removed, and despite the summer sunshine, the streets were pretty much deserted.

Next day on Friday, June 27, the planned tea party for the older generation and poor of the town at the Co-operative Hall also went ahead. Around 500 guests enjoyed food prepared by caterer Mr S. Derbyshire, although the organised entertainment was postponed as it was not felt appropriate due to the King's grave condition.

The 'coronation bonfire' was eventually set alight on the evening of July 1. At 10.00pm, the Mayor lit the fuse in front of a crowd of around 10,000. The structure was 35 feet in height and consisted of 40 tons of timber. A number of barrels of tar placed in the middle of the bonfire, surrounded by straw and shavings, resulted in the glare of the fire visible for miles. It burnt long after midnight and many watched until the final embers had died away.

On July 5 (a week later than normal due to the planned coronation), a total of 420 Railway Volunteers made their way to Aldershot for a week long training programme. Lieutenant Lemon again won the officers cup and the men excelled in their work, especially the building of brushwood field defences and entrenchments. During the holiday period, the townsfolk of Crewe bought upwards of 10,000 railway tickets, with the most popular destinations being Blackpool, Rhyl, Colwyn Bay, Llandudno, Isle of Man, New Brighton, Scarborough, Aberystwyth, Morecambe and Southport.

In July, the directors of Crewe Alexandra Football Club appealed to fans to purchase their season tickets (7s.6d) for the coming season, with the team playing in the Birmingham & District League. The response however, was not very encouraging, due to lack of new signings, retirements, departing players and the poor performances of the previous season.

On Saturday, July 19, members of the Loyal Excelsior Lodge of the Grand United Order of Oddfellows assembled at the Hop Pole Hotel to celebrate the return of prominent member Sapper G. H. Wearne, who had been invalided home. He left Crewe with the first draft of the Railway Reserve in October 1899 (8th Railway Company). During the evening all enjoyed a music and dance show.

Also in July, the Patriotic Committee at Crewe contacted the War Office, in the hope of acquiring a 'trophy of war' for the town, due to the amount of men who served. They had requested two guns that had been used in action and were hoping to place them next to the new war memorial.

On July 22, a statement issued by the War Office reached Crewe Engineers HQ, informing them that Lieutenant Davenport and 43 members of the Volunteer Service Sections were aboard S.S. *Malta*. She had departed South Africa for the homeward voyage on July 14. Estimations put their arrival at Southampton around the first week of August. Upwards of 179 Railway Volunteers were still in South Africa, with no news of their return date, although several had agreed to remain in South Africa after agreeing lucrative contracts (mainly fitters, turners and millwrights).

Next day, James Kellett of the Crewe Engineers was buried in Crewe following a long illness. He was the brother-in-law of Sapper Cunningham, who had been serving in South Africa, and it was his dying wish that he should live long enough to see him return (Cunningham would not return until the end of August). With the King's coronation approaching, the Crewe Engineers were honoured with the news that they were to be represented by a detachment, under the command of Captain J. N. Jackson. The Crewe Ambulance Brigade were also to be present and 1st Class Sergeant A. Coope and Privates Davies, Earnshaw, Fisher, Jervis, E. J. Jones, T. Potter and W. T. Jones would be among the lucky ones picked to represent the Brigade.

On Monday, August 4, news again quickly spread through the town regarding the return of the two Volunteer Service Sections, who had been the last Crewe Engineers to leave town in April 1901. They had arrived at Southampton on Sunday, August 3. Here the men were afforded a magnificent reception on the docks. Lieutenant Davenport communicated with Colonel Cotton-Jodrell on the estimated time of arrival home next day, and immediately plans were put in place to welcome them home.

On the Tuesday at 4.00pm, a message was received at the Crewe HQ that the men had reached Stafford. The officials at Crewe Station (Mr Lowndes and Mr Glenister) wired officials at Stafford to run the Crewe Engineers home by a special train, so their carriages were detached and a fresh engine coupled on. This steamed into Crewe station just about the same time as the evening buzzer sounded. The station authorities wisely arranged for the train to be directed into a siding near the approach to the old goods warehouse, which turned out to be a safe measure, as the station was already in danger of being overrun by enthusiastic and excited townsfolk. Colonel Cotton-Jodrell, fellow officers and the Engineers Band were first to be let through the goods yard gates.

The Colonel greeted Lieutenant Davenport, then shook hands with all who had returned. The gates were then opened and the men were swallowed up by the hordes who descended onto the platform. The men themselves were a picture of health, looking fit and bronzed. Many had ostrich feathers in their slouch hats and none seemed effected by the hustle and bustle of the large crowd, although Sergeant D. Pearson and Detective Inspector Smart were on hand to ensure things didn't get out of hand. After the initial welcome had died down, they formed up as best they could and the Engineers Band struck up with *Sons Of The Empire*. This was a signal for the crowd waiting outside and in Nantwich Road to begin a loud and vociferous cheer. When the men marched into the streets, some were lifted shoulder high. Progress to the Market Square was a slow affair, but no one seemed to care. The town was again a sea of bunting, streamers and flags and the local church bells rang out as the men made their way down Mill Street. Eventually they reached the square amid chaotic scenes, where upwards of 25,000 were waiting to greet them. Colonel Cotton-Jodrell made his way onto the Post Office balcony to say a few words, but after a while, gave up as the noise of the crowd made it impossible for anybody to hear him. Slowly the men drifted away to their homes, followed through the streets by individual groups of family and friends, intent on prolonging celebrations. It had been a magnificent homecoming. It would not be the last.

Next day, the returning men were inspected at 10.00am by Colonel Cotton-Jodrell, who drove in a carriage from Reaseheath Hall, accompanied by Lieutenant Davenport, his guest for the night. Of No.1 Section, Sapper E. B. Fox had yet to return and Corporal W. Worrall, Lance Corporal T. Wale and Sappers C. Fox and J. J. Lewis had already been invalided home. From No.2 Section, Sappers R. Rhead, J. W. Thompson and W. D. Thomas remained in South Africa. Captain Collins, who had taken over No.2 Section after the death of Lieutenant Trotter, also remained, after being appointed in a government position.

Before the excitement of the returning men had died down, news reached the Armoury that the majority of the remaining 173 members of the Railway Reserve were on their way home, having left Cape Town on August 4 on the S.S. *Moravian*. It was estimated they would be back on British soil by the end of the month and for many, this would be the first time home for nearly three years.

On Friday, August 8, a party of Railway Volunteers proceeded to Willesden to take part in the King's coronation, which was taking place next day. The detachment enjoyed supper in the Enginemen's Barracks, before retiring early to bed, as next morning, at 5.25am, they left for

Euston. From here they marched to the rest camp in Hyde Park, where they joined up with the 5th Brigade. Marching from Hyde Park, they proceeded to The Mall, where they took up their positions at 8.00am. After the royal procession had passed, the detachment returned to Euston, where they again entrained for Willesden. Here they enjoyed another first class dinner, before returning to Crewe on the 5.25pm train, arriving home around 9.00pm. The following men attended: Captain J. N. Jackson, (commanding officer in charge), CSM Brooke, Corporal G. T. Butterworth ("D" Company), Corporal J. F. Brownsword ("A" Company), Corporal F. Dutton, Sapper E. Vickers ("B" Company), Lance Corporal A. Bimson ("C" Company), Sapper J. B. Spencer, Sapper W. H. Vickerman ("E" Company), and Sapper W. Jordan ("F" Company). During the ceremony, the town was also represented at Westminster Abbey by the Mayor Alderman McNeill and Mr J. Tomkinson, member of parliament of the Crewe Division.

On the day in Crewe, even though the streets and town were decorated, most of the festivities had already taken place, so the town remained quiet. The railway workers did however, get their paid holiday.

If the streets were quiet on August 9, the opposite could be said the following week when Crewe once again dressed up and put on a show, that very few towns could equal. On August 16, another Great Patriotic Demonstration took place to raise further funds for the memorial. The highlight of the day was again the procession, and as before, the individual railway workshops had gone overboard with their costumes and float designs. However, pride of place in this procession would be the men who had returned from South Africa. The 100 or so sections stretched well over a mile in length, and would take 45 minutes to pass any given point. Of all the railway sections, the 'Living Wheel' constructed by the Smithy (Old Works) was one of the most impressive. It was 20 feet in height and in the wheel staves were small boys dressed in sailor suits. The streets again were a picture of flags, bunting and streamers and among them were banners proclaiming the return of the men. *'Welcome To Our Brave Crewe Engineers'* and *'Honour To Our Citizen Soldiers'* were seen all along the procession route, and in Mill Street, a most impressive arch had been erected by Mr H. Clews, opposite his shop. At 2.00pm the procession started, under the watchful eye of chief marshal, Mr J. A. Dutton. The front started on Merrill's Bridge and ended somewhere down Wistaston Road. The popular George E. Morgan again portrayed 'Lord Kitchener' and W. Mossford looked resplendent on horseback as 'Lord Roberts.' The band of the Crewe Engineers followed closely behind and then came the President of the Patriotic Demonstration, Dr. Atkinson, accompanied by his family. It was also a popular move by the Mayor Alderman McNeill to take part, following the previous year's snub. Then came the sections, again dominated by the railway workshops, although the clothing factories of the town were also well represented. As usual, prizes were handed out to the best sections and among the winners were the Crewe North Sheds (Best Workshop Section) who won £1.1s. Harding's factory won the Best Ladies Workshop Section, dressed as Japanese girls. The Crewe Carriage Works Silver Band walked off with the £1 prize money as best band and the most comical band was won by the Erecting Shop workmen as 'The Blue Hungry Band.' After the procession, several events took place in Crewe Hall Park, including a military tournament, which was witnessed by around 25,000 people. As day turned to night, the festivities continued all over town, which by now was illuminated by coloured lights and Chinese lanterns. In the Town Hall a fancy dress ball was held and around 100 revellers enjoyed a programme of music and dance until midnight.

Although the return of the Volunteer Service Sections had caused great celebration in Crewe, the arrival home of the first and second drafts was even more eagerly anticipated. At 10.00am on Wednesday, August 27, the S.S. *Moravian* docked at Southampton. The men landed, but half were sent to Chatham and the rest to Aldershot, due to the lack of accommodation at Chatham - which was significant in the fact that the men would now not all travel home together.

Next day in Crewe, at around 1.00pm, a telegram was received at Crewe Engineers HQ informing them that upwards of 40 men under the command of Sergeant Scragg were on their way back to the town, the majority of which had served in the 45th Fortress (Steam Road Transport) Company - and best of all was that they'd be home by early evening.

Around 30,000 townsfolk lined the streets from the station to the Market Square in anticipation of their arrival on the 7.48pm train. Bandmaster Coen and the Engineers Band were also ready to greet the men at the station, but it was reported that they had missed their connection at Willesden and would now not arrive at Crewe until 9.10pm. Despite the disappointment, very few left their places. Dead on time, the train pulled into the station, with the men occupying a specially reserved central carriage, which had been arranged at Euston. Outside, the streets were packed with people eager to get a first glimpse of the returning heroes. Eventually, among chaotic scenes, the column reached the Square and there to greet them was a crowd in excess of

20,000. At first, only 12 actually made it through to a specially cleared area, as the rest were swallowed up. The idea of a formal welcome home therefore was abandoned and after the singing of the National Anthem, the men were allowed to leave for home. Among the returning Engineers were Corporals Boughey, Eyres, Swinney and Sudlow, 2nd Corporals Dixon, Bickerton, Prince, and Groom, Lance Corporals Morgan, Mottram, Butterworth, and Bimson, Sappers Ankers, Beckett, Buckley, Cliffe, Conquest, Cornes, Cox, Dale, Dunn, Edwards, Garbett, Grime, Heap, Hoban, F. Jones, M. Jones, Lewis, Lloyd, J. Morris (1), J. Morris (2), Nield, Nicholson, Pearson, Phillips, Pointon, Porter, Roberts, Rowbottom, Upton, Weston, Wheatman, Williams and Wrench.

On Friday, August 29, the remaining men of the Crewe Engineers (8th, 10th and 31st Companies) made the journey home, but once again the predicted time of arrival did not materialise (around 8.00pm) and to make matters worse, the men were to arrive in two batches. At around 7.00pm, heavy rain fell, soaking through the waiting crowds. By the time the first batch arrived at the station, the rain fell in torrents and many of the crowd went home, especially when it was learnt that the men would not be marched to the Market Square, owing to the logistics of marching two different sections arriving at different times, especially after the scenes of the previous night. The first group, of around 40, reached the station at 9.10pm and were given a fantastic reception on the station top. With formalities over, Colonel Kennedy made the decision to dismiss them, and the majority boarded cabs to beat the wet weather. Then at 10.20pm, the remaining men arrived, and after similar scenes of congratulations, were again dismissed by Colonel Kennedy. These under the command of Sergeants Wadkins and Ellson included Corporal Wolfe, Lance Corporals Davies, Stanway and Furphy, Sappers Beeston, Butt, Cross, Evans, Godkin, Greenwood, Hassall, Hough, Harris, A. Jones, J. Jones, Maybury, Noden, Parr, Pratt, Rowley, Rowe and Russell.

Three officers of the Corps, Collins, Tweedy and Sidgwick, had decided to stay in South Africa. Collins accepted a job as the locomotive superintendent in the Central South African Railway at Bloemfontein; Tweedy, a role of superintendent in the Road Transport Company (known during the war as the Steam Road Transport) and Sidgwick a job as locomotive superintendent at Pretoria.

In Crewe, many events were held to celebrate the homecoming. On September 1, Sapper Cunningham, along with several comrades and their wives, were entertained in a field off Wistaston Road. The event, held in the evening, included the Carriage Works Band and a number of Morris Dance troupes. While on the field, the houses of the men were decorated with flags and streamers.

At 3.30am in the early hours of Wednesday, September 3, one of England's most prominent soldiers - Lord Kitchener - found himself stranded at Crewe station. At the time, the platform was deserted and Kitchener and his servant were given rooms at the Crewe Arms Hotel. At 9.30am, he checked out and walked back to the station, where this time he was instantly recognised, much to the disbelief of many in the vicinity. After a short and rousing reception, he boarded the 9.35am train to Welshpool, where he was to be a guest of Lord Powys.

Over the next few days, Crewe Station was a hive of activity with more Reservists returning from South Africa. On Thursday, September 4, Thomas H. Bailey, Civil Surgeon of the Surgeons Rhodesian Field Force and son of the late Doctor Bailey, arrived back after a month long voyage on the S.S. *Braemar Castle*.

However, among all the excitement, a Crewe man died on his way home. Private John Adnitt of 25, Richard Moon Street (2nd Cheshire Regiment), had been invalided home early August, suffering with enteric fever, but while onboard ship, seemed to make a good recovery, until a second bout rendered him in a critical state. On arrival in Southampton, he was taken to Netley Hospital, but died almost immediately.

On Monday, September 8, Lord Kitchener was again stranded on the platform at Crewe Station, when travelling home from Welshpool. It was close on midnight when he arrived, with an hour's wait for the Irish mail train. At this time there were still passengers and mail workers about and again he was instantly recognised, but Kitchener was keen to avoid any fuss and spent the hour waiting at the end of the platform until his train arrived, where he promptly entered the sleeping saloon of the Holyhead express.

The cost of the memorial had been calculated at £1,050 and it was also planned that a brass plaque would be erected in the Garrison Church of St. Paul's to honour the fallen of the Railway Volunteers. On October 2, about 200 Railway Volunteers held a smoking party at the Old Vaults public house in High Street, to celebrate their return home. The 'smoker' was also attended by other Reservists and a few Royal Navy personnel. The chair for the evening was held by QMS Gibson, who congratulated the men on their achievements and safe return and also proposed that the event should be an annual celebration. Special guest was the popular humorist, Mr Frank Crawford, who was also a member of the Crewe Engineers Band. Before the close, the men drank a silent standing toast to their fallen comrades.

By now, plans for the Crewe (South Africa) Volunteers and Reservists Memorial were at an advanced stage and designs for the new memorial were put on public display in the council chambers of the Mechanics Institute from October 23, for two days. The committee of the fund also requested that all men from Crewe who had served were to submit their names and regiments to Mr W. E. Dutton and Mr S. Simpson for inclusion on the cast tablets. In October, statistics were released from the LNWR Company that 1,760 of their employees had served in the war and 99 had fallen, of which 76 had been Reservists. During the same month, the Crewe Reservists and Volunteer fund was finally wound up. While in existence, £2,738.7s.7½d had been raised, with the expenditure calculated at £2,675.10s.1½d. A total of 3 men, 180 women and 281 children had benefited. The remaining money was donated to the Soldiers and Sailors Families Association, to which Colonel Cotton-Jodrell's wife was President. QMS George Riddle Gibson, secretary of the fund, would be presented with a gold watch for all his efforts, which was inscribed:

'South African War, 1899-1902. Presented to George Riddle Gibson, in recognition of his services as honorary secretary of the Crewe Reservists Fund – 27th October, 1902.'

The fund had been a massive success but there had been instances of deception and false claims. One wife of a Railway Volunteer continued to claim, even though her husband had returned home and to work.

An unusual incident occurred on Tuesday, October 21, when Chester military authorities sent an escort to Crewe Works and arrested Sapper Harry Thompson, a fitter of Chetwode Street, who had served during the war in the 8th Railway Company, and was among the first draft of the Railway Reserve to leave town. While away he had married at Pietermaritzburg in June 1901. Unfortunately he hadn't asked the permission of his wife living in Crewe! Sapper Thompson was immediately conveyed to Chester, where he was transferred to Chatham. After a long drawn out affair, he was tried in Pretoria and sentenced to six months in jail.

On Sunday, October 26, the Bishop of Chester visited the town to preach to the returning men at St. Paul's. Two days later, they were guests of honour at a party in the Town Hall held by Colonel Cotton-

Jodrell. Over the main platform in the main room were banners which read *'Honour To The Crewe Engineers Who Have Fought For The Flag'* and *'Welcome Home.'* Among the invited guests were the Mayor Alderman McNeill, Dr. Wilson and Councillor John Jones, who was the Mayor when the first draft had left town. Reverend D. McVarish was also in attendance, but there was great disappointment that Francis William Webb could not attend. The lavish cold supper (no establishment in the town could serve 300 men with a hot meal) was provided by Richard Dickeson and Co. of Liverpool. While the men ate, the Engineers Band, occupying the galleries, played several popular tunes. After supper, the usual speeches were made. During the rest of the evening, a programme of entertainment kept the men amused, which included an artist drawing portraits of prominent British soldiers. It was noted that during his act that the Crewe men cheered louder for the drawing of General Buller than of Lord Roberts, and also called out repeatedly for one of General French.

On Wednesday afternoon, November 5, the town paid homage to a Railway Volunteer, who had been killed on November 1, in Crewe Works. CSM Edwin Fleet, who had been a member of "B" Company, was buried with full military honours and thousands lined the route from his home to St. Paul's Church. The incident in the Works happened just a few minutes before he was due to leave on the previous Saturday morning. He was in the Millwright's Shop, when a shunted wagon jumped the rails and pinned him to a wall, killing him instantly. He was forty years of age and resided at 85, Flag Lane with his wife and three children. He had attended the get together at the Town Hall and the service by the Bishop of Chester, only days previous and was one of the most respected members of the Corps.

Following the viewing of the designs for the Boer War memorial, six were left in the running for the contract. They were: Whitehead & Sons of London, M. Cliffe of Crewe, Boddis & Co. of Aberdeen, W. Mossford of Crewe, Alton Iron Co. of London and John Bennett & Co. of London. In mid-November, more good news regarding the conduct of the Railway Volunteers who had served was received at Crewe Engineers HQ. In the Corps orders, Colonel Cotton-Jodrell wrote:

> *'It is with great gratification that the commanding officer places on record the fact that General Lord Kitchener, in his despatch, dated 25th June, 1902, mentions the names of Lieutenant C. K. D. Sidgwick and Sergeant H. W. Hitchcock of the 2nd Cheshire Royal Engineers (Railway Volunteers) for special and meritorious service in the field.'*

The following also appeared in *The London Gazette*:

> 'The King has been graciously pleased to give orders for the appointment to the Distinguished Service Order, in recognition of their service during the operations in South Africa, the whole to bear date 22nd August 1902, except where otherwise stated: Royal Engineers (Volunteers) to be a companion of the Distinguished Service Order – Lieutenant Charles Kater Dury Sidgwick, 2nd Cheshire.'

A few days after news of his award, Lieutenant Sidgwick resigned his commission in the Railway Volunteers.

When members of the Crewe Engineers had gone to war, 31 were employees of the boilermaker's department of Crewe Works. When these men left town, their shopmates gave them a fitting 'send off,' so it was only appropriate that the 'welcome home party' should be just as impressive. On November 15, at 5.00pm, a large party gathered at the Co-operative Hall, where the guests enjoyed a 'knife and fork' dinner, courtesy of Mr J. Williams of Nantwich Road. The gathering then proceeded to the Imperial Hotel, where a smoking party was held. Mr H. Cooper, chief foreman of the Boiler Shop, presided over the whole affair.

On Monday, November 17, a meeting in the Mechanics Institute reported the statement of accounts in connection with the Patriotic Demonstration on August 16. The sum raised was £303.5s.11d which brought the fund total to £832.17s.9½d. Further donations were then received from Francis William Webb (£25) and the Mayor Alderman McNeill (£5 5s).

On November 29, it was announced that Francis William Webb was about to retire from his position in the LNWR Company. Mr George Whale of Crewe or Mr Park of Wolverton were tipped to take over the role.

It was also reported towards the end of November that the contract for the memorial had been awarded to J.Whitehead & Sons (Sculptors of the Imperial Works) of 74, Rochester Row, Westminster, London. It was to be sited in Queens Park at the end of the main avenue leading from the entrance gates (initial plans were for it to be placed on the Market Square). Meanwhile another call was made for all Crewe men who had served in South Africa to submit their names for the memorial tablets.

Towards the end of December, a letter from Major Scholfield, who had commanded the Steam Road Transport during the war, was received at Crewe Engineers HQ, in relation to the conduct of the Crewe men who served under his command. Thirty-six Sappers were commended and of Lieutenant N. H. Brierley his comments were:

> '*I cannot speak too highly of this officer's energy and excellent work done during the last year.*'

Christmas was celebrated for the first time in four years, with Britain at peace. The Crewe Engineers Ball took place on Friday, December 26 in the Town Hall, with 200 in attendance. The music was again supplied by the Engineers Band and the MC's for the evening, QMS Gibson and Sergeant Shaw, ensured the night ran smoothly.

Chapter Five - 1903
-Honour The Citizen Soldiers-

With the serving men back in their workplaces - the majority doing the same jobs and working with the same workmates - all was now geared towards the erection and unveiling of the war memorial. In March, it was proposed that the monument was to be erected on the present site of the park bandstand, with the bandstand moved to the centre of the lawn tennis ground.

On March 4, Surgeon Captain James Reginald Atkinson resigned his commission in the Railway Volunteers and was replaced by QMS J. Williamson of the Cheshire Regiment.

Crewe residents received quite a shock in the dinner hour of Tuesday, March 24, when the town was subjected to a minor earthquake, which caused much panic, especially among the older fraternity.

Two days later, a distinguished visitor was spotted in a railway carriage which had halted for a few moments at Crewe Station. King Edward VII, on the way to Knowsley Hall, arrived in Crewe at 5.28pm, but even though there was a large presence on the platforms, very few caught a glimpse of their monarch.

At much debate and planning, Saturday, August 8 was the date chosen for the unveiling of the war memorial, and by the end of March, 460 names had been forwarded for inclusion on the cast plaques.

Accidents and deaths were a common occurrence in the railway workshops in the town and on April 20, an explosion in the Crewe Steel Works, left five men badly burned. Approximately twenty tons of molten metal was in the process of being transferred to the moulds from the

(**ABOVE**) *Private Thomas Wareham of the 1st King's Dragoon Guards, who died of disease at Kroonstad on February 20, 1902. (**BELOW**) His memorial card.*

In Loving Memory of

Thomas,

The beloved son of George and Jane Wareham.

Who died at Kroonstad, South Africa,
February 20th, 1902.

AGED 26 YEARS 11 MONTHS;

1st. King's Dragoon Guards.

*(**ABOVE**) Another Boer farm burns. (**BELOW**) A stone blockhouse. This substantial structure was built by railway bridges and important stretches of the line and proved most effective, as no bridges were blown where one was sited.*

(ABOVE) Lance Corporal W. W. Morgan of 9, Cotterill Street, who left Crewe with the second draft of the Railway Reserve. He is pictured here at Winburg on March 9, 1902, outside this 'Rice' blockhouse, which had been designed in 1901 by Major S. R. Rice, commander of the 23rd Field Company, Royal Engineers. This type (nicknamed 'Pepper Pots') consisted of a double skin of corrugated sheet with loopholed walls, with a filling of stones and rubble between the sheets. The interior diameter was 13 feet and the gabled roof provided standing space of 6 feet. It could be erected in just 6 hours by six trained men at a cost of £16. (BELOW) Sapper Richard Chesters (standing right) with train '53' of the Imperial Military Railways.

*(**ABOVE**) Railway Volunteers advance party for Aldershot in 1902.*

*(**ABOVE**) 1901 Carnival participants.*

'The Great Patriotic Demonstration.' (**ABOVE**) *Men who had served, march proudly in the procession.* (**BELOW**) *'The Living Wheel' constructed by members of the Smithy (Old Works) proceeds on its journey, watched by children sitting on the wall around 'Hillock House' on Hightown.*

Bessemer furnaces, when a stopper problem caused the metal to explode. The five men were William Farr, William Yeomans, Allen Beckett, William Evanson and George Cornthwait. William Farr, aged 59, died from his injuries in the Railway Company's hospital at around 7.00pm on Monday, April 27. A resident of Bradfield Road, Coppenhall, he was buried in Coppenhall Churchyard on Saturday, May 2.

As other Boer War memorials throughout the country were unveiled, it was only fitting that the LNWR Company should honour their dead, by unveiling a tribute to the 99 employees who had fallen. On Wednesday, April 8, an order was issued by Captain F. D. Stones for all Crewe Engineers who had served to parade at the Armoury for the purpose of selecting a number of them to act as a guard of honour to Lord Roberts at Euston, for the unveiling of the LNWR tablet. The tallest and smartest men were picked and the following two officers and 50 men were chosen to represent them (their ranks were now those held in their own Corps): Lieutenants Davenport and Brierley, Sergeants A. Scragg and D. Heap, Corporals W. P. Roscoe, W. Bickerton, A. J. Boughey, J. Brookes, J. Swinney, A. Ross, 2nd Corporals R. T. Upton, R. Dixon, J. H. Dodd, W. Spilsbury, Lance Corporals W. Goodwin, J. Stanway, W. H. Phillips, Sappers J. Edwards, B. Pointon, T. Winder, H. J. Parr, C. Ralphs, W. Kent, W. Cox, E. Weston, W. Champion, J. Wareham, W. Cooke, W. Barnes, E. Fox, W. Manning, W. Sumner, J. Guest, A. E. Ankers, C. H. Bennett, G. Wearne, W. Godkin, J. Jones, H. Hubbard, J. Walley, J. O'Neil, G. W. Noden, W. D. Thomas, F. Rowe, F. Francis, H. Beckett, G. Harris, W. Capper, W. Pugh, W. Mottram, F. Beeston and L. Kirkham.

On Thursday morning, April 23, the party assembled on the Market Square at 11.15am in their new uniforms, specially produced for the occasion by Compton's factory. The body of men all wore their war medals which had arrived just before departure. They then marched to the railway station and were applauded along the route by a large number of townsfolk who had turned out to see them off. Here, a special train was waiting on the horse landing platform, which steamed out of the station at 12.20pm. It was ironic that the driver of the train, was the very same who had taken the first draft to Chatham in October 1899. Once again the Railway Volunteer contingent performed their duties with impeccable thoroughness and were commended on their turn out when Lord Roberts unveiled the tablet in the Great Hall at Euston.

In May, another impressive illuminated address was presented, this time to the directors of the LNWR from the railway workers of the town who had served, in appreciation of the kindness shown to their families while they were away. The address was made by Mr W. Ellis of Crewe and when it was put on public display at Mr W. Hamilton's shop in Market Street, it attracted much attention.

With the closing of the Holmes Chapel rifle range by the War Office, the Railway Volunteers had nowhere to practice. A search in the immediate area unearthed a site at Coppenhall Moss, but the War Office rejected the 600 yard range. Another piece between Crewe and Barthomley was also rejected, so to ensure the men had somewhere to shoot, a deal was struck with the North Staffordshire Volunteers, to rent their range at Newcastle.

The month of June saw the unveiling of a brass tablet in St. Paul's Church which commemorated the ten members of the Railway Volunteers who had lost their lives during the conflict. The tablet was designed by Mr T. J. Gawthorp of London.

The Railway Volunteers continued their normal annual routine by attending a week long summer encampment. This year some 600 members left Crewe on Saturday, June 27, for Chatham. Rumours meanwhile, circulated in the town that George Whale would take over Francis William Webb's role in the LNWR. The appointment was expected to take place on July 1.

After much organisation, the day of the memorial unveiling finally arrived. A number of special trains were laid on by the LNWR to ferry passengers from Rugby and Horwich and trains packed with daytrippers had been booked from as far north as Carlisle and far south as London. In Crewe, the railway works was shut for the day and the shops closed for a few hours in the afternoon. The favourable weather soon saw the streets of the borough congested. Tradesmen and private residents vied with one another in their displays of bunting, flags, streamers and patriotic banners, which invoked all kinds of tributes to the citizen soldiers of the town. A major feature of the unveiling would again be the procession. Well over 100 sections were to take part, and the railway workshops were all hoping to win the 25s for the best section prize.

Between the morning hours of 11.00 and 12.00 o'clock, frantic preparations took place in Goddard Street and Richard Moon Street, as the sections took up their respective positions, and by the time all were in place, the line stretched over a mile. At exactly 12.30pm, the great line moved into West Street. The designated route then took them into Hightown, Victoria Street, Market Street, Henry Street, Hall O' Shaw Street, Earle Street, Market Street, Coppenhall Terrace, High

Street, Mill Street, Nantwich Road, Edleston Road, Stalbridge Road, Walthall Street, Wistaston Road, Victoria Avenue and finally to Queens Park. It was no small task to organise the vast line, but once again chief marshals, Mr J. A. Dutton and Mr G. E. Morgan, both mounted on magnificent chargers, kept the sections in perfect order, with Mr Morgan again attired as 'Lord Roberts.' Near the front of the parade were around fifty war veterans under the command of Sergeant G. Jones of the 2nd King's Shropshire Light Infantry. The sections were too many to mention individually, but several had spent weeks on their preparation. One such section was the North Steam Sheds, who were represented by around forty members in red and yellow African costumes with tall hats to match, who walked down either side of the road, with a further dozen ladies down the centre, carrying red parasols. To the strains of the Crewe Steam Sheds Band, led by Mr J. Skellern, they danced the 'cake-walk' much to the amusement of the vast crowds who lined the route.

At around 3.15pm, the first sections arrived at Queens Park, along with the full compliment of the Railway Volunteers. It was estimated that around 45,000 were present to witness the unveiling. As the time approached, all eyes were on the memorial, which at this time was covered by a large Union flag. It had been constructed of the best Aberdeen granite, stood 31 feet high, and was surmounted by a life-size figure of 'Tommy Atkins.' Either side of the monument was guarded by a lion and where the pedestal met the base, there was a model of F.W. Webb's latest locomotive - No.1942 'King Edward VII.' This had been specially designed and constructed by Crewe Works fitter Mr J. H. Lightfoot of Buxton Avenue and Mr R. Bebbington, with the four foot long model conveyed to the park on a milk float! Also on the four faces were the cast plaques which recorded the names of those who had left Crewe to serve, including the 26 who had died during the campaign.

Prior to the unveiling a number of speeches were delivered; the first by Dr. Atkinson, who then handed over to the Chairman of the LNWR, Lord Stalbridge. Among his words were some interesting statistics regarding the service of LNWR men during the war.

> "Out of 1,760 men who went to war, 99 fell, and their names are inscribed on the tablet at Euston. Of the remaining 1,661, 1,393 availed themselves of the opportunity of returning to the service of the company. Of the remainder, 191 took up other employment, with some preferring to stay in South Africa, with 35 re-engaging themselves for public service in the Army.....With regards to the wives and families, no less than 1,538 wives, children and dependants of

railway men who went out were assisted at a cost to the company of no less than £19,000."

Then the moment finally arrived for the unveiling, performed by Lord Stalbridge himself, and a deathly hush fell over the park. As the memorial was finally revealed, cheers and applause rang out. The Crewe Engineers Band then played the National Anthem and the Bishop of Chester dedicated the memorial with the words:

"...the memorial of men who in an hour of great need went forth from this place to fight the battles of their country in South Africa. Grant that the record of their patriotism may inspire like zeal and constancy and self-sacrifice in the hearts of beholders for many generations."

Major Whale, the newly appointed Chief Mechanical Engineer of the LNWR Company then said a few words before officially handing over the memorial to the Mayor and town councillors. Further speeches followed by the Mayor himself, Lieutenant Colonel Sir Frederick Harrison (General Manager of the LNWR Company) and Mr Frank Ree (Chief of the Goods Department at Euston), before Major General Sir Thomas Fraser, Honourable Colonel of the Engineer Corps, presented DCM's to Sappers Jones and Pugh of the Railway Volunteers, as well as the King's South Africa medal to a number of the Crewe Engineer Reservists. Then Mrs Holford, daughter of Lord Stalbridge, awarded special bronze medals to the ambulance men of the town (Superintendent Oldham and Privates Dixon, Holland, Measures and Burgess) who had served. The most poignant moment during this presentation was when she handed similar medals to Mr Powell and Mr Thornton, the fathers of Charles Powell and Private Thornton, who had died of disease during the campaign. Both fathers openly wept when receiving the awards. After this ceremony, there was a brief speech from Colonel Cotton-Jodrell, and then Councillor John Jones thanked the committee of the memorial fund, namely Dr. Atkinson (President), Mr J. A. Dutton (Chairman), Mr W. E. Dutton and Mr S. Simpson (Secretaries), Mr H. Lynes (Financial Secretary) and Mr Eardley (Honourable Treasurer). After a brief reply by Dr. Atkinson, speaking on behalf of the committee, a large number of dignitaries, visitors and friends were entertained in a large marquee by Dr. Atkinson, where tea was served. In the park various entertainments kept the large crowd amused until the events of the day were finally wound up. It had been a proud and emotive day in the history of Crewe and one that would be long remembered.

The committee offered cash prizes for the procession participants in their respective categories - the majority of which had been donated by Crewe tradesmen. The following winners were:-

Best Workshop Section
1st - Crewe North Sheds 'Florida Coons' (25s)
2nd - Crewe South Sheds 'Dutch Wedding' (17s 6d)
3rd - Fitting Shop 'Hornpipe Dancers' (10s)
4th - Millwright Shop 'Original Straw Men' (7s 6d)
Judges: Mr Fletcher and Mr Wilkinson of Stockport.

Ladies' Business Section
1st - Compton's 'Lady Serpentine Dancers' (12s 6d)
2nd - Harding's 'The Law' (7s 6d)
Judges: Mr D. Froggatt and Mr E. Hill.

Gentleman Morris Dancers
1st - Betley Morris Dancers (20s)
2nd - Crewe Royal Morris Dancers (10s)

Most Artistically Dressed Gentleman on Horseback
1st - Mr A. Milton 'Cavalier' (15s)
2nd - Mr Dutton 'Brigand' (5s)
Judges: Councillor H. Hoptroff and Mr W. Hamilton.

Most Artistically Dressed Gentleman on Foot
1st - Mr J. W. Capper of Wistaston Road (5s)
Judges: Councillor H. Hoptroff and Mr W. Hamilton.

Most Artistically Dressed Lady on Foot
1st - Miss F. Griffin of Bridle Road (7s 6d)
2nd - Miss E. Bloss of Broad Street (2s 6d)
Judges: Councillor H. Hoptroff and Mr W. Hamilton.

Most Artistically Dressed Gentleman on a Cycle
1st - Mr W. J. Kirk (10s 6d), prize donated by Mr. P. P. Johnson
Judges: Councillor H. Taylor and Mr C. Vickers.

Most Comically Dressed Gentleman on Foot
1st - Mr R. H. Ashley of St. Clair Street (10s 6d)

Judges: Councillor H. Hoptroff and Mr W. Hamilton.

Most Comical Turnouts (Not Attached)
1st - 'Diamond Convict Gang' (10s)
Judges: Councillor C. Wilson and Mr W. Hurstfield.

Most Effective Tableau
1st - Crewe Baths and Hospital Laundry (7s 6d)
Judges: Councillor C. Wilson and Mr W. Hurstfield.

Most Comical Band
1st - Sousa's 'Millinary' Band, No.5 and 6 Erecting Shops (15s)
2nd - 'Blue Hungry Band,' No.2 Erecting Shop (7s 6d)
Judges: Councillor C. Wilson and Mr W. Hurstfield.

Best Quick-Step Band
1st - Crewe Carriage Works Band (30s)
2nd - Moulton Verdin Institute Band (15s)
3rd - Crewe Temperance Band (7s 6d)
Judge: Mr Guy of Abergavenny.

Fire Brigades Smartest Turnout
1st - Crewe Corporation Fire Brigade (20s)
2nd - Audlem Fire Brigade (10s)
Judges: Mr J. Knott and Mr T. Keeley.

Ladies Collecting Most Money in the Streets
1st - Miss L. Hill of Mill Street who collected £2 18s 4d (7s 6d)
2nd - Miss G. Spokes who collected £2 3s 9½d (5s)
3rd - Miss G. Dutton of Stalbridge Road who collected £1 11s 10½d (3s 6d)
4th - Miss F. Ankers of Alexandra Street who collected £1 11s 9½d (2s 6d)
5th - Miss L. Cooke of Adelaide Street who collected £1 11s 6d (2s 6d)
6th - Miss G. Farmer of West Street who collected £1 11s 1½d (2s 6d)
Special Prize - Lady (committee) collecting most money on the streets was Miss Spokes of Beech Street who collected £1 5s.

Gentleman Collecting Most Money on the Streets (Boxes only)
1st - Mr A. Antill of Edleston Road who collected £2 8s 10½d
2nd - Mr J. Evans of Rose Terrace who collected £1 11s 8½d
3rd - Mr E. J. Cooper of Lincoln Street who collected £1 2s 6½d.

Gentleman Collecting Most Money on the Streets (Purse Poles)
1st - Mr C. Cole of Moss Square who collected £2 1s 6½d
2nd - Mr G. Jones of Nantwich Road who collected £2.

A few months after the unveiling, letters appeared in the local papers, stating that names had been missed off the memorial. Two such men were Sergeant J. Adams and Private J. Malone, who had originated from the town, but had worked in South Africa for a number of years.

It had been hoped that the War Office would donate a number of old artillery pieces to stand by the memorial, but with none spare, the request was denied. So it was decided that three R.M.I. 9 - pounders would be purchased by Dr. James Atkinson, Mr Wilmot Eardley and Mr J. A. Dutton, which were delivered to Queens Park in September 1904. Each piece had an inscription on it which read: *'This gun was presented to the town of Crewe by....*(followed by the name of the purchaser). No history of the guns were submitted, but they were believed to be only training pieces. Official confirmation was received in a letter from Woolwich (written on September 9, 1904), in reply to one sent by Mr W. E. Dutton.

'Dear Sir, In reply to your letter of the 28th ult. re the history of the three R.M.I. guns recently purchased by you. I have to inform you that the guns in question have only been used for practice purposes in this country. Yours, Smith Cooper, Captain for Principal Ordnance Office.'

When the public learnt that the guns had no significant military history, many resented their place by the memorial. Letters of complaint soon appeared in the local papers and echoed the voice of one such protester who stated:

'They hadn't been used in South Africa, so did not represent the men who did.'

On June 4, 1906, the instigator of the Railway Volunteers, Francis William Webb, died in Bournemouth, aged 70. With the formation of the Territorial Army in 1908, numbers in the Railway Volunteers diminished to such a level, that their continuation was even discussed in the House of Commons on July 27, 1910. The strength of the Corps had dwindled to just 213 and Viscount Valentia had proposed that a new Territorial battalion should be formed. However, the Secretary of State for War (who had initiated the formation of the Territorial Army in 1908) Richard Haldane, had not yet decided on the duties of railway troops in time of war, but concluded that under no circumstances should the Crewe Engineers recruit up to its former strength, which had stood at 716 in 1908. This sounded the death knell for the Corps. Despite desperate attempts to save the Railway Volunteers, a letter from the War Office - dated March 4, 1912 - signalled the end. It read:

> *'I am commanded by the Army Council to inform you that his Majesty the King has now graciously approved of the disbandment of the Cheshire Railway Battalion, Royal Engineers (Territorial Force). R. H. Brade.'*

The order was to be carried out immediately, and instructions were issued for the return of all government property. Officers, NCO's and men were given the option of transferring to another Territorial unit.

So on a miserable day, on Sunday March 17, 1912 the Railway Volunteers had one final church parade. They assembled on the Market Square for 10.10am, together with 100 veterans, including Bugler H. Settle, who in 1887 blew the first call. In front of a sizeable audience, their commanding officer, Colonel Howard C.B. (Colonel Cotton-Jodrell had relinquished the role in 1908) presented long service medals* to seven serving members and ten retired. They were: (serving) Sergeant E. W. Newton, Lance Corporal J. Simpson, Lance Corporal C. F. Clewes, Sapper W. E. Allcock, Sapper A. Bailey, Sapper F. Mullock, Sapper A. Perkins. The retired men included Corporal W. Bickerton, Corporal L. E. Tirrell, Lance Corporal T. Conquest, Sapper M. Coupe, Sapper W. K. Mcilwraith, Sapper R. Trow, Sapper A. H. Upton, Sapper A. Williams, Sapper J. W. Wrench and Sapper C. W. Wright. (*Territorial Efficiency Medals in *The Crewe Guardian*.)

After the presentation, the battalion, headed by the Regimental band, under the command of Bandmaster Stear, proceeded to Christ Church, where a special service was held. Officers present included Colonel Howard, Adjutant Captain Greig, Major Jackson, Captains Black, Beaumont, Beames and Lieutenant Davenport. Following the conclusion, the men marched to the Armoury, via Victoria Street and Flag Lane. On arrival at the Carriage Works, they were photographed by the Corps photographer Mr Slight. Then the ensemble entered a large room at the Armoury, where Colonel Howard and Mr Bowen-Cooke addressed the men before dismissing them one last time. Many in the room were visibly upset by the final order.

Two years later, and nearly eleven years to the day of the unveiling of the Queens Park memorial, the declaration of war with Germany signalled the start of what would be known as the Great War. Again the men of

Crewe answered the call (around 5,500), including many who had served in South Africa. Unfortunately not all would return to collect their medals to pin alongside their tokens earned during the Boer War. Among the fallen would be Sapper Fred Francis, 1st Field Company, Royal Engineers, who died of wounds on July 30, 1915, at Gallipoli.

Many more would receive wounds and suffer the nightmares of combat. As the years progressed the Boer War veterans would continue to meet-up, until there was no-one left to talk about the adventures in South Africa. According to *The Crewe Chronicle*, the last Crewe Boer War veteran to pass away was Haslington man Charles William Tandy of 12, Wellesley Avenue, who died aged 93, on June 19, 1974 - the very last of the Cheshire Boer War survivors. He had worked for many years as a Parcels Foreman for British Rail, and had also been the Vice-President of the Crewe Green and Haslington British Legion.

As for Colonel Edward Cotton-Jodrell, he died on October 13, 1917 in a Manchester nursing home, following a seizure three weeks previous. After the Boer War, he had been made a Companion of the Bath in 1902 and in 1906, was appointed Assistant Director of the Volunteer Services on the staff of the Director of Auxiliary Forces. In 1911, his name appeared in the list for Coronation honours when he was made Knight Commander of the Bath. As a much travelled man, he had visited nearly every corner of the globe. His interest in education saw him appointed one of the foundation managers of Worleston School, and following his retirement from politics in 1900 (he was M.P. for the Wirral Division from 1885), he threw his heart and soul into the Red Cross movement, where he held the position of County Director for the Cheshire Branch. He was also a Justice of the Peace and sat at Nantwich, where he was one of the senior magistrates, and was also a Deputy Lieutenant for Cheshire. His funeral took place at Manchester Crematorium on Tuesday, October 16 and a memorial service was held next day at Acton Church - attended by representatives of the Red Cross, the miltary, and other societies he was associated with, as well as many residents of Nantwich. Military duties accounted for the absence of many of his friends and comrades, but even so, the colour of khaki was still prominent in the large gathering.

It has now been over a hundred years since the end of the Boer War, and the five hundred Crewe men who served are long gone. We should never forget their efforts, hardships and sacrifices.

(ABOVE) The procession on August 8, 1903, turning into Henry Street after passing under the Cumberland Bridge. In the photo are the Over Silver Band and the Hornpipe Dancers of the Fitting Shop. (LEFT) The memorial, complete with lions, model train and 'Tommy Atkins.'

(ABOVE) The memorial c1905, surrounded by the three artillery pieces.

(ABOVE) The Crewe town crest featuring the motto 'Never Behind.' It is situated on the north face of the memorial and is the last known surviving crest found in the town.

*Reminders of the Boer War, now in the Municipal Buildings in the town. (**ABOVE**) The model of 'King Edward VII' which adorned the memorial for over 70 years. (**BELOW**) The St. Paul's plaque to the members of the Railway Volunteers who lost their lives.*

Francis William Webb's grave in the Wimbourne Road Cemetery, Bournemouth.

*The last parade of the 2nd Cheshire Royal Engineers (Railway Volunteers) on March 17, 1912. (**ABOVE**) Members (left) line up on a wet Market Square ready for Sunday service, with retired members of the Corps behind them. The photograph has been taken from the Labour Exchange balcony, formerly the old Post Office. The buildings in the background are (from left to right) the Manchester & Liverpool District Bank, Post Office and Telegraph Office.*

*(**ABOVE**) A final photograph in the Carriage and Wagon Works yard, Wistaston Road.*

-The Men Who Served-

Spellings are as memorial plates. Men in bold lost their lives during the campaign.

Private	Adams W.M.	North Staffordshire Regiment
Private	**Adnitt J.**	**2nd Bn. Cheshire Regiment**
Private	Alcock J.	22nd Cheshire Regiment
Private	Alcroft G.H.	22nd Cheshire Regiment
1st Gr.Ord	Allen H.W.	St. John Ambulance Brigade
Sapper	Allen W.	2nd Cheshire Roy. Eng. (Railway Vol.)
Sgt.	Allman G.E.	Shropshire Light Infantry
Private	Allman J.	22nd Cheshire Regiment
Sapper	Ankers A.E.	2nd Cheshire Roy. Eng. (Railway Vol.)
Sapper	**Ankers F.**	**2nd Cheshire Roy. Eng. (Railway Vol.)**
Private	Arrowsmith H.	Shropshire Light Infantry
Trooper	Ash P.H.O.	Imperial Yeomanry
Private	Astles J.	22nd Cheshire Regiment
Private	Astley A.T.	Shropshire Light Infantry
Sapper	Atherton E.	2nd Cheshire Roy. Eng. (Railway Vol.)
Trooper	Atkinson A.W.	South African Constabulary
Surg. Capt.	Atkinson J.R.	2nd Cheshire Roy. Eng. (Railway Vol.)
Sapper	Attwood I.	2nd Cheshire Roy. Eng. (Railway Vol.)
Private	Badrock J.T.	22nd Cheshire Regiment
Surg. Capt.	Bailey E.C.	Surgeons, Rhodesian Field Force
Sapper	Bailey S.J.	Volunteer Service Section
Civil Surg.	Bailey T.H.	Surgeons, Rhodesian Field Force
Private	**Bamford L.**	**2nd Bn. King's Own Royal Lancasters**
Private	Banks S.	22nd Cheshire Regiment
Sapper	Barker E.M.	2nd Cheshire Roy. Eng. (Railway Vol.)
Private	Barker H.	Shropshire Light Infantry
Lance Corp.	Barlow H.	2nd Cheshire Roy. Eng. (Railway Vol.)
Sapper	Barnes J.T.	2nd Cheshire Roy. Eng. (Railway Vol.)
Sapper	Barnes W.	2nd Cheshire Roy. Eng. (Railway Vol.)
Private	Bateman J.	Lancashire Fusiliers
Sapper	Batt F.G.	2nd Cheshire Roy. Eng. (Railway Vol.)
Sapper	Battison W.H.	Volunteer Service Sections
Lance Corp.	Baystone T.	Royal Welsh Fusiliers
Trooper	Beames H.B.F.	Imperial Yeomanry
Sapper	Bebbington E.	2nd Cheshire Roy. Eng. (Railway Vol.)

Driver	**Bebbington J.**	**Royal Horse Artillery**
Private	Bebbington J.	Grenadier Guards
Corp	Bebbington K.	22nd Cheshire Regiment
Sgt	Beckett G.	2nd Cheshire Roy. Eng. (Railway Vol.)
Sapper	Beckett H.	2nd Cheshire Roy. Eng. (Railway Vol.)
Sapper	Beeston F.W.	2nd Cheshire Roy. Eng. (Railway Vol.)
Sapper	Bennett C.H.	Volunteer Service Sections
Private	Bentley G.W.	North Staffordshire Regiment
Sapper	Berry E.	2nd Cheshire Roy. Eng. (Railway Vol.)
Private	Bevan A.	Shropshire Light Infantry
2nd Corp	Bickerton W.	2nd Cheshire Roy. Eng. (Railway Vol.)
Sapper	Biggs W.G.	2nd Cheshire Roy. Eng. (Railway Vol.)
Private	Billington G.W.	22nd Cheshire Regiment
Lance Corp	Bimson J.J.	2nd Cheshire Roy. Eng. (Railway Vol.)
Sapper	Bird G.	2nd Cheshire Roy. Eng. (Railway Vol.)
Private	Blakemore A.	North Staffordshire Regiment
Private	Blaze J.	22nd Cheshire Regiment
Sapper	Boden H.	Volunteer Service Sections
Sapper	Boote G.	2nd Cheshire Roy. Eng. (Railway Vol.)
Corp	Boughey A.J.N.	2nd Cheshire Roy. Eng. (Railway Vol.)
Sapper	Boulton J.H.	2nd Cheshire Roy. Eng. (Railway Vol.)
Private	Brayford G.W.	Grenadier Guards
Lance Corp	**Brennan J.**	**Royal Army Medical Corps**
Sapper	Brereton W.S.	2nd Cheshire Roy. Eng. (Railway Vol.)
Sapper	Brett E.J.	Volunteer Service Sections
Sgt	Brett T.W.	2nd Cheshire Roy. Eng. (Railway Vol.)
Lt	Brierley N.H.	2nd Cheshire Roy. Eng. (Railway Vol.)
Sapper	Broach E.	2nd Cheshire Roy. Eng. (Railway Vol.)
Sapper	Broady T.	2nd Cheshire Roy. Eng. (Railway Vol.)
Sapper	Brocklehurst C.H.	2nd Cheshire Roy. Eng. (Railway Vol.)
Corp	Brookes J.	2nd Cheshire Roy. Eng. (Railway Vol.)
Sapper	Brookshaw J.	Volunteer Service Sections
Private	Broster W.	22nd Cheshire Regiment
Trooper	Brown F.C.	Grenadier Guards
Gunner	Brown J.R.	Royal Field Artillery
Sapper	Buckley A.E.	2nd Cheshire Roy. Eng. (Railway Vol.)
Trooper	Buckley S.	Imperial Yeomanry
Private	**Burgess A.**	**King's Royal Rifles**
Private	Burgess J.	Royal Army Medical Corps
Private	Burgoyne E.	Lancashire Fusiliers

Sapper	Butt A.W.	2nd Cheshire Roy. Eng. (Railway Vol.)
Sapper	Butt H.W.	2nd Cheshire Roy. Eng. (Railway Vol.)
Lance Corp	Butterworth J.H.	2nd Cheshire Roy. Eng. (Railway Vol.)
Private	Cade W.	Northumberland Fusiliers
Sapper	Calderbank R.P.	2nd Cheshire Roy. Eng. (Railway Vol.)
Sapper	Capper G.	2nd Cheshire Roy. Eng. (Railway Vol.)
Sapper	Capper W.	2nd Cheshire Roy. Eng. (Railway Vol.)
Sapper	Carron W.A.	2nd Cheshire Roy. Eng. (Railway Vol.)
Private	Castree J.W.	Gordon Highlanders
Corp.	Ceats T.	Imperial Yeomanry
Sapper	Champion T.	2nd Cheshire Roy. Eng. (Railway Vol.)
Sapper	Champion W.	2nd Cheshire Roy. Eng. (Railway Vol.)
Private	Charlton G.	9th Lancers
Sapper	Chesters R.	Volunteer Service Sections
Sapper	Cliffe F.G.	2nd Cheshire Roy. Eng. (Railway Vol.)
Private	Clough W.	22nd Cheshire Regiment
Private	**Cole C.G.**	**King's Shropshire Light Infantry**
Sapper	Coleman A.J.	2nd Cheshire Roy. Eng. (Railway Vol.)
Private	Colley T.	Shropshire Mounted Infantry
Sapper	Collier E.	2nd Cheshire Roy. Eng. (Railway Vol.)
Lt	Collins F.R.	2nd Cheshire Roy. Eng. (Railway Vol.)
Lance Corp	Compton J.F.	Manchester Regiment
Sapper	Conquest T.	2nd Cheshire Roy. Eng. (Railway Vol.)
Private	Cooke J.E.	22nd Cheshire Regiment
Sapper	Cooke W.	Volunteer Service Sections
Sapper	Cookson A.	2nd Cheshire Roy. Eng. (Railway Vol.)
Corp/Trum	Cooper E.	Imperial Yeomanry
Private	Cooper J.	Shropshire Mounted Infantry
Private	Cooper R.M.	Army Post Office Corps
Sapper	**Coops T.**	**2nd Cheshire Roy. Eng. (Railway Vol.)**
Sapper	Cornes W.	2nd Cheshire Roy. Eng. (Railway Vol.)
Sapper	Coupe M.	2nd Cheshire Roy. Eng. (Railway Vol.)
Sapper	Cox W.	2nd Cheshire Roy. Eng. (Railway Vol.)
Sapper	Coxsey F.	2nd Cheshire Roy. Eng. (Railway Vol.)
Sapper	Crank E.	2nd Cheshire Roy. Eng. (Railway Vol.)
Sapper	Crawley A.	Volunteer Service Sections
Sapper	Crawley G.H.	Volunteer Service Sections
Lance Corp	Crimes G.	2nd Cheshire Roy. Eng. (Railway Vol.)
Corp	Crimes T.	2nd Cheshire Roy. Eng. (Railway Vol.)
Sapper	Cross A.E.	2nd Cheshire Roy. Eng. (Railway Vol.)

Sapper	Cunningham W.	2nd Cheshire Roy. Eng. (Railway Vol.)
Sapper	Curbishley T.	2nd Cheshire Roy. Eng. (Railway Vol.)
Sapper	Dale A.	2nd Cheshire Roy. Eng. (Railway Vol.)
Gunner	Dalton J.	Royal Horse Artillery
Private	Daniels A.	Royal Welsh Fusiliers
Sapper	**Darlington J.J.**	**2nd Cheshire Roy. Eng. (Railway Vol.)**
Lt	Davenport E.	2nd Cheshire Roy. Eng. (Railway Vol.)
Private	Davies C.	South Wales Borderers
Lance Corp	Davies E.J.	2nd Cheshire Roy. Eng. (Railway Vol.)
Private	Davies S.	22nd Cheshire Regiment
Private	**Davies S.**	**King's Royal Rifles**
Sapper	Davies T.	2nd Cheshire Roy. Eng. (Railway Vol.)
Private	Dawson J.	West Yorkshire Regiment
Sergt.	Day C.T.	Imperial Yeomanry
Trooper	Day J.F.	Imperial Yeomanry
Sergt.	Day W.A.J.	Imperial Yeomanry
Corp.	Dean R.	2nd Cheshire Roy. Eng. (Railway Vol.)
Private	Dickenson E.	Army Service Corps
1st Gr.Ord	Dickson I.	St. John Ambulance Brigade
2nd Corp	Dixon R.	2nd Cheshire Roy. Eng. (Railway Vol.)
Sapper	Dodd A.M.	Volunteer Service Sections
Sapper	Dodd J.H.	2nd Cheshire Roy. Eng. (Railway Vol.)
Corp.	Dodd J.W.	Durham Light Infantry
Sapper	Doughty T.	2nd Cheshire Roy. Eng. (Railway Vol.)
Private	Dudley J.	22nd Cheshire Regiment
Private	Dunn J.	Shropshire Light Infantry
Sapper	Dunn J.H.	2nd Cheshire Roy. Eng. (Railway Vol.)
Sapper	Dunn T.	2nd Cheshire Roy. Eng. (Railway Vol.)
Corp	Dunn W.	22nd Cheshire Regiment
Trooper	Dunning J.W.	Cape Mounted Police
Private	Dyer A.F.	Shropshire Light Infantry
Sapper	Eakins W.H.	2nd Cheshire Roy. Eng. (Railway Vol.)
Sapper	Edge W.P.	Volunteer Service Sections
Private	Edgington W.	Leicester Regiment
Private	Edwards G.	East Lancashire Regiment
Sapper	Edwards G.H.	2nd Cheshire Roy. Eng. (Railway Vol.)
Sapper	Edwards J.	2nd Cheshire Roy. Eng. (Railway Vol.)
Sapper	Egerton A.	2nd Cheshire Roy. Eng. (Railway Vol.)
Sapper	Ellis A.	2nd Cheshire Roy. Eng. (Railway Vol.)
Sapper	Ellis F.	2nd Cheshire Roy. Eng. (Railway Vol.)

Sgt	Elson C.	2nd Cheshire Roy. Eng. (Railway Vol.)
Sapper	Elson P.	2nd Cheshire Roy. Eng. (Railway Vol.)
Sgt	Emery J.	2nd Cheshire Roy. Eng. (Railway Vol.)
Sapper	Etheridge W.H.	2nd Cheshire Roy. Eng. (Railway Vol.)
Sapper	**Evans F.J.**	**2nd Cheshire Roy. Eng. (Railway Vol.)**
Private	Evans H.	South Wales Borderers
Sapper	Evans J.L.	2nd Cheshire Roy. Eng. (Railway Vol.)
Sapper	Evans W.	2nd Cheshire Roy. Eng. (Railway Vol.)
Sapper	Evans W.H.	2nd Cheshire Roy. Eng. (Railway Vol.)
Sapper	Evanson J.T.	2nd Cheshire Roy. Eng. (Railway Vol.)
Corp	Eyers C.	2nd Cheshire Roy. Eng. (Railway Vol.)
Sapper	Fairbrother R.	2nd Cheshire Roy. Eng. (Railway Vol.)
Private	Farrell W.	East Lancashire Regiment
Private	Faulkner G.	King's Own (Royal Lancaster Regiment)
Private	Felton S.	North Staffordshire Regiment
Civil Surg	Felton W.B.	Surgeons, Rhodesian Field Force
Private	Ferrington H.J.	King's Own (Royal Lancaster Regiment)
Trooper	Fincken F.C.	Imperial Yeomanry
Bombardier	Fitzgerald J.A.	Royal Field Artillery
Private	Follows W.	North Staffordshire Regiment
Private	Ford H.	Royal Army Medical Corps
Sapper	Forrest A.	2nd Cheshire Roy. Eng. (Railway Vol.)
Private	Foulkes T.G.	Royal Welsh Fusiliers
Sapper	Fox A.	Volunteer Service Sections
Sapper	Fox C.	Volunteer Service Sections
Sapper	Fox E.B.	Volunteer Service Sections
Sapper	**Foy A.H.**	**2nd Cheshire Roy. Eng. (Railway Vol.)**
Sapper	Francis F.	2nd Cheshire Roy. Eng. (Railway Vol.)
Sapper	Friend R.	Volunteer Service Sections
Sapper	Froome W.D.J.	2nd Cheshire Roy. Eng. (Railway Vol.)
Lance Corp	Furphy G.F.	2nd Cheshire Roy. Eng. (Railway Vol.)
Sapper	Galliard R.H.	2nd Cheshire Roy. Eng. (Railway Vol.)
Sapper	Ganner S.	2nd Cheshire Roy. Eng. (Railway Vol.)
Sapper	Garbett J.H.	2nd Cheshire Roy. Eng. (Railway Vol.)
Private	Gibbon A.W.	22nd Cheshire Regiment
Sapper	Gibbons F.M.	2nd Cheshire Roy. Eng. (Railway Vol.)
Private	Gibson T.	Royal Army Medical Corps
Corp	Giles E.	Shropshire Mounted Infantry
Private	Gilmore C.	King's Liverpool Regiment
Sapper	Godkin W.	2nd Cheshire Roy. Eng. (Railway Vol.)

Lance Corp..	Goode W.	Middlesex Regiment
Private	Goodwin H.	22nd Cheshire Regiment
Sapper	Goodwin W.	2nd Cheshire Roy. Eng. (Railway Vol.)
Sapper	Green B.	2nd Cheshire Roy. Eng. (Railway Vol.)
Sapper	Greenhalgh J.H.	2nd Cheshire Roy. Eng. (Railway Vol.)
Sapper	Greenwood T.	2nd Cheshire Roy. Eng. (Railway Vol.)
Sapper	Grime C.	2nd Cheshire Roy. Eng. (Railway Vol.)
Sapper	Grime J.T.	2nd Cheshire Roy. Eng. (Railway Vol.)
Private	Grindley H.	Shropshire Light Infantry
Private	Grocott G.H.	22nd Cheshire Regiment
Sadler	Groom A.	Shropshire Mounted Infantry
2nd Corp	Groom J.	2nd Cheshire Roy. Eng. (Railway Vol.)
Lance Corp	Guest G.E.	Lancashire Fusiliers
Sapper	Guest J.T.	2nd Cheshire Roy. Eng. (Railway Vol.)
Private	Gunning W.	Shropshire Light Infantry
Private	Hall G.	Shropshire Light Infantry
Sapper	Hallows E.	2nd Cheshire Roy. Eng. (Railway Vol.)
Private	Hammond S.	South Staffordshire Regiment
Private	Hampton G.	Durham Light Infantry
Private	Hampton S.	Durham Light Infantry
Private	Hampton W.	Worcestershire Regiment
Gunner	Hankey W.	Royal Garrison Artillery
Private	Hanmer J.	Shropshire Light Infantry
Sapper	Harris G.	2nd Cheshire Roy. Eng. (Railway Vol.)
Sapper	Harrison A.A.	2nd Cheshire Roy. Eng. (Railway Vol.)
Lance Corp	Hart F.W.	Volunteer Service Sections
Sapper	Harvey G.A.	2nd Cheshire Roy. Eng. (Railway Vol.)
Sapper	Harvey S.	2nd Cheshire Roy. Eng. (Railway Vol.)
Sapper	Hassall C.	2nd Cheshire Roy. Eng. (Railway Vol.)
Sgt	Haughton W.J.	Volunteer Service Sections
Private	**Hayes J.**	**3rd Bn. King's Own Royal Lancasters**
Sapper	Healey C.H.	2nd Cheshire Roy. Eng. (Railway Vol.)
Sgt	Heap D.	2nd Cheshire Roy. Eng. (Railway Vol.)
Sapper	Heap I.	2nd Cheshire Roy. Eng. (Railway Vol.)
Sapper	Heap J.	2nd Cheshire Roy. Eng. (Railway Vol.)
Private	Heath J.	North Staffordshire Regiment
Private	Heath T.	North Staffordshire Regiment
Private	Hesketh A.T.	East Lancashire Regiment
Sapper	Hewitt W.J.	Volunteer Service Sections
Sapper	Hewlett T.H.	Volunteer Service Sections

Sapper	Higgins J.	2nd Cheshire Roy. Eng. (Railway Vol.)
Sapper	Hill G.J.	Volunteer Service Sections
Private	Hill H.R.	Coldstream Guards
Private	Hill W.A.	Royal Army Medical Corps
Trooper	Hills W.C.	Imperial Yeomanry
Sapper	Hinett H.	Volunteer Service Sections
Sgt	Hitchcock H.W.	Volunteer Service Sections
Sapper	Hoban P.	2nd Cheshire Roy. Eng. (Railway Vol.)
Gunner	Hodgkinson T.	Royal Field Artillery
Private	**Hodson C.**	**North Staffordshire Regiment**
Sapper	Hodson J.H.	2nd Cheshire Roy. Eng. (Railway Vol.)
Private	Hodson J.T.	North Staffordshire Regiment
Sgt	Holland J.	Lord Loch's Scouts
Sapper	Hollinshead A.	2nd Cheshire Roy. Eng. (Railway Vol.)
Sapper	Hough A.	2nd Cheshire Roy. Eng. (Railway Vol.)
Trooper	House C.	Baden-Powell Police
Private	Howard W.	South Lancashire Regiment
Sapper	Hubbard H.	2nd Cheshire Roy. Eng. (Railway Vol.)
Sgt	Hughes G.	Imperial Yeomanry
Sgt	Hughes L.	Cameronian Scottish Rifles
Sgt	Huson P.	22nd Cheshire Regiment
Sapper	Jackson W.H.	2nd Cheshire Roy. Eng. (Railway Vol.)
2nd Corp	Johnson W.	2nd Cheshire Roy. Eng. (Railway Vol.)
Private	Jones A.	King's Royal Rifle Corps
Sapper	Jones A.J.	2nd Cheshire Roy. Eng. (Railway Vol.)
Private	Jones C.	9th Lancers
Gunner	Jones C.	Royal Horse Artillery
Trooper	Jones D.	Baden-Powell Police
Corp	Jones D.	Imperial Yeomanry
Sapper	Jones F.	2nd Cheshire Roy. Eng. (Railway Vol.)
Sgt	Jones G.	Shropshire Light Infantry
Private	Jones H.	King's Own Yorkshire Regiment
Sapper	Jones J.	Volunteer Service Sections
Sapper	Jones Jno.	2nd Cheshire Roy. Eng. (Railway Vol.)
Sapper	Jones Jos.	2nd Cheshire Roy. Eng. (Railway Vol.)
Sapper	Jones M.	2nd Cheshire Roy. Eng. (Railway Vol.)
Gunner	Jones R.	Royal Field Artillery
Private	Jones R.	Royal Welsh Fusiliers
Sapper	Joyce S.	2nd Cheshire Roy. Eng. (Railway Vol.)
Sapper	Kent W.	2nd Cheshire Roy. Eng. (Railway Vol.)

Sapper	Key J.	Volunteer Service Sections
Sapper	Kirkham L.	2nd Cheshire Roy. Eng. (Railway Vol.)
Sapper	Lakin W.W.	2nd Cheshire Roy. Eng. (Railway Vol.)
Private	Latham J.	Grenadier Guards
Sapper	Latham W.	2nd Cheshire Roy. Eng. (Railway Vol.)
Trooper	Lawrence C.J.M.	South African Constabulary
Sapper	Lawson W.T.	2nd Cheshire Roy. Eng. (Railway Vol.)
Private	Leigh G.E.	22nd Cheshire Regiment
Sapper	Lewis F.A.	2nd Cheshire Roy. Eng. (Railway Vol.)
Sapper	Lewis J.J.	Volunteer Service Sections
Sgt	Lewis T.	22nd Cheshire Regiment
Private	Lloyd A.	Shropshire Light Infantry
Sapper	Lloyd C.	2nd Cheshire Roy. Eng. (Railway Vol.)
Sapper	Lloyd J.H.	2nd Cheshire Roy. Eng. (Railway Vol.)
Sapper	Lloyd T.	2nd Cheshire Roy. Eng. (Railway Vol.)
Sapper	Long A.R.	2nd Cheshire Roy. Eng. (Railway Vol.)
Private	Lowndes H.	King's Own (Royal Lancaster Regiment)
Sapper	Lydiart T.	2nd Cheshire Roy. Eng. (Railway Vol.)
Sapper	Maddocks R.	Volunteer Service Sections
Sapper	**Madeley W.**	**2nd Cheshire Roy. Eng. (Railway Vol.)**
Private	Mahony T.	King's Royal Rifle Corps
Sapper	Manning W.	2nd Cheshire Roy. Eng. (Railway Vol.)
Private	Mansell H.	Duke Of Cornwall's Light Infantry
Private	Marsh A.	Shropshire Light Infantry
Sapper	Mason A.	2nd Cheshire Roy. Eng. (Railway Vol.)
Sapper	Mason C.E.	2nd Cheshire Roy. Eng. (Railway Vol.)
Private	**Maude W.**	**Grenadier Guards**
Sapper	Maybury A.W.	2nd Cheshire Roy. Eng. (Railway Vol.)
Private	McEvoy J.	22nd Cheshire Regiment
Sapper	Mcilwraith W.K.	2nd Cheshire Roy. Eng. (Railway Vol.)
Trooper	Meakin V.	Imperial Yeomanry
1st Gr. Ord	Measures W.M.	St. John Ambulance Brigade
Private	Merricks W.	South Staffordshire Regiment
Private	Milley M.	Lancashire Fusiliers
Trooper	Moody S.B.	Imperial Yeomanry
Private	Moores J.	22nd Cheshire Regiment
Sapper	Morbey J.D.	2nd Cheshire Roy. Eng. (Railway Vol.)
Private	Morbey S.	22nd Cheshire Regiment
Lance Corp	Morgan W.W.	2nd Cheshire Roy. Eng. (Railway Vol.)
Trooper	**Morris A.C.**	**Imperial Yeomanry**

Sapper	Morris Jos.	2nd Cheshire Roy. Eng. (Railway Vol.)
Sapper	Morris Jos.	2nd Cheshire Roy. Eng. (Railway Vol.)
Private	Morris M.	22nd Cheshire Regiment
Corp.	Morris S.	Royal Welsh Fusiliers
Private	Morris W.H.	Shropshire Light Infantry
Private	**Moses C.**	**Wiltshire Regiment**
Corp.	Moss F.S.	South Lancashire Regiment
Sapper	Moss J.T.	2nd Cheshire Roy. Eng. (Railway Vol.)
Private	Mostyn A.	Durham Light Infantry
Sapper	Mottram J.H.	2nd Cheshire Roy. Eng. (Railway Vol.)
2nd Corp	Mottram P.	2nd Cheshire Roy. Eng. (Railway Vol.)
Sapper	Mottram W.	Volunteer Service Sections
Private	Mountford T.	Manchester Regiment
Private	Nagle P.	22nd Cheshire Regiment
Lance Corp	Newnes G.	Royal Welsh Fusiliers
Sapper	Newton G.W.	2nd Cheshire Roy. Eng. (Railway Vol.)
Sapper	Nicholson J.W.	2nd Cheshire Roy. Eng. (Railway Vol.)
Private	Nicholson T.	Wiltshire Regiment
Sapper	Nield J.M.	2nd Cheshire Roy. Eng. (Railway Vol.)
Private	Nixon J.	22nd Cheshire Regiment
Sapper	Noden G.W.	2nd Cheshire Roy. Eng. (Railway Vol.)
Private	Oakes M.	Grenadier Guards
Trooper	Oakley R.	Imperial Yeomanry
Sapper	Ogbourn F.G.	2nd Cheshire Roy. Eng. (Railway Vol.)
1st CS Off	Oldham F.H.	St. John Ambulance Brigade
Private	Oliver H.	Shropshire Light Infantry
Sapper	O'Neil J.	2nd Cheshire Roy. Eng. (Railway Vol.)
Sapper	Osborn T.	2nd Cheshire Roy. Eng. (Railway Vol.)
2nd Corp	Owen T.	2nd Cheshire Roy. Eng. (Railway Vol.)
Private	Pace E.	22nd Cheshire Regiment
Private	Page E.	Worcestershire Regiment
Gunner	Palmer E.B.	Royal Field Artillery
Sapper	Parr H.J.	2nd Cheshire Roy. Eng. (Railway Vol.)
Private	Parry W.	Royal Welsh Fusiliers
2nd Corp	Parsonage A.C.	Volunteer Service Sections
Trooper	Pattison W.	Cape Mounted Police
Sapper	Pearson J.G.	2nd Cheshire Roy. Eng. (Railway Vol.)
Sapper	Penlington G.	2nd Cheshire Roy. Eng. (Railway Vol.)
Sh.Smith	Perry W.H.	Imperial Yeomanry
Sapper	Pettinger R.D.L.	2nd Cheshire Roy. Eng. (Railway Vol.)

Sapper	Phillips J.	2nd Cheshire Roy. Eng. (Railway Vol.)
Sapper	Phillips W.H.	2nd Cheshire Roy. Eng. (Railway Vol.)
Private	Plant E.	22nd Cheshire Regiment
Sapper	Pointon B.	2nd Cheshire Roy. Eng. (Railway Vol.)
Private	Pooley W.	Manchester Regiment
Corp.	Porter F.	Lancashire Fusiliers
Sapper	Porter S.F.	2nd Cheshire Roy. Eng. (Railway Vol.)
Private	Potts H.	7th Dragoon Guards
Sapper	Potts W.	2nd Cheshire Roy. Eng. (Railway Vol.)
1st Gr.Ord.	**Powell C.H.**	**St. John Ambulance Brigade**
Sapper	Powell P.	Volunteer Service Sections
Sapper	Pratt A.	2nd Cheshire Roy. Eng. (Railway Vol.)
Sapper	Preston C.D.	Volunteer Service Sections
Private	Preston W.	King's Own (Royal Lancaster Regiment)
Sapper	Price H.	Volunteer Service Sections
2nd Corp	Prince J.	2nd Cheshire Roy. Eng. (Railway Vol.)
Sapper	Prince J.	Volunteer Service Sections
Private	Prince W.	South Staffordshire Regiment
Private	Proctor W.	Royal Marines
Sapper	Pugh W.	2nd Cheshire Roy. Eng. (Railway Vol.)
Sapper	Purcell T.E.	Volunteer Service Sections
Private	Quiggin A.	Shropshire Light Infantry
Sapper	Ralphs C.	2nd Cheshire Roy. Eng. (Railway Vol.)
Private	Randle G.	Cameronian Scottish Rifles
Sapper	Reade J.	Volunteer Service Sections
Sapper	Reed E.A.	2nd Cheshire Roy. Eng. (Railway Vol.)
Sapper	Reeves J.E.	2nd Cheshire Roy. Eng. (Railway Vol.)
Sapper	Reeves W.	2nd Cheshire Roy. Eng. (Railway Vol.)
Sapper	Rhead R.	Volunteer Service Sections
Private	Richards J.	Shropshire Light Infantry
Sgt	Riley T.W.	2nd Cheshire Roy. Eng. (Railway Vol.)
Sapper	Roberts G.T.	2nd Cheshire Roy. Eng. (Railway Vol.)
Sapper	Roberts R.	2nd Cheshire Roy. Eng. (Railway Vol.)
Sapper	**Roberts T.H.**	**2nd Cheshire Roy. Eng. (Railway Vol.)**
Sapper	Robinson E.	Volunteer Service Sections
Sapper	**Robinson S.**	**2nd Cheshire Roy. Eng. (Railway Vol.)**
Private	Roles C.	Shropshire Light Infantry
Sapper	Roscoe W.P.	2nd Cheshire Roy. Eng. (Railway Vol.)
Corp	Ross A.	Volunteer Service Sections
Sapper	Rowbottom J.	2nd Cheshire Roy. Eng. (Railway Vol.)

Sapper	Rowbottom R.	2nd Cheshire Roy. Eng. (Railway Vol.)
Sapper	Rowe F.	2nd Cheshire Roy. Eng. (Railway Vol.)
Sapper	Rowley J.F.	2nd Cheshire Roy. Eng. (Railway Vol.)
Private	Rush G.T.	South Wales Borderers
Sapper	Russell W.	2nd Cheshire Roy. Eng. (Railway Vol.)
Private	Ryan J.	Royal Dublin Fusiliers
Sapper	Sanders A.J.	2nd Cheshire Roy. Eng. (Railway Vol.)
Lance Corp	Sanders J.	22nd Cheshire Regiment
Sapper	Saunders W.H.	2nd Cheshire Roy. Eng. (Railway Vol.)
Sapper	Scoffin D.	2nd Cheshire Roy. Eng. (Railway Vol.)
Sgt	Scragg A.	2nd Cheshire Roy. Eng. (Railway Vol.)
Private	Scragg J.	Shropshire Light Infantry
Private	Shaw J.E.	22nd Cheshire Regiment
Sapper	Shaw T.	Volunteer Service Sections
Trooper	Sherwin H.	Imperial Yeomanry
Lt	Sidgwick C.K.D.DSO	2nd Cheshire Roy. Eng. (Railway Vol.)
Sapper	Simon J.	Royal Engineers
Private	Simpson T.J.	Volunteer Service Corps Cheshire Reg.
Private	Skerratt T.	King's Liverpool Regiment
Sapper	Smith F.	2nd Cheshire Roy. Eng. (Railway Vol.)
Private	Smith T.H.	Shropshire Light Infantry
Sapper	Spilsbury W.	2nd Cheshire Roy. Eng. (Railway Vol.)
Private	Stanier G.	King's Own (Royal Lancaster Regiment)
Trooper	Stanley J.E.	South Nottingham Hussars
Lance Corp	Stanway J.	2nd Cheshire Roy. Eng. (Railway Vol.)
Private	Steele R.J.	22nd Cheshire Regiment
Sapper	Steele T.	2nd Cheshire Roy. Eng. (Railway Vol.)
Sapper	Stevenson E.	2nd Cheshire Roy. Eng. (Railway Vol.)
Sapper	Stockton A.	Volunteer Service Sections
Sapper	Stockton G.	2nd Cheshire Roy. Eng. (Railway Vol.)
Private	Stones T.	22nd Cheshire Regiment
Private	Stubbs E.	3rd Scots Guards
Corp	Sudlow R.S.	2nd Cheshire Roy. Eng. (Railway Vol.)
Sapper	Sumner W.	2nd Cheshire Roy. Eng. (Railway Vol.)
Sapper	Surridge G.W.	2nd Cheshire Roy. Eng. (Railway Vol.)
Private	Swindells J.	22nd Cheshire Regiment
Private	Swindles R.	King's Royal Rifle Corps
Gunner	Swindley J.	Royal Field Artillery
Corp	Swinney J.	2nd Cheshire Roy. Eng. (Railway Vol.)
Sapper	Swinwood J.	2nd Cheshire Roy. Eng. (Railway Vol.)

Private	Tagg G.	Shropshire Light Infantry
Sapper	**Talbot W.**	**2nd Cheshire Roy. Eng. (Railway Vol.)**
Sapper	Tandy C.W.	Volunteer Service Sections
Sapper	Taylor A.	2nd Cheshire Roy. Eng. (Railway Vol.)
Private	Taylor J.	Shropshire Light Infantry
Sgt	Taylor W.	Shropshire Light Infantry
Sapper	Theirs H.	2nd Cheshire Roy. Eng. (Railway Vol.)
Sapper	Thomas W.D.	Volunteer Service Sections
Private	**Thomason J.**	**King's Shropshire Light Infantry**
Sapper	Thompson H.	2nd Cheshire Roy. Eng. (Railway Vol.)
Sapper	Thompson J.W.	Volunteer Service Sections
Sgt	Thompson R.	King's Own (Royal Lancaster Regiment)
Col. Sgt	Thorley F.	22nd Cheshire Regiment
Sapper	Thorndyke F.E.	2nd Cheshire Roy. Eng. (Railway Vol.)
1st Gr. Ord	**Thornton W.**	**St. John Ambulance Brigade**
Sapper	Thurstan A.T.	Volunteer Service Sections
Trooper	Timmis R.S.	South African Constabulary
Private	Timperley J.	22nd Cheshire Regiment
Sapper	Tirrell L.E.	2nd Cheshire Roy. Eng. (Railway Vol.)
Sapper	Tomkins W.A.	Volunteer Service Sections
Private	Tonks G.T.	Royal Welsh Fusiliers
Corp	Topham A.J.	22nd Cheshire Regiment
Sapper	Towers A.	2nd Cheshire Roy. Eng. (Railway Vol.)
Gunner	Towers T.	Royal Horse Artillery
Lt	**Trotter C.M.F.**	**Volunteer Service Sections**
Sapper	Trow R.	2nd Cheshire Roy. Eng. (Railway Vol.)
Private	Tudor S.	Shropshire Light Infantry
Private	Tunnicliffe G.	North Staffordshire Regiment
Sapper	Turner J.	Royal Engineers
Lt	Tweedy A.C.	2nd Cheshire Roy. Eng. (Railway Vol.)
Sapper	Upton A.H.	2nd Cheshire Roy. Eng. (Railway Vol.)
2nd Corp	Upton R.T.	Volunteer Service Sections
Sgt	Wadkins H.	2nd Cheshire Roy. Eng. (Railway Vol.)
Gunner	Wainwright J.	Royal Field Artillery
Lance Corp	Wale T.	Volunteer Service Sections
Sapper	Walker B.	2nd Cheshire Roy. Eng. (Railway Vol.)
Private	Walker F.	Royal Warwickshire Regiment
Private	Walley H.	22nd Cheshire Regiment
Sapper	Walley J.H.	2nd Cheshire Roy. Eng. (Railway Vol.)
Private	Walley J.H.	Grenadier Guards

Sapper	Walley Jno.	2nd Cheshire Roy. Eng. (Railway Vol.)
Private	Walton J.	Manchester Regiment
Sapper	Warham*J.	Volunteer Service Sections
Private	**Wareham T.**	**1st King's Dragoon Guards**
Sapper	Wearne G.H.	2nd Cheshire Roy. Eng. (Railway Vol.)
Sapper	Weston E.	2nd Cheshire Roy. Eng. (Railway Vol.)
Sapper	Weston F.	2nd Cheshire Roy. Eng. (Railway Vol.)
Sapper	Weston G.B.	2nd Cheshire Roy. Eng. (Railway Vol.)
Sapper	Wheatman H.R.	2nd Cheshire Roy. Eng. (Railway Vol.)
Private	White F.	22nd Cheshire Regiment
Trooper	Whitehead A.R.	Imperial Yeomanry
Sapper	Wickham J.G.	Royal Engineers
Sapper	Wilkinson A.	2nd Cheshire Roy. Eng. (Railway Vol.)
Trooper	Wilkinson A.	Imperial Yeomanry
Sapper	Williams H.	2nd Cheshire Roy. Eng. (Railway Vol.)
Sapper	Williams J.R.	2nd Cheshire Roy. Eng. (Railway Vol.)
Sapper	Winder T.	Volunteer Service Sections
Sapper	Witter E.W.	2nd Cheshire Roy. Eng. (Railway Vol.)
Corp	Wolfe S.	2nd Cheshire Roy. Eng. (Railway Vol.)
Sapper	Wood G.	2nd Cheshire Roy. Eng. (Railway Vol.)
Corp	Worrall W.	Volunteer Service Sections
Sapper	Wrench J.W.	2nd Cheshire Roy. Eng. (Railway Vol.)
Sapper	Wright C.W.	2nd Cheshire Roy. Eng. (Railway Vol.)
Sapper	Young A.	2nd Cheshire Roy. Eng. (Railway Vol.)
Trooper	Young B.J.	South African Constabulary

*Should be Wareham.

Men of the Railway Reserve, who went out with the first two drafts. **(LEFT)** Ralph P. Calderbank **(MIDDLE)** Arthur Scragg and **(RIGHT)** Alfred Joseph Coleman, who also served in the 10th Service Battalion, Cheshire Regiment, during World War One.

·In Memoriam·

3453 Private **J. Adnitt**, 2nd Cheshire Regiment, died of enteric fever in Netley Hospital, England, in September 1902. This man possibly served under another name, as there is no record of his death date.

1443 Sapper **F. Ankers**, 10th (Railway) Company, Royal Engineers, died of disease at Bloemfontein, on May 29, 1900. Buried in the President Avenue Cemetery, Bloemfontein, South Africa.

3586 Private **L. Bamford**, 2nd King's Own (Royal Lancaster) Regiment, killed in action during the Battle of Spion Kop, on January 24, 1900. Buried on Spion Kop, South Africa.

78083 Driver **J. Bebbington**, Royal Horse Artillery (Ammunition Column), died of enteric fever at Kimberley, on May 30, 1900. Buried Kimberley West End Cemetery (Grave B.A.7), South Africa.

16898 Lance Corporal **J. Brennan**, Royal Army Medical Corps, died of disease at Harrismith, on May 20, 1902. Buried Harrismith Town Cemetery, South Africa.

3251 Private **A. Burgess**, 1st King's Royal Rifles, died of enteric fever on July 21, 1900. Buried Newcastle Cemetery (Grave A34), South Africa.

1662 Private **C.G. Cole**, 2nd King's Shropshire Light Infantry, died of disease at Middleburg, on January 23, 1902. Buried Middleburg Cemetery, South Africa.

1565 Sapper **T. Coops**, 31st (Fortress) Company, Royal Engineers, killed in an armoured train crash at Burgersdorp, on January 31, 1902. Buried Burgersdorp Cemetery, South Africa.

3589 Sapper **J.J. Darlington**, 45th (Fortress) Company, Royal Engineers, accidentally killed at Bloemfontein, on May 11, 1901.* Buried President Avenue Cemetery, Bloemfontein, South Africa. *May 18 on gravestone.

7019 Private **S. Davies**, 3rd King's Royal Rifles, died of wounds on January 23, 1900, following the Battle of Colenso. Buried Chieveley Cemetery, South Africa.

27830 Sapper **F.J. Evans**, 31st (Fortress) Company, Royal Engineers, died of enteric fever at Modder River, on April 15, 1900. Buried Kimberley West End Cemetery, South Africa.

2558 Sapper **A.H. Foy**, 8th (Railway) Company, Royal Engineers, died of enteric fever at the Orange River Station, on April 15, 1900. Buried Kimberley West End Cemetery, South Africa.

6593 Private **J. Hayes**, 3rd King's Own Royal Lancaster Regiment, died of the plague at Cape Town, on October 23, 1901.

2671 Private **C. Hodson**, 2nd North Staffordshire Regiment, died of dysentry at Wakkerstroom, on June 3, 1901. Buried Wakkerstroom Cemetery, South Africa.

57 Sapper **W. Madeley**, 10th (Railway) Company, Royal Engineers, died of enteric fever at Bloemfontein, on April 20, 1900. Buried President Avenue Cemetery, Bloemfontein, South Africa.

5272 Private **W. Maude**, 3rd Grenadier Guards, died of dysentry at Orange River Station, on February 13, 1900. Buried Kimberley West End Cemetery, South Africa.

1221 Trooper **A.C. Morris**, 5th Company, Imperial Yeomanry, died of enteric fever at Kroonstad, on July 8, 1900. Buried North Road Cemetery, Kroonstad, South Africa.

6378 Private **C. Moses**, 3rd Wiltshire Regiment, died of enteric fever at Kroonstad, on December 7, 1901. Buried North Road Cemetery, Kroonstad, South Africa (Grave 590).

118 1st Grade Orderly **C. H. Powell**, St. John Ambulance Brigade, died of enteric fever (and pneumonia) in Netley Hospital, England, on January 4, 1901. Buried Coppenhall Cemetery, Crewe, Cheshire, England.

27831 Sapper **T. H. Roberts**, 31st (Fortress) Company, Royal Engineers, killed near Naboomspruit, on July 4, 1901. Buried Pietersburg Cemetery, South Africa.

1803 Sapper **S. Robinson**, 10th (Railway) Company, Royal Engineers, died of enteric fever at Bloemfontein, on May 27, 1900. Buried President Avenue Cemetery, Bloemfontein, South Africa.

1551 Sapper **W. Talbot**, 45th (Fortress) Company, Royal Engineers, accidentally killed at Kroonstad, on February 10, 1902. Buried North Road Cemetery, Kroonstad, South Africa.

1984 Private **J. Thomason**, 2nd Shropshire Light Infantry, died of disease at Pretoria, on February 6, 1901. Buried Pretoria Cemetery, South Africa (Grave 572).

1702 Private **W. Thornton**, St. John Ambulance Brigade, died of enteric fever at Elandsfontein, on March 1, 1901. Buried Primrose Cemetery, Germiston, South Africa.

Lieutenant **C. M. F. Trotter**, 2nd Cheshire (Railway) Royal Engineers, died at Chatham, on April 10/11, 1901. Buried Polesworth Vicarage, England.

3539 Private **T. Wareham**, 1st King's Dragoon Guards, died of disease at Kroonstad, on February 20, 1902.* Buried North Road Cemetery, Kroonstad, South Africa. *February 21 on grave marker.

Summary of deaths: Disease/Medical - 19, Accidents - 4, KIA/DOW - 3.

(ABOVE) The South Africa Arch at Brompton Barracks, Chatham, which commemorates all Royal Engineers lost during the campaign. *(BELOW)* Kroonstad Old Cemetery, the final resting place for four Crewe men. Note the razor wire which rings the cemetery boundaries.

(**ABOVE**) The main memorial in Kimberley West End Cemetery. In 1907 many British Boer War casualties were re-interred in more centralised cemeteries. These large block memorials are above sandwich graves, where hundreds of bodies are buried in layers to save space. Among the Crewe men buried here are Driver J. Bebbington, Sapper F. J. Evans, Sapper A. H. Foy, and Private W. Maude. (**LEFT**) The grave of Sapper J. J. Darlington in the President Avenue Cemetery, Bloemfontein. Originally broken in half by vandals, it has been crudely restored.

The vandalised grave of Sapper W. Talbot at Kroonstad. This cemetery and the one at De Aar are amongst the worst in terms of broken headstones and missing grave markers.

(ABOVE) Grave marker for 1662 Private C. Cole of the 2nd King's Shropshire Light Infantry. He is buried in Middleburg Cemetery. (BELOW) Grave roundel for 3539 Private Thomas Wareham of the 1st King's Dragoon Guards in North Road Cemetery, Kroonstad. The date of death is different by one day to his memorial card (page 155).

Railway Volunteers Medal Roll and Drafts

The following from the Railway Volunteers are listed in the relevant drafts (and Companies) that left Crewe along with their medal entitlement (with bars). This information has been taken from local newspapers and *The Medal Roll of the Corps of Royal Engineers, Volume V, Queen's and King's South Africa Medals 1899-1902*. Both sources are known to contain errors, so this list cannot be deemed 100% accurate. A total of 26 bars were awarded for the Boer War, of which 24 were awarded to members of the Royal Engineers. Bars awarded to the Crewe Engineers include CC=Cape Colony, OFS=Orange Free State, TVL=Transvaal, BELM=Belmont, MR=Modder River, ROL=Relief of Ladysmith, NAT=Natal, BELF=Belfast, SA01=South Africa 1901, SA02=South Africa 1902. Other medals on the list are the KSA=King's South Africa Medal, DSO=Distinguished Service Order and DCM=Distinguished Conduct Medal. The abbreviations on the list are as follows. (No.)=Service Number, (R)=Rank, (Reg.)=RR for Railway Reserve or VSS for Volunteer Service Sections, C=Company. For members of "G" or "E" Companies, their attached Company follows their letter. For members of the Volunteer Service Sections (Sections 1 and 2), their attached Company follows their Section number. For example, 1442 Sapper W. Allen, was a member of G Company, attached to the 10th Railway Company (G,10). 8531 Sapper W.H. Battison, was a member of No.1 Section of the Volunteer Service Sections, attached to the 8th Railway Company (1,8). D=Drafts to leave Crewe. (1) was on October 16, 1899, (2) was on February 25, 1901 and (3) on April 3, 1901. QSA Bars and Other Medals=Medals and bars awarded.

No.	R	Name	Reg.	C	D	QSA Bars and Other Medals.
1442	Sap.	Allen, W	RR	G,10	2	CC, OFS, TVL, SA01, SA02.
24399	Sap.	Ankers, A.E.	RR	45	1	CC, OFS, SA01, SA02.
1443	Sap.	Ankers, F.	RR	10	1	CC, OFS.
958	Sap.	Atherton, E.	RR	31	1	BELM, MR.
1459	Sap.	Attwood, I.	RR	31	1	CC, BELM, MR, OFS, SA01, SA02.
8554	Sap.	Bailey, S.J.	VSS	2,10	3	CC, OFS, TVL, SA01, SA02.
1285	Sap.	Barker, E.M.	RR	10	1	CC, OFS, TVL, KSA.
2207	L/C	Barlow, H.	RR	8	1	BELM, MR, OFS, TVL. KSA.
28036	Sap.	Barnes, J.T.	RR	G,45	2	CC, SA01, SA02.
25333	Sap.	Barnes, W.	RR	8	1	BELM, MR, OFS, TVL, SA01.
2209	Sap.	Batt, F.G.	RR	31	1	BELM, OFS.
8531	Sap.	Battison, W.H.	VSS	1,8	3	CC, OFS, TVL, SA01, SA02.
1195	Sap.	Bebbington, E.	RR	37	1	ROL.
73	Sgt.	Beckett, G.	RR	G,45	2	CC, OFS, SA01, SA02.
2224	Sap.	Beckett, H.	RR	45	1	CC, ROL, OFS, TVL. KSA

27158	Sap.	Beeston, F.W. .... RR	G,8	2	CC, OFS, TVL, SA01, SA02.
8555	Sap.	Bennett, C.H. .... VSS	2,10	3	CC, OFS, TVL, SA01, SA02.
780	Sap.	Berry, E .... RR	G,10	2	CC, OFS, TVL, SA01, SA02.
3592	2/C	Bickerton, W. .... RR	G,45	2	CC, OFS, SA01, SA02.
3225	Sap.	Biggs, W.G. .... RR	10	1	CC, OFS, TVL.
1460	L/C	Bimson, J.J. .... RR	45	1	CC, ROL, OFS, TVL. KSA.
28189	Sap.	Bird, G. .... RR	G,45	2	CC, OFS, TVL, SA01.
8530	Sap.	Boden, H. .... VSS	1,8	3	CC, OFS, TVL, SA01, SA02.
1876	Sap.	Boote, G. .... RR	31	1	BELM, MR, OFS, TVL. KSA.
56	Cpl.	Boughey, A.J.N. .... RR	G,45	2	CC, OFS, SA01, SA02.
1563	Sap.	Boulton, J.H. .... RR	8	1	BELM, MR, OFS. KSA.
1453	Sap.	Brereton, W.S. .... RR	10	1	CC, OFS.
8532	Sap.	Brett, E.J. .... VSS	1,8	3	CC, OFS, TVL, SA01, SA02.
23974	Sgt.	Brett, T.W. .... RR	8	1	BELM, MR, OFS, TVL, SA01, SA02. KSA.
None	Lt.	Brierley, N.H. .... RR	45	2	CC, OFS, TVL, SA01, SA02.
1286	Sap.	Broach, E. .... RR	10	1	CC, OFS, KSA.
1877	Sap.	Broady, T. .... RR	G,8	2	CC, OFS, TVL, SA01, SA02.
2347	Sap.	Brocklehurst, C.H. .. RR	31	1	BELM, MR, OFS, TVL. KSA.
27828	Cpl.	Brookes, J. .... RR	31	1	BELM, MR, OFS, TVL. KSA.
8529	Sap.	Brookshaw, J. .... VSS	1,8	3	CC, OFS, TVL, SA01, SA02.
1562	Sap.	Buckley, A.E. .... RR	G,45	2	CC, OFS, SA01, SA02.
443	Sap.	Butt, A.W. .... RR	8	1	BELM, MR, OFS, TVL. KSA.
27469	Sap.	Butt, H.W. .... RR	10	1	CC, OFS, TVL. KSA.
959	L/C.	Butterworth, J.H. .... RR	G,45	2	CC, OFS, SA01, SA02.
24401	Sap.	Calderbank, R.P. ...... RR	10	1	CC, OFS, TVL.
28882	Sap.	Capper, G. .... RR	37	?	NAT.
1446	Sap.	Capper, W. .... RR	10	1	CC, OFS, TVL. KSA.
2226	Sap.	Carron, W.A. .... RR	G,45	2	CC, OFS, TVL, SA01, SA02.
24394	Sap.	Champion, T. .... RR	G,10	2	CC, OFS, TVL, SA01, SA02.
25349	Sap.	Champion, W. .... RR	8	1	BELM, MR.
8533	Sap.	Chesters, R. .... VSS	1,8	3	CC, OFS, TVL, SA01, SA02.
1564	Sap.	Cliffe, F.G. .... RR	G,45	2	CC, OFS, SA01, SA02.
1176	Sap.	Coleman, A.J. .... RR	10	1	CC, OFS.
1550	Sap.	Collier, E. .... RR	G,45	2	CC, OFS, SA01, SA02.
None	Lt.	Collins, F.R. .... VSS	10	3	CC, OFS, TVL, SA01, SA02.
214	Sap.	Conquest, T. .... RR	G,45	2	CC, SA01, SA02.
8536	Sap.	Cooke, W. .... VSS	1,8	3	CC, OFS, TVL, SA01, SA02.
28497	Sap.	Cookson, A. .... RR	8	1	BELM, MR, OFS, TVL, SA01.
1565	Sap.	Coops, T. .... RR	31	1	MR, OFS, TVL. KSA.
1277	Sap.	Cornes, W. .... RR	G,45	2	CC, OFS, TVL.
3587	Sap.	Coupe, M. .... RR	8	1	BELM, MR, SA01.
960	Sap.	Cox, W. .... RR	G,45	2	CC, OFS, SA01, SA02.
28499	Sap.	Coxsey, F. .... RR	8	1	BELM, MR, OFS, TVL.
2348	Sap.	Crank, E. .... RR	8	1	BELM, MR.
8534	Sap.	Crawley, A. .... VSS	1,8	3	CC, OFS, TVL, SA01, SA02.
8535	Sap.	Crawley, G.H. .... VSS	1,8	3	CC, OFS, TVL, SA01, SA02.
28492	L/C	Crimes, G. .... RR	G,8	2	CC, OFS, TVL, SA01, SA02.
24397	Cpl.	Crimes, T. .... RR	8	1	BELM, MR, OFS, TVL. KSA.
2227	Sap.	Cross, A.E. .... RR	G,8	2	CC, OFS, TVL, SA02.
26611	Sap.	Cunningham, W. .... RR	10	1	CC, OFS, TVL. KSA.
3588	Sap.	Curbishley, T. .... RR	8	1	BELM, MR.
29702	Sap.	Dale, A. .... RR	G,45	2	CC, OFS, SA01, SA02.
3589	Sap.	Darlington, J.J. .... RR	G,45	2	CC, OFS, SA01.

None	Lt.	Davenport, E.	VSS	45	3	CC, OFS, TVL, SA01, SA02.
1106	L/C	Davies, E.J.	RR	8	1	BELM, MR, OFS, TVL. KSA.
3231	Sap.	Davies, T.	RR	8	1	BELM, MR, OFS, TVL. KSA.
25347	Cpl.	Dean, R.	RR	8	1	BELM, MR, OFS, TVL. KSA.
1445	2/C	Dixon, R.	RR	G,45	2	CC, SA01, SA02.
8537	Sap.	Dodd, A.M.	VSS	1,8	3	CC, OFS, TVL, SA01, SA02.
1177	Sap.	Dodd, J.H.	RR	8	1	BELM, MR, OFS, TVL. KSA.
3599	Sap.	Doughty, T.	RR	E,45	2	CC, SA01.
29703	Sap.	Dunn, J.H.	RR	G,45	2	CC, OFS, SA01, SA02.
23101	Sap.	Dunn, T.	RR	G,45	2	CC, SA01.
1178	Sap.	Eakins, W.H.	RR	8	1	BELM, MR, OFS, TVL. KSA.
8538	Sap.	Edge, W.P.	VSS	1,8	3	CC, OFS, TVL, SA01, SA02.
25324	Sap.	Edwards, G.H.	RR	8	1	BELM, MR.
26615	Sap.	Edwards, J.	RR	G,45	2	CC, OFS, SA01, SA02.
1790	Sap.	Egerton, A.	RR	10	1	CC, OFS.
1279	Sap.	Ellis, A.	RR	10	1	CC, OFS.
1280	Sap.	Ellis, F.	RR	10	1	CC, OFS.
1179	Sgt.	Elson, C.	RR	8	1	BELM, MR, OFS, TVL. KSA.
25346	Sap.	Elson, P.	RR	8	1	BELM, MR.
24056	Sgt.	Emery, J.	RR	G,45	2	CC, OFS, SA01, SA02.
1197	Sap.	Etheridge, W.H.	RR	10	1	CC, OFS, TVL.
27830	Sap.	Evans, F.J.	RR	31	1	BELM, MR.
2349	Sap.	Evans, J.L.	RR	8	1	BELM, MR, OFS, TVL. KSA.
23100	Sap.	Evans, W.	RR	G,45	2	CC, OFS, SA01.
1878	Sap.	Evans, W.H.	RR	10	1	CC, OFS, TVL. KSA.
1894	Sap.	Evanson, J.T.	RR	10	1	CC, OFS.
1128	Cpl.	Eyers, C.	RR	G,45	2	CC, SA01, SA02.
2350	Sap.	Fairbrother, R.	RR	10	1	CC, OFS, TVL. KSA.
25328	Sap.	Forrest, A.	RR	8	1	BELM, MR.
8539	Sap.	Fox, A.	VSS	1,8	3	CC, OFS, TVL, SA01, SA02.
8540	Sap.	Fox, C.	VSS	1,8	3	CC, OFS, TVL, SA01, SA02.
8541	Sap.	Fox, E.B.	VSS	1,8	3	CC, OFS, TVL, SA01, SA02.
2558	Sap.	Foy, A.H.	RR	8	1	BELM, MR.
1288	Sap.	Francis, F.	RR	8	1	BELM, MR.
8542	Sap.	Friend, R.	VSS	1,8	3	CC, OFS, TVL, SA01, SA02.
3004	Sap.	Froome, W.D.J.	RR	10	1	CC, OFS, TVL. KSA.
1879	L/C	Furphy, G.F.	RR	8	1	BELM, MR, OFS, TVL. KSA.
2228	Sap.	Galliard, R.H.	RR	10	1	CC.
23103	Sap.	Ganner, S.	RR	G,8	2	CC, OFS, TVL, SA01, SA02.
4346	Sap.	Garbett, J.H.	RR	45	?	CC, OFS, SA01, SA02.
1268	Sap.	Gibbons, F.M.	RR	G,10	2	CC, OFS, TVL, SA01, SA02.
25352	Sap.	Godkin, W.	RR	8	1	BELM, MR, OFS, TVL. KSA.
1187	Sap.	Goodwin, W.	RR	10	1	CC, OFS, TVL. KSA.
29086	Sap.	Green, B.	RR	8	1	BELM, MR, OFS, TVL.
2210	Sap.	Greenhalgh, J.H.	RR	8	1	BELM, MR, OFS, TVL.
1119	Sap.	Greenwood, T.	RR	G,8	2	CC, OFS, SA01.
1108	Sap.	Grime, C.	RR	G,45	2	CC, OFS, SA01, SA02.
25353	Sap.	Grime, J.T.	RR	8	2	CC, OFS, TVL.
1791	2/C	Groom, J.	RR	10	1	CC, OFS, TVL. KSA.
29480	Sap.	Guest, J.T.	RR	10	1	CC, OFS.
2211	Sap.	Hallows, E.	RR	10	1	CC, OFS, TVL. KSA.
1188	Sap.	Harris, G.	RR	8	1	BELM, MR, OFS, TVL. KSA.
28186	Sap.	Harrison, A.A.	RR	G,45	2	CC, OFS, SA01.

8553	L/C	Hart, F.W. .... VSS	2,10	3	CC, OFS, TVL, SA01, SA02.
3005	Sap.	Harvey, G.A. .... RR	10	1	CC, OFS, TVL. KSA.
1895	Sap.	Harvey, S. .... RR	10	1	CC, OFS.
2212	Sap.	Hassall, C. .... RR	8	1	BELM, MR, OFS, TVL. KSA.
8525	Sgt.	Haughton, W.J. .... VSS	1,8	3	CC, OFS, TVL, SA01, SA02.
27839	Sap.	Healey, C.H. .... RR	G,45	2	CC, OFS, SA01, SA02.
444	Sgt.	Heap, D. .... RR	G,45	2	CC, OFS, SA01, SA02.
449	Sap.	Heap, I. .... RR	G,45	2	CC, OFS, SA01, SA02.
29087	Sap.	Heap, J. .... RR	8	1	BELM, MR, OFS, TVL.
8544	Sap.	Hewitt, W.J. .... VSS	1,8	3	CC, OFS, TVL, SA01, SA02.
8545	Sap.	Hewlett, T.H. .... VSS	1,8	3	CC, OFS, TVL, SA01, SA02.
28515	Sap.	Higgins, J. .... RR	G,45	2	CC, OFS, TVL, SA01.
8543	Sap.	Hill, G.J. .... VSS	1,8	3	CC, OFS, TVL, SA01, SA02.
8546	Sap.	Hinett, H. .... VSS	1,8	3	CC, OFS, TVL, SA01, SA02.
8550	Sgt.	Hitchcock, H.W. ...... VSS	2,10	3	CC, OFS, TVL, SA01, SA02.
29092	Sap.	Hoban, P. .... RR	G,45	2	CC, SA01, SA02.
1198	Sap.	Hodson, J.H. .... RR	G,45	2	CC, OFS, TVL, SA01, SA02.
2213	Sap.	Hollinshead, A. .... RR	10	1	CC, OFS, TVL. KSA.
1793	Sap.	Hough, A. .... RR	8	1	BELM, MR, OFS, TVL. KSA.
2229	Sap.	Hubbard, H. .... RR	10	1	CC, OFS, TVL. KSA.
1880	Sap.	Jackson, W.H. .... RR	8	1	BELM, MR.
24275	2/C	Johnson, W. .... RR	8	1	BELM, MR, OFS, TVL. KSA.
1129	Sap.	Jones, A.J. .... RR	G,8	2	CC, OFS, TVL, SA01, SA02.
29705	Sap.	Jones, F. .... RR	G,45	2	CC, OFS, TVL, SA01, SA02.
8556	Sap.	Jones, J. .... VSS	2,10	3	CC, OFS, TVL, SA01, SA02.
1795	Sap.	Jones, Jno. .... RR	8	2	CC, OFS, TVL, SA01, SA02.
1794	Sap.	Jones, Jos. .... RR	10	1	CC, OFS, TVL. KSA. DCM.
2230	Sap.	Jones, M. .... RR	G,45	2	CC, SA01, SA02.
27832	Sap.	Joyce, S. .... RR	31	1	BELM, MR, OFS, TVL. KSA.
1120	Sap.	Kent, W. .... RR	G,45	2	CC, OFS, SA01.
8557	Sap.	Key, J. .... VSS	2,10	3	CC, OFS, TVL, SA01, SA02.
1796	Sap.	Kirkham, L. .... RR	G,45	2	CC, OFS, TVL, SA01, SA02.
27845	Sap.	Lakin, W.W. .... RR	G,45	2	CC, OFS, SA01, SA02.
450	Sap.	Latham, W. .... RR	10	1	CC, OFS, TVL, SA01.
1269	Sap.	Lawson, W.T. .... RR	G,45	2	CC, OFS, TVL, SA01.
1797	Sap.	Lewis, F.A. .... RR	G,45	2	CC, SA01, SA02.
8547	Sap.	Lewis, J.J. .... VSS	1,8	3	CC, OFS, TVL, SA01, SA02.
3065	Sap.	Lloyd, C. .... RR	31	1	MR, OFS, TVL. KSA.
29091	Sap.	Lloyd, J.H. .... RR	8	2	CC, OFS, TVL, SA01.
1881	Sap.	Lloyd, T. .... RR	G,45	2	CC, OFS, SA01, SA02.
1798	Sap.	Long, A.R. .... RR	31	1	MR, OFS, TVL. KSA.
1461	Sap.	Lydiart, T. .... RR	31	1	MR, OFS, TVL. KSA.
8558	Sap.	Maddocks, R. .... VSS	2,10	3	CC, OFS, TVL, SA01, SA02.
57	Sap.	Madeley, W. .... RR	10	1	CC, OFS.
1799	Sap.	Manning, W. .... RR	10	1	CC, OFS, TVL. KSA.
1190	Sap.	Mason, A. .... RR	10	1	CC, OFS.
451	Sap.	Mason, C.E. .... RR	10	1	CC, OFS, TVL. KSA.
454	Sap.	Maybury, A.W. .... RR	G,8	2	CC, OFS, TVL, SA01, SA02.
3232	Sap.	Mcilwraith, W.K. ...... RR	10	1	CC, OFS, TVL. KSA.
2331	Sap.	Morbey, J.D. .... RR	E,8	2	CC, OFS, TVL, SA01, SA02.
446	L/C	Morgan, W.W. .... RR	G,45	2	CC, OFS, SA01, SA02.
453	Sap.	Morris, Jos. .... RR	E,45	2	CC, OFS, TVL, SA01, SA02.
1282	Sap.	Morris, Jos. .... RR	G,45	2	CC, OFS, SA01, SA02.

(LEFT) The QSA medal of 1288 Sapper Fred Francis of the 8th Railway Company, showing Belmont and Modder River bars.

(RIGHT) 8525 Sergeant W. J. Haughton's QSA with five bars awarded, showing the reverse of the medal. He served in the Volunteer Service Sections (No.1), attached to the 8th Railway Company.

72	Sap.	Moss, J.T. .... RR	G,45	2	CC, SA01.
1200	Sap.	Mottram, J.H. .... RR	G,45	2	CC, OFS.
28870	2/C	Mottram, P. .... RR	G,45	2	CC, OFS, SA01, SA02.
8548	Sap.	Mottram, W. .... VSS	1,8	3	CC, OFS, TVL, SA01, SA02.
1181	Sap.	Newton, G.W. .... RR	8	1	BELM, MR, OFS, TVL. KSA.
1121	Sap.	Nicholson, J.W. .... RR	E,45	2	CC, OFS, TVL, SA01, SA02.
29479	Sap.	Nield, J.M. .... RR	E,45	2	CC, OFS, TVL, SA01, SA02.
3233	Sap.	Noden, G.W. .... RR	8	1	BELM, MR, OFS, BELF. KSA.
3066	Sap.	Ogbourn, F.G. .... RR	31	1	MR, OFS, TVL. KSA.
26621	Sap.	O'Neil, J. .... RR	E,45	2	CC, OFS, SA01, SA02.
1182	Sap.	Osborn, T. .... RR	10	1	CC, OFS, TVL. KSA.
27730	2/C	Owen, T. .... RR	E,45	2	CC, SA01.
3234	Sap.	Parr, H.J. .... RR	E,8	2	CC, OFS, TVL, SA01.
8527	2/C	Parsonage, A.C. .... VSS	1,8	3	CC, OFS, TVL, SA01, SA02.
1454	Sap.	Pearson, J.G. .... RR	E,45	2	CC, SA01, SA02.
25350	Sap.	Penlington, G. .... RR	E,10	2	CC, OFS, TVL, SA01, SA02.
1191	Sap.	Pettinger, R.D.L. ..... RR	8	1	BELM, MR, OFS, TVL.
9644	Sap.	Phillips, J. .... RR	45	?	CC, SA02.
1462	Sap.	Phillips, W.H. .... RR	E,45	2	CC, OFS, TVL, SA01, SA02.
1801	Sap.	Pointon, B. .... RR	E,45	2	CC, SA01, SA02.
3235	Sap.	Porter, S.F. .... RR	E,45	2	CC, OFS, TVL, SA01, SA02.
1110	Sap.	Potts, W. .... RR	E,10	2	CC, OFS, TVL, SA01, SA02.
8560	Sap.	Powell, P .... VSS	2,10	3	CC, OFS, TVL, SA01, SA02.
3236	Sap.	Pratt, A. .... RR	8	1	BELM, MR, OFS, TVL. KSA.
8562	Sap.	Preston, C.D. .... VSS	2,10	3	CC, OFS, TVL, SA01, SA02.
8561	Sap.	Price, H. .... VSS	2,10	3	CC, OFS, TVL, SA01, SA02.
1122	2/C	Prince, J. .... RR	E,45	2	CC, OFS, TVL, SA01, SA02.
8549	Sap.	Prince, J. .... VSS	1,3	3	CC, OFS, TVL, SA01, SA02.
1183	Sap.	Pugh, W. .... RR	10	1	CC, OFS, TVL. KSA. DCM.
8559	Sap.	Purcell, T.E. .... VSS	2,10	3	CC, OFS, TVL, SA01, SA02.
455	Sap.	Ralphs, C. .... RR	10	1	CC, OFS, TVL. KSA.
8563	Sap.	Reade, J. .... VSS	2,10	3	CC, OFS, TVL, SA01, SA02.
25337	Sap.	Reed, E.A. .... RR	E,45	2	CC, SA01.
3067	Sap.	Reeves, J.E. .... RR	10	1	CC, OFS, TVL.
28187	Sap.	Reeves, W. .... RR	E,10	2	CC, OFS, TVL, SA01.
8565	Sap.	Rhead, R. .... VSS	2,10	3	CC, OFS, TVL, SA01, SA02.
24352	Sgt.	Riley, T.W. .... RR	E,45	2	CC, SA01, SA02.
1802	Sap.	Roberts, G.T. .... RR	E,45	2	CC, SA01, SA02.
24000	Sap.	Roberts, R. .... RR	E,10	2	CC, OFS, TVL, SA01.
27831	Sap.	Roberts, T.H. .... RR	31	1	MR, OFS, TVL, SA01.
8564	Sap.	Robinson, E. .... VSS	2,10	3	CC, OFS, TVL, SA01, SA02.
1803	Sap.	Robinson, S. .... RR	10	1	CC, OFS.
12366	Sap.	Roscoe, W.P. .... RR	10	1	CC, OFS, TVL. KSA.
8551	Cpl.	Ross, A. .... VSS	2,10	3	CC, OFS, TVL, SA01, SA02.
28871	Sap.	Rowbottom, J. .... RR	E,45	2	CC, OFS, SAO1, SA02.
1123	Sap.	Rowbottom, R. .... RR	E,45	2	CC, OFS, SAO1, SA02.
2351	Sap.	Rowe, F. .... RR	8	1	BELM, MR, OFS, TVL. KSA.
2214	Sap.	Rowley, J.F. .... RR	8	1	BELM, MR, OFS, TVL. KSA.
2352	Sap.	Russell, W. .... RR	E,8	2	CC, OFS, TVL, SA01, SA02.
29495	Sap.	Sanders, A.J. .... RR	10	1	CC, OFS.
3237	Sap.	Saunders, W.H. .... RR	10	1	CC, OFS, TVL. KSA.
1805	Sap.	Scoffin, D. .... RR	10	1	CC, OFS, TVL, SA01.
1124	Sgt.	Scragg, A. .... RR	E,45	2	CC, SA01, SA02.

8566	Sap.	Shaw, T.	VSS	2,10	3	CC, OFS, TVL, SA01, SA02.
None	Lt.	Sidgwick, C.K.D.	RR	45	2	CC, OFS, TVL, SA01, SA02. DSO.
28864	Sap.	Smith, F.	RR	E,10	2	CC, OFS, TVL, SA01.
1271	Sap.	Spilsbury, W.	RR	10	1	CC, OFS, TVL, SA01.
1192	L/C	Stanway, J.	RR	8	1	BELM, MR, OFS, TVL. KSA.
29704	Sap.	Steele, T.	RR	10	1	CC, OFS, TVL. KSA.
28188	Sap.	Stevenson, E.	RR	E,45	2	CC, OFS, TVL, SA01.
8567	Sap.	Stockton, A.	VSS	2,10	3	CC, OFS, TVL, SA01, SA02.
29984	Sap.	Stockton, G.	RR	E,8	2	SA01.
781	Cpl.	Sudlow, R.S.	RR	E,45	2	CC, OFS, TVL, SA01, SA02.
1804	Sap.	Sumner, W.	RR	10	1	CC, OFS, TVL. KSA.
1270	Sap.	Surridge, G.W.	RR	10	1	CC, OFS.
1463	Cpl.	Swinney, J.	RR	E,45	2	CC, SA01, SA02.
29078	Sap.	Swinwood, J.	RR	8	1	BELM, MR.
1551	Sap.	Talbot, W.	RR	E,45	2	CC, OFS, SA01, SA02.
8568	Sap.	Tandy, C.W.	VSS	2,10	3	CC, OFS, TVL, SA01, SA02.
58	Sap.	Taylor, A.	RR	10	1	CC, OFS, TVL, SA01.
3226	Sap.	Theirs, H.	RR	31	2	CC, OFS, TVL, SA01.
8572	Sap.	Thomas, W.D.	VSS	2,10	3	CC, OFS, TVL, SA01, SA02.
3227	Sap.	Thompson, H.	RR	8	1	BELM, MR, OFS, BELF. KSA.
8570	Sap.	Thompson, J.W.	VSS	2,10	3	CC, OFS, TVL, SA01, SA02.
2215	Sap.	Thorndyke, F.E.	RR	E,10	2	CC, OFS, TVL, SA01, SA02.
8569	Sap.	Thurstan, A.T.	VSS	2,10	3	CC, OFS, TVL, SA01, SA02.
1552	Sap.	Tirrell, L.E.	RR	8	1	BELM, MR, OFS, TVL. KSA.
8571	Sap.	Tomkins, W.A.	VSS	2,10	3	CC, OFS, TVL, SA01, SA02.
215	Sap.	Towers, A.	RR	10	1	CC, OFS, TVL. KSA.
None	Lt.	Trotter, C.M.F.	VSS	2	3	Died before going to South Africa.
3238	Sap.	Trow, R.	RR	31	1	MR, OFS.
None	Lt.	Tweedy, A.C.	RR	45	2	CC, OFS, TVL, SA01, SA02.
2216	Sap.	Upton, A.H.	RR	E,45	2	CC, OFS, SA01, SA02.
8552	2/C	Upton, R.T.	VSS	2,10	3	CC, OFS, TVL, SA01, SA02.
25345	Sgt.	Wadkins, H.	RR	E,10	2	CC, OFS, TVL, SA01, SA02.
8528	L/C	Wale, T.	VSS	1,8	3	CC, OFS, TVL, SA01, SA02.
1806	Sap.	Walker, B.	RR	10	1	CC, OFS, TVL. KSA.
1807	Sap.	Walley, J.H.	RR	31	?	CC, OFS, TVL. KSA.
1441	Sap.	Walley, Jno.	RR	10	1	CC, OFS.
8573	Sap.	Wareham, J.	VSS	2,10	3	CC, OFS, TVL, SA01, SA02.
2559	Sap.	Wearne, G.H.	RR	8	1	BELM, MR, OFS, TVL. KSA.
28058	Sap.	Weston, E.	RR	E,10	2	CC, OFS, TVL, SA01, SA02.
2217	Sap.	Weston, F.	RR	8	1	BELM, MR, OFS. KSA.
1447	Sap.	Weston, G.B.	RR	E,45	2	CC, OFS, SA01, SA02.
1272	Sap.	Wheatman, H.R.	RR	E,45	2	CC, OFS, SA01, SA02.
1184	Sap.	Wilkinson, A.	RR	8	1	BELM, MR.
1455	Sap.	Williams, H.	RR	E,45	2	CC, OFS, SA01, SA02.
2283	Sap.	Williams, J.R.	RR	45	1	CC, ROL, OFS. KSA.
8574	Sap.	Winder, T.	VSS	2,10	3	CC, OFS, TVL, SA01, SA02.
1113	Sap.	Witter, E.W.	RR	E,10	2	CC, OFS, TVL, SA01, SA02.
27471	Cpl.	Wolfe, S.	RR	8	1	BELM, MR, OFS. KSA.
1553	Sap.	Wood, G.	RR	31	1	BELM, MR, OFS, TVL. KSA.
8526	Cpl.	Worrall, W.	VSS	1,8	3	CC, OFS, TVL.
3590	Sap.	Wrench, J.W.	RR	E,45	2	CC, OFS, TVL, SA01, SA02.
2354	Sap.	Wright, C.W.	RR	8	1	BELM, MR, OFS, TVL.
28867	Sap.	Young, A.	RR	8	1	BELM, MR, OFS, TVL.

Diary of Sapper Arthur William Maybury

During the South Africa War, it was difficult to monitor the exact locations of the serving men from Crewe, especially members of the Railway Reserve and Volunteer Service Sections, who were often split into smaller units and sent all over South Africa. As far as we can ascertain, there were no records kept to help identify their whereabouts, but a diary belonging to Sapper Arthur William Maybury (see page 126), who was a member of the second draft of the Railway Reserve, gives us some insight into their work, diet and places where they were employed. In 1901, Sapper Maybury was 31 years-of-age and married with four children, residing at 79, Middlewich Street. The diary starts after a fortnight's training at Brompton Barracks, Chatham, and ends just before his return to Crewe. Place names and spellings etc. are as recorded.

1901

Thursday, March 14th - 'Parade at Coffee tavern, St. Mary's Barracks for breakfast at 6 o'clock a.m. Fell in prior to sailing to South Africa at 7.30 a.m. Entrained 10 a.m. for Albert docks, London. Arrived 1 p.m. Met a few Crewe friends. Went in the S.S. St. Andrew for embarkment to South Africa, setting sail at 4 o'clock amidst a lot of cheering and counter cheers from the troops. Dinner at 3.30, bread and meat. Tea, bread and butter. Slung hammocks at 6 p.m. Weather rough. Got a wetting through someone opening porthole window. Got up and slept on the table the remainder of the night.'

Saturday 16th - 'Arrived at Queenstown at 4 p.m. amidst cheers from the people gathered around. As soon as we anchored there came several people to the ship in boats and before you could ask them what they had to sell they had climbed on the deck with all sorts of things from easy chairs to oranges until darkness set in. Slung hammocks at 6 p.m. Lights out at 8 o'clock.'

Sunday 17th - 'St. Patrick's Day. Unslung hammocks 6 a.m. Went on deck, saw a lot of people selling all kinds of articles such as mufflers, handkerchiefs, pencils, oranges, cakes, tobacco, cigarettes and pocket books. The troops were receiving them by hauling a rope in with a basket attached amidst a lot of laughter. Sometimes the money dropping in the dock and sometimes the articles through the basket tipping over. Received a section of Munster Militia on board and a quantity of eatables for the troops. Setting sail from Queenstown at 4 o'clock amidst cheers. Diet, stew, bread, margarine, meat, potatoes and plum duff.'

Tuesday 19th - 'Parade at 10 a.m. for ship inspection by Captain. Warned for main guard, 24hrs. 2 on and 4 off. Weather rough.'

Thursday 21st - 'Parade 10 a.m. for orders. Received orders to parade for 12 hrs military watch. Held a concert at 8 o'clock by permission of the Captain of the S.S. St. Andrew and military officers on board until 10 p.m.'

Monday 25th - 'Fell in 6.45, roll call. Parade 10 a.m. bare feet with chest bare for medical inspection. Shooting match 2 o'clock. 7 shots each at a rope ball drawn behind the ship by a rope. Passed Cape Vurn at 3.30, saw shoals of porpoise at 6 p.m.'

Friday 29th - 'Parade 6.45. Fatigue 8.30 cleaning washhouses and latrine. Fatigue 2 o'clock drawing forage for horses consisting of hay, oats & carrots. Sports field 5.30. Prizes given by the officers on the ship. First prize 5/-, second prize 3/6, third prize 2/6, fourth prize 1/6. Sports pillow fight, two of the troops to sit facing one another on a pole and the one who knocks the other off to be the winner but not allowed to touch the pole with your hands. Pillow filled with hay.'

Saturday 30th - 'One of the Munster Militia men died. We buried him 5.30 p.m.'

Monday April 1st - 'Parade for the company physical drill. Parade at 4 o'clock for kit inspection. Passed the night with a song amongst ourselves. Weather splendid.'

Tuesday 2nd - 'Parade 10 a.m. for inspection of the ship by the captain and officers. Parade 12.30 for hammock inspection. Parade 2 o'clock for pay. During the day experiments by the troops and crew for prize of £3 offered by the officers for the best design of a target for use to shoot at from a vessel.'

Wednesday 3rd - 'Rifle drill parade 10 a.m. Drew stuff for plum duff and made it up. Concert at 8 o'clock promoted by Serg. Birch held on the top deck.'

Thursday 4th - 'Parade 6.45 for company rifle drill. Parade 11 a.m. for strap inspection. During the afternoon had a lie down when there came a rush of water through the porthole and got a good soaking.'

Friday 5th - 'Independent shooting match between Greys, 12th Lancers, Engineers, Dragoons & Munster Militia. Engineers won. First prize 1 large bottle of beer per man. Second prize 1 small bottle of beer per man. I was one of the selected team.'

Saturday 6th - 'Went to fetch coffee for breakfast, coming down stairs fell and spilled coffee over me, scalding my thigh and had to be attended to by doctor.'

Sunday 7th - 'Troops busy getting all their accoutrements out of the hold on to the top deck ready for disembarkation. Parade 4 o'clock to receive a present of half a pound of tobacco given by the owners of the ship. Prayer meeting 7 p.m.'

Monday 8th - 'Unslung hammocks 5am. Sighted Green Point camp at 5.15. Arrived close in 5.30. Awaiting orders had a look round and saw Table Mountain, and very nice scenery all round. Saw a few transport with troops on. Received orders at noon to start for Port Elizabeth for further orders. Started at 6.30 at night.'

Wednesday 10th - 'Troops busy swabbing and cleaning prior to disembarkation. When on deck saw a small pilot boat being tossed about. Sea washing over deck. Weather rough. Arrived Port Elizabeth 6.30. Troops all left the boat with the exception of the Engineers.'

Friday 12th - 'Went on deck, saw some of the troops passing time by fishing. Saw a 2 funnel ship come in with a further consignment of troops. Kaffirs very busy unloading and loading goods for Cape Town. Left port at 5.15 p.m. Off duty 6p.m. Went on top deck and saw a beautiful sight like the water lit up by electricity, the shoals of fish looked beautiful.'

Sunday 14th - 'Arrived Greenpoint and Table Mountain 5.15. Parade 2 o'clock for disembarkation. Landed 4.20. Saw between 2 and 3 thousand prisoners, guards over them. Arrived Greenpoint camp 5.30. Tents pitched for us 11 men and 2 of "N" Co. Lights out 9 o'clock. Very hot.'

Tuesday 16th - 'Engineers supplied guard of 36 over Boer prisoners.'

Wednesday 17th - 'Had a walk down to Cape Town and saw some fine buildings and went on the station.'

Thursday 18th - 'Parade for troops that was warned to go up country to Pretoria, Bloemfontein and Kroonstad. Gave them a good English cheer. Fell in for the night turn. Marched to post close to invalids being entertained by the ladies and gentlemen of Cape Town. After they had a feast there was a concert. Everyone seemed to be enjoying themselves.'

Friday 19th - 'Came off duty 7.30. Parade 10 o'clock for fatigue. Parade 4 o'clock for strap inspection and check. After parade for pay. Weather showery and lightning. Walked to Cape Town, had some refreshments in soldiers home.'

Sunday 21st - 'Commenced duties as cook. 11 o'clock warned to proceed to Pretoria by 2 o'clock. Entrained in trucks at 3 o'clock. Started at 4 o'clock. 40 troops in one truck, and baggage.'

Monday 22nd - 'Arrived Prince Albert Road. Started again at 11.15. Arrived Fraserburg at 12.15. Passed several graves with stones erected. Arrived Beaufort West 4.30. Told off for rear of the train to guard and keep a look out for snipers.'

Tuesday 23rd - 'Arrived De Aar 6 a.m., had breakfast. Left 8.15, arrived Naauwpoort 1.30. Left 6.30.'

Wednesday 24th - 'Arrived Norvals Pont. Weather very hot in day time and very cold at night.'

Thursday 25th - 'Left Norvals Pont 7.30 a.m. Arrived Springfontein 10.25, arrived Bloemfontein. Passed a lot of dead horses and Kaffir Kraals. Very nice scenery around. Passed several poor chaps graves.'

Friday 26th - 'Left Bloemfontein 7.30. Arrived Brandfort. Heard an account of fighting on the 24th. Passed wreck caused by the Boers. Arrived Ventersburg 5 o'clock. Went to concert held in a large tent and there passed the night.'

Saturday 27th - 'Left Ventersburg 6.45. Passed wreck caused by Boers on the 24th. Arrived Kroonstad.'

Sunday 28th - 'Arrived Pretoria. Diet during the journey, corned beef, biscuits, tea & coffee.'

Tuesday 30th - 'Had a walk as far as town. Went in the Museum and saw a lot of curios and model of a ship.'

Friday May 3rd - 'Left Pretoria to join 8th company R.E. at Vereeniging. Met some townies.'

<u>Sunday 5th</u> - 'Busy packing kits and camp stores for Voker to build bridges.'
<u>Monday 6th</u> - 'Left for Voker at 7 o'clock. Struck camp at 5 o'clock. Went to Pretoria and stayed the night.'
<u>Tuesday 7th</u> - 'Left Pretoria about 8 o'clock. Landed at Middleburg 5 o'clock having been ill all day. Admitted to hospital suffering from dysentery.'
<u>Wednesday 15th</u> - 'Left for General hospital in Red Cross train at 9 o'clock.'
<u>Sunday 19th</u> - 'Better.'
<u>Monday 27th</u> - 'Fell in 9 o'clock for fatigue. Left for R.A. barracks to join 26th comp. R.E. awaiting orders to join unit.'
<u>Wednesday 29th</u> - 'Warned to return to unit.'
<u>Thursday 30th</u> - 'Awakened 5.30 to get ready for 7 o'clock train for Avoca. Received 3 day rations. Arrived Middleburg, stayed the night in Rest camp.'
<u>Friday June 1</u> - 'Commenced journey to Avoca. At 10 o'clock arrived Waterval Point. Slept in van.'
<u>Saturday 2nd</u> - 'Left Waterval Point at 7 o'clock, arrived at Nooiteideacht. Stayed 1 hr through Boers sniping at block-house. Armoured train cleared way. Arrived Kaapmuiden and stayed night.'
<u>Sunday 3rd</u> - 'Left Kaapmuiden at 10 o'clock, arrived at Avoca. Warned for guard.'
<u>Monday 4th</u> - 'Came off guard at 6 o'clock. Commenced work at 9 o'clock until 12 and from 12.45 to 4 o'clock.'
<u>Wednesday 6th</u> - 'Arrival of 25 Crewe Engineers.'
<u>Thursday 7th</u> - 'Saw Artillery Battery cross the river.'
<u>Friday 8th</u> - 'Commenced work on the bridge.'
<u>Thursday 14th</u> - 'Received letter dated April 25. 1 Sentinel dated April 20, 1 Sentinel dated May 4, 1 Chronicle dated April 20 and 1 Chronicle dated May 4.'
<u>Wednesday 20th</u> - 'Commenced drilling and retapping rollers for bridge.'
<u>Friday 22nd</u> - 'Fetching other parts belonging to rollers and cleaning ready for use again. Sale of one of the Sappers kit belonging to the 8th who died at Barberton Hospital on June 16th 1901 for benefit of widowed mother.'
<u>Tuesday July 2nd</u> - 'Working on bridge. Saw train load of refugees going to Barberton.'
<u>Thursday 4th</u> - 'Working on bridge. One of the lucky ones in a draw for a present from the field force canteen.'
<u>Thursday 18th</u> - 'Working on bridge. Received a letter from home. Received 1lb butter from canteen funds.'
<u>Wednesday 24th</u> - 'Working on bridge. Received present from Cape Town given by Colonel Cotton Jodrell, a writing case.'
<u>Friday August 2nd</u> - 'On guard at 6 p.m. off at 6 a.m. Report came in that Boers (120) were within a few miles, travelling in a South East direction. Camp all in readiness for attack but did not have any sight of them.'
<u>Thursday 15th</u> - 'Working on camp. Took a sick Volunteer to station on Trolley.'
<u>Tuesday 20th</u> - 'Off guard 6 a.m. Sick with injured hand. Received parcel from home.'
<u>Friday 23rd</u> - 'Still sick. Company had photo taken.'
<u>Saturday 24th</u> - 'Still sick. First engine with train passed over bridge safely.'

Thursday 29th - 'Sick. Saw doctor. Received orders to go to Barberton. Arrived Barberton, had wounds dressed awaiting for ambulance cart and went to hospital in ambulance drawn by oxen.'

Friday 30th - 'Ordered to be detained. Gave clothes in stores and received hospital dress.'

Friday September 6th - 'Still in hospital. Was alarm during night. Ringing of bells to take up position in case of attack.'

Tuesday 10th - 'Improving. Asked doctor to make ointment. Left hospital 4.30 and stayed with Hants the night.'

Wednesday 11th - 'Left Barberton to join company 1.30.'

Sunday 15th - 'Struck tents. Commenced journey at 9 o'clock. Arrived Waterval Point and stayed night.'

Wednesday 18th - 'Arrived Kroonstad.'

Thursday 19th - 'Commenced work (trenching).'

Friday 20th - 'Trenching. Entertained by a section of Crewe Engineers on transport to Kroonstad to a smoke.'

Monday 23rd - 'Escort with traction wire for fencing. Slept in blockhouse between Jordan and America sidings.'

Wednesday October 2nd - 'Started to trek for Vredefort Road. Stayed America siding the night.'

Thursday 3rd - 'Commenced journey. Stayed the night at Honingspruit.'

Saturday 5th - 'Arrived Vredefort Road.'

Thursday 10th - 'Turned out at 12 o'clock as Boers were firing at a blockhouse.'

Saturday 19th - 'Stood to arms, heavy firing from blockhouse close to the station.'

Friday 25th - 'Received orders to return to Kroonstad.'

Friday November 1st - 'Working on bridge. Received letter from wife and children.'

Saturday 16th - 'Working on bridge. Played in afternoon in cricket match between 1st team v 16 of 2nd - Score 1st team 72, 2nd team 64.'

Tuesday 19th - 'Attending hospital with abscesses on arm.'

Saturday 23rd - 'Attending hospital. Playing in a cricket match between first eleven v R.A.M.C. Lost match - 1st XI, 71, R.A.M.C. 94. Stumping, gave no extras. Myself made 4.'

Tuesday 26th - 'Received discharge from attending hospital.'

Saturday 30th - 'Working on bridge. Cricket match in afternoon, return match between R.A.M.C. and R.E. - R.A.M.C. 74, R.E. 70. Stumping, gave no extras, made 5 runs.'

Saturday December 7th - 'Playing in cricket match. Post Office v R.E. Post Office 98 R.E. 68. 24 extras against me. Made 33 not out.'

Sunday 8th - 'Attending hospital through accident in the match.'

Wednesday 25th - (Christmas Day.) 'Church parade. Diet, fowl, duck, geese, plum pudding, beans, pomkins, ham, blancmange, pickles, minerals, cheese, tea, coffee, bread and jam.'

Saturday 28th - 'Preparing tressels for loading girders for Vet River Bridge. Cricket match in afternoon between Post Office and 38th Coy R.E. - Post Office

63, R.E. 36. Stumping, 7 extras, runs nil, rain stopped play.'
<u>Monday 30th</u> - 'Working on work for Vet River Bridge. Received present sent out from England consisting of 1lb tobacco, 1 pipe and 1 plum duff.'

1902

<u>Wednesday January 1st</u> - 'Holiday. Saw natives cricketing also native women and men playing and dancing in their style.'
<u>Monday 6th</u> - 'Saw funeral of P.M.O. Colonel Wood and 5 soldiers. No work.'
<u>Friday 17th</u> - 'Returning all useless things to A.O.C. Arrival of detachment belonging to company.'
<u>Monday 20th</u> - 'Commenced journey for Harrismith 2.30. Arrived at Elandsfontein and stayed the night.'
<u>Tuesday 21st</u> - 'Commenced journey, arrived at Charlestown and stayed the night.'
<u>Wednesday 22nd</u> - 'Arrived Ladysmith and stayed the night.'
<u>Thursday 23rd</u> - 'Arrived Harrismith. Diet, biscuits and bully. Weather showery.'
<u>Wednesday 29th</u> - 'Unloading stores. Football match - R.E. 2 South Stafford 4.'
<u>Saturday February 1st</u> - 'In charge of natives on new line.'
<u>Monday 17th</u> - 'On camp fatigue. Football match - Married 1 Single 5.'
<u>Saturday 22nd</u> - 'In charge of natives. Football match - R.A.M.C. 1 R.E. 1. Match unfinished through one of R.A.M.C. breaking his arm.'
<u>Saturday March 8th</u> - 'In charge of natives. Football match - R.E. 2 Black Watch 2nd Batt. 0.'
<u>Tuesday April 15th</u> - 'Working in yard fitting on brakes.'
<u>Monday May 12th</u> - 'Working on engine, night as well.'
<u>Saturday 17th</u> - 'In charge of natives at Elands River.'
<u>Monday June 2nd</u> - 'Working on bridge. Diet, stew, onions, bread, jam, rum and bacon. Peace declared. All troops extra rum issued to the value of 1/6.'
<u>Thursday 12th</u> - 'No work. Too cold.'
<u>Monday 16th</u> - 'Volunteers left for home (Sunday). Working on bridge.'
<u>Wednesday 25th</u> - 'Working on bridge until 1.30 and then proceed to Harrismith for coronation on leave.'
<u>Monday 30th</u> - 'Return to Elands River working on bridge. Received orders for home.'
<u>Tuesday July 1st</u> - 'Packed kit for home. Left Elands River for Harrismith.'
<u>Wednesday 2nd</u> - 'Commenced journey. Arrived Ladysmith.'
<u>Friday 4th</u> - 'Arrived Elandsfontein.'
<u>Monday 7th</u> - 'Cooking for remainder of men on platelaying.'
<u>Wednesday 9th</u> - 'On visit to Johannesburg.'
<u>Tuesday 29th</u> - 'Left Elandsfontein for home.'
<u>Saturday August 2nd</u> - 'Arrived Cape Town.'

Monday 4th - 'Cooking. Busy prior to embarkation on S.S. Moravian. Set sail at 4.00.'
Saturday 9th - 'With mess. Diet, Breakfast, porridge, meat, potatoes, fried fish, tea, bread and butter. Dinner, stew, Irish stew, cheese, potatoes, boiled meat, pudding, pickles. Tea, bread, potatoes, boiled mutton, pigs head, and cakes. Ball at night for officers and concert amongst troops, being coronation day. August 9th 1902.'
Wednesday 20th - 'Arrived Tenerife 8 o'clock at night.'
Thursday 21st - 'Commenced journey at 4 a.m.'
Wednesday 27th - 'Fish and sardines for tea.'

Arthur Maybury retired from the Brass Finishing Shop in 1934, after 50 years service in Crewe Works. When WW2 broke out in 1939, he volunteered as an Air Raid Warden. He died on August 6, 1942, aged 72.

·Summary of Events·

1899

October 7 - Members of the Army Reserve from Crewe receive their orders to mobilise.
October 8 - A total of 105 men from the Crewe Railway Reserve are told to prepare for South Africa.
October 11 - War officially declared with the Boers.
October 13 - Twenty men attached to the Shropshire Light Infantry leave the town.
October 14 - Nineteen more members of the Railway Reserve notified. General Buller and his Army Corps leave Southampton for South Africa.
October 16 - Railway Reserve leave Crewe for Chatham.
October 21 - Men belonging to the 10th Railway Company leave Southampton on the S.S. *Goorkha*.
October 22 - 8th Railway Company and 31st Fortress Company leave home shores aboard S.S. *Malta*.
November 15 - S.S. *Goorkha* docks at Cape Town. Winston Churchill captured by the Boers.
November 16 - S.S. *Malta* docks at Cape Town.
November 23 - Battle of Belmont.
November 25 - Further action involving Crewe men at Graspan.
November 28 - Battle of Modder River. First Crewe casualty when Sapper A. Wilkinson is wounded.
December 11 - Battle of Magersfontein.

December 28 - Another 100 men from the Railway Reserve from Crewe depart for Chatham.

1900

January 2 - Men of the Railway Reserve return to Crewe on an initial one month furlough.
January 6 - A further 330 men from the Crewe Engineers volunteer.
January 10 (approx) - 10th Railway Company join up with the 8th and 31st Companies at Modder River to help re-construct blown-up bridge.
January 23 - First death of a Crewe man in war zone when Private S. Davies dies of wounds suffered at Colenso.
January 24 - Private L. Bamford of 81, Ridgway Street, killed in action during the Battle of Spion Kop.
February 13 - Private W. Maude dies at Orange River.
February 15 - A Crewe man drives the first train into Kimberley, following the relief of the town.
February 28 - Ladysmith relieved.
March 13 - Lord Roberts enters Bloemfontein.
April 3 - Modder River bridge completed.
April 15 - Two Railway Volunteers die of enteric fever. Sapper Foy dies at Orange River and Sapper Evans at Modder River.
April 20 - Sapper W. Madeley dies of enteric fever at Bloemfontein.
May 17 - Relief of Mafeking.
May 27 - Death of Sapper Septimus Robinson, also at Bloemfontein.
May 29 - Sapper F. Ankers becomes another victim of enteric fever.
May 30 - Driver J. Bebbington dies of enteric fever.
June 5 - The fall of Pretoria, capital of the Transvaal.
June 9 - The Crewe Works Carnival & Patriotic Demonstration takes place.
June 14 - Sappers B. Walker and W. Goodwin captured at Leeuw Spruit.
June 16 - The 4,000th loco rolls off the production line at Crewe Works.
July 8 - Trooper A. C. Morris succumbs to enteric fever.
July 21 - Private A. Burgess dies at Newcastle.
November 7 - Queen Victoria passes through Crewe station.
December 11 - Lord Roberts sails for home.

1901

January 2 - General Sir Redvers Buller arrives in Crewe.

January 4 - Death of 1st Grade Orderley Charles Powell in Netley Hospital.
January 22 - Queen Victoria dies.
February 2 - Funeral of Queen Victoria.
February 6 - Private J. Thomason of the Shropshire Light Infantry dies in Pretoria.
February 25 - Second draft of Railway Reserve leave Crewe for Chatham.
March 1 - Private W. Thornton dies of enteric fever at Elandsfontein.
March 14 - Second draft of the Railway Reserve set sail for war-zone on S.S. *St. Andrew*.
April 3 - Volunteer Service Sections leave town for Chatham.
April 10/11 - Death of Lieutenant Trotter at Chatham.
April 14 - Funeral of Lieutenant Trotter. S.S. *St. Andrew* finally docks at Cape Town.
April 27 - Volunteer Service Sections leave for South Africa on the S.S. *Pinemore*.
May 11 - Sapper J. J. Darlington accidentally shot dead at Bloemfontein.
May 21 - Volunteer Service Sections land at Cape Town.
June 3 - Private C. Hodson dies of dysentery at Wakkerstroom.
July 4 - Sapper Tom Roberts murdered by the Boers.
August 31 - The Crewe Patriotic Carnival Demonstration takes place.
October 23 - Private J. Hayes dies of the plague in Cape Town.
November 1 - Baden-Powell visits Nantwich.
December 7 - Private Charles Moses dies of enteric fever at Kroonstad.

1902

January 4 - Grand banquet in Town Hall for wives and children of men serving in South Africa.
January 23 - Private C. G. Cole of Gladstone Street dies at Middleburg.
January 31 - Sapper T. Coops is killed in an armoured train crash at Burgersdorp.
February 6 - Lord Kitchener begins sweeps with four 'super columns.'
February 10 - Another Crewe Engineer loses his life when Sapper W. Talbot dies at Kroonstad.
February 20 - Private Thomas Wareham also dies at Kroonstad.
March 7 - Lord Methuen wounded and captured at Tweebosch.
May 20 - Medical man Lance Corporal J. Brennan becomes another victim of enteric fever.
May 31 - End of the war.
July 5 - Railway Volunteers at home proceed to Aldershot.

July 14 - S.S. *Malta* leaves South Africa with a number of Crewe men aboard.
August 3 - The two Volunteer Service Sections arrive at Southampton.
August 4 - Volunteer Service Sections return to Crewe among chaotic scenes. On the same day, S.S. *Moravian* leaves Cape Town with many Railway Reserve members aboard.
August 9 - A number of Crewe Engineers take part in King Edward VII's coronation.
August 16 - Another Patriotic Demonstration takes place in Crewe to raise further funds for the proposed war memorial.
August 27 - S.S. *Moravian* docks at Southampton.
August 28 - First group of the Railway Reserve return to Crewe.
August 29 - The remaining men return home in two groups.
September 3 - Lord Kitchener spends the night at The Crewe Arms Hotel.
October 2 - Over 200 Crewe Engineers who had served in South Africa enjoy a 'smoking party.'

1903

April 23 - A section of Railway Volunteers attend the unveiling of the LNWR tablet to the fallen at Euston.
August 8 - Unveiling of the South Africa war memorial in Queens Park.

1906

June 4 - Death of Francis William Webb at Bournemouth.

1912

March 17 - Final parade of the Railway Volunteers.

1917

October 13 - Colonel Cotton-Jodrell dies in a Manchester nursing home.

1974

June 19 - The last Crewe man to serve in the Boer War, Charles William Tandy, dies aged 93.

(TOP LEFT) QMS Gibson c1907. (TOP RIGHT) Robert Kilshaw, also of the Railway Volunteers.

(ABOVE) Crewe Engineers practising on land in Victoria Avenue c1909.

(ABOVE) Members of the Railway Volunteers on the Victoria Avenue training ground c1909. Standing far left if Lance Corporal Harry Twiss. He would serve during World War One, as would many of the Corps. (BELOW) The Volunteers at Chatham in July 1909. Among the men is William John Wilford (standing centre).

Three more who served in both the Boer and Great Wars. (**ABOVE LEFT**) *Private William Kent (see page 126).* (**ABOVE RIGHT**) *Corporal Jack Walley (see page 12), who served in the Cheshire Regiment during the 1914-18 campaign. He is pictured (seated) with Frank Pickford Snr., Gertrude Pickford (nee Walley), and children Gertrude, Frank and Elsie. Frank would serve in India during World War Two.* (**BELOW**) *Second Lieutenant John Guest (seated centre), formerly of 15, Somerville Street, who won the Croix de Guerre in France in 1918.*

*Robert John Steele (far right) - another Crewe man to serve in two major campaigns (see page 49). (**ABOVE**) Whilst serving with the Liverpool Pals in WW1. (**BELOW**) Company Sergeant Major Steele (sitting second right) now in the 1/5th Bn. East Lancashire Regiment. He would win the DCM and MM during the Great War, thus becoming one of the most decorated local men of the war. He resided at 23, West Street and would later lose his left leg following an accident in Crewe Works.*

(**ABOVE**) A re-union of several members of the Railway Volunteers in March 1942, to commemorate the 30th anniversary of the last parade of the Crewe Engineers. Robert Kilshaw is seated far right.
(**LEFT**) Charles Henry Healey, who went to South Africa with the second draft of the Railway Reserve. He is standing in the backyard of his home at 13, Dorfold Street.

Joseph Henry Lloyd on the footplate, during the latter years of his working life. During the Boer War, he left the town on February 25, 1901, with the second draft of the Railway Reserve. Resided at 39, South Street (c1900) and later at 30, Laura Street.

*For various reasons (not living in the town at the time of war, name not submitted etc.), not all Crewe men who served during the Boer War are commemorated on the South Africa memorial in Queens Park. Some omissions are (**TOP LEFT**) Richard Rowlands of the Shropshire Light Infantry, who is pictured (far right) many years later in the Crewe South Junction box, where he worked for 23 years. (**BELOW LEFT**) Private Thomas Elson of Ludford Street, who also served during the Great War in the 1st Bn. South Wales Borderers. He was killed in action at Langemarck on October 22, 1914. (**BELOW RIGHT**) 6822 Corporal William 'Danny' James Dyer of the Norfolk Regiment. He moved to the town in 1930 to become stage manager of the Crewe Lyceum.*

In Remembrance.

In remembrance raise your fountain,
Let its waters
Tell the daughters,
And the sons of Crewe
That o'er Africa's veldt or mountain,
When war raged
Well engaged
Were the men of Crewe!

In remembrance, raise some token
Which may stand
A centre grand
Through the distant age,
And may tell in lines unbroken
How your sons
By their guns
Stood in battle rage.

In remembrance, keep the story
Fresh and full,
You may cull
Flowers there to twine
Round about your heroes' glory,
In those days
When men praise
Crewe! such men as thine!

The memorial in 2008, still one of the most impressive Boer War monuments in the country.

Bibliography

SOCIAL & ECONOMIC DEVELOPMENT OF CREWE 1780-1923 by W. H. Chaloner.
THE HISTORY OF THE CORPS OF ROYAL ENGINEERS VOLUME III by Colonel Sir Charles M. Watson.
OUR REGIMENTS IN SOUTH AFRICA by John Stirling.
THE BOER WAR by Thomas Pakenham.
THE GREAT BOER WAR by Byron Farwell.
IN MEMORIAM - ROLL OF HONOUR IMPERIAL FORCES ANGLO-BOER WAR 1899-1902 by Steve Watt.
THE NATIONAL ARMY MUSEUM BOOK OF THE BOER WAR by Field Marshal Lord Carver.
THE CREWE & NANTWICH ROLL OF HONOUR 1914-1945 by Mark Potts and Tony Marks.
THE MEDAL ROLL OF THE CORPS OF ROYAL ENGINEERS, VOLUME V, QUEEN'S AND KING'S SOUTH AFRICA MEDALS 1899-1902 by Graham Hornby.